PRAYERS
BASED ON THE EPISTLES OF PAUL

PRAYERS
BASED ON THE EPISTLES OF PAUL

Romans
through
Philemon

D. D. LEWIS

XULON PRESS

Xulon Press
2301 Lucien Way #415
Maitland, FL 32751
407.339.4217
www.xulonpress.com

Unless otherwise indicated, Scripture quotations taken from the Holy Bible, New International Version (NIV). Copyright © 1973, 1978, 1984, 2011 by Biblica, Inc.™. Used by permission. All rights reserved.

Scripture quotations taken from the English Standard Version (ESV). Copyright © 2001 by Crossway, a publishing ministry of Good News Publishers. Used by permission. All rights reserved.

Paperback ISBN-13: 978-1-66284-697-7
Ebook ISBN-13: 978-1-66284-698-4

TABLE OF CONTENTS

INTRODUCTION

Background story

ABOUT TWO YEARS ago, Mark, my friend for over thirty years, invited me over to his mother's home to have dinner with him and his wife. I had not seen Mark or his family for over five years. I had a wonderful evening with Mark, his wife, and his mother. We had a great time as we testified to the goodness and faithfulness of God in our lives. The evening was mutually encouraging, and we concluded the evening in prayer for one another. I was greatly encouraged and thanked God for my friends.

The next day, I received a text from Mark. Mark told me he began to send out daily prayers approximately three years ago. The prayers came from his daily readings of Scripture. He asked me if I wanted to receive them. Of course, I said yes. I quickly came to see these prayers as a powerful ministry opportunity. I strongly desired to speak the Gospel more regularly into the lives of my family and friends. A few days later, I called Mark. I wanted to know how he began this ministry? What was the scope of this ministry? And how effective this ministry had been? Mark told me how he started this ministry by sending daily prayers to his youngest son after he left to pursue a career in New York City. As Mark told others what he was doing, many asked to be on his list. Mark's prayer list grew to over 160 people! Mark told me that he did not send his prayers out as a group but individually, and he prayed for each one specifically. I was impressed and very encouraged to follow in his steps.

I immediately started writing prayers on my phone and sending them out as a text as Mark had done. I told everyone that they could reply stop if they did not wish to receive the prayers. Their acceptance was

100%. As I told others what I was doing, many asked me to add them to the list.

I have the privilege and the joy of serving as a pastor at Providence Church in Pittsburgh, Pa., along with three other men. (Rob, Nate, and Ryan.) After a few months, Rob, our head pastor, ask me to consider posting my prayers on Slack, a tool we use to communicate and encourage our members. I have sent these prayers out to a diverse audience, from mature Christians to unbelievers. I sent them to four pastors which I deeply respect and work with closely. I wanted to bless them and solicit their input. I also sent them to many friends and family. I have been amazed and encouraged by the positive responses from people with very different beliefs. It has been a blessing for me to write these prayers, edit them, and reread them many times. Therefore, I began praying about the possibility of publishing these prayers with the hope of blessing a larger audience.

Two years ago, I was engaged in a program to read through the Bible in a year. I was reading and meditating on 2 Timothy. When I started writing prayers from 2nd Timothy, my reading plan slowed to a crawl. I began a two-year journey through the Epistles, beginning in 2 Timothy and continuing through Jude. I skipped Revelation, which I am currently studying and meditating on in preparation for writing. I went back to 1 Corinthians and continued through 1 Timothy. Then, I finished by writing prayers based on the great book of Romans. Dedicating the past two years to writing these prayers has been very rewarding. Writing these prayers has caused me to grow in my knowledge and love for God. I have also grown in my love and appreciation for the apostles. I also had many conversations with family, friends, and coworkers about the Gospel, which I would not of had if I had not studied the Epistles and written these prayers. God is good in all He does!

Intent and Purpose

I hope this introduction is helping you to see my heart and motivation for writing and publishing this book. The rewards I spoke of in the last paragraph have been great, and I desire you to experience the same. May you grow in your knowledge and love for God. And in your love, respect, and appreciation for Paul. May you be more equipped to live and speak the Gospel accurately and boldly into the lives of others. My prayer is that God would use this book to bring many into a closer walk with Christ and his bride (the Church).

There have been many good commentaries written. I did not write this book to be another commentary. In writing these prayers, I am committed not to teach or give any opinions, either my own or someone else's. I only want to proclaim the truth clearly taught in Scripture. I strive to be clear, concise, and accurate. I know that I am accountable to God for the way I handle His Word, and I take that responsibility very seriously. (2 Timothy 2:15)

This book is not a replacement for a commentary . There will be more proclaiming than explaining. I will ask more questions than I answer. My goal is to drive you deeper into the study of the Word of God. I have added questions at the end of the prayers that are open-ended and are written to help you get more out of the text and apply it to your life. I also believe it is good and right to ask direct, challenging questions.

If a Scripture is confusing and often easily misinterpreted, I will present some background information and context necessary for understanding. I am not interested in promoting clever details that will not contribute to understanding an application. The prayers will begin with stating the main point, followed by a prayer of exaltation and thanks. The middle section will be commentary and background necessary for understanding the truth presented. They will end with a prayer of petition.

I believe that Scripture is true and sufficient. We should not profess anything contrary to Scripture. I pray that this book will challenge any beliefs that contradict Scripture. I will not proclaim anything to be true without having strong support from Scripture. You will find many Scriptural references in these daily prayers, especially when the passage is implicit. Explicit Scriptures that support the implied truth are then listed.

I pray that this introduction has served you well. I want you to know my heart and my intentions for writing and living. I have written for my Lord and Savior and for the purpose of spurring you on in the faith. Take care, my friends. I do not know you yet, but I hope to meet you someday soon. If not here, then in heaven. Amen.

Acknowledgments

I AM SO thankful and grateful for all the encouragements and prayers that I have received in the process of writing this book. For two years, I never had a single day without some encouragement. God is so good! He knows how weak I am and how easily I give up. The support of believers and even some unbelievers was nothing short of amazing. There were many days when I wrestled with the Scriptures and did not know what to write. I learned to trust God's provisions and be quick and specific in asking for prayer. I am so grateful for the many who prayed for me to be faithful to His Word.

First, I would like to thank Mark Corbin, who I mentioned in the intro, for setting me on this journey and for the many encouragements and prayers, along the way. I am also thankful for Jody Dausey, who just sent me another encouraging text, just as I was writing this. She has been a daily encouragement and a faithful, prayerful friend. I am thankful for Mick McGinnis, who I sat under for six years, and Sally, his wife. They both cared for me through some troubling years, and I am very grateful. They have been faithful Friends for over 30 years. I greatly appreciate their encouragement and support Not only in writing this book but in many other ways as well. My friend, Nate Rutman is a faithful Barnabas. He is always encouraging and willing to help anyone. He has volunteered to design a web page for this book ministry. I could go on and list dozens of new friends that have been very supportive. When I say a new friend, I mean someone I have known for less than a decade. May God richly bless you with many Christian friends who know you well and show their love for their Lord and Savior by living in obedience to His Word. There is no greater Joy than seeing others walk in the Lord. (3 John 1:4) Amen.

Prayer for a new year

Father, May we continue to grow in our knowledge and love for You. You are infinitely glorious, beyond anything we could imagine or think. Make us more aware of Your sustaining grace in our lives. The more we acknowledge and experience Your daily work in our lives, the more we will rejoice in who You are and what You have done! May we grow in our knowledge of You and love for You. At the end of this year, may we be more in love with You than we have ever been! May we not be discouraged because we have not arrived, but may we, like Paul, press on to the high calling in Christ Jesus! (Philippians 3:12-17) Amen.

ROMANS

Prayer based on Romans 1:1-7

A Word about calling, purpose, and commitment to God and His Gospel:

Father, We thank You for calling Paul and giving him a powerful ministry to the Gentiles. You called him to be Your chosen instrument, to carry Your name before the Gentiles, kings, and the children of Israel. (Acts 9:15)

Paul introduces himself to Your Church in Rome as a bondservant of Your Son, set apart for Your Gospel. Paul saw himself as a bondservant because he knew he was not his own but bought with a price. (1 Corinthians 6:19-20) Paul declares that Jesus is the promised Messiah from the line of David. (Isaiah 9:6-7, 11:1) Paul then boldly proclaims that Jesus is Your Son, for You raised Him from the dead by the power of Your Holy Spirit. Paul also claims that he has received grace and his apostleship from Jesus, whom he met traveling on the road to Damascus. (Acts 9-1-17) Paul then claims he was taught directly by Your Son for three years, just like the other apostles. (Galatians 1:11-18)

Father, we thank You for giving us a great example of a man who lives for one purpose, to declare Your name among the nations. May we learn from Paul what it means to be on mission for You. Give us eyes to see, ears to hear, and hearts that will obey so that we may join with all the saints in proclaiming Your Gospel as You commanded us to do in (Matthew 28:18-20). May we pray and live as You taught us in (Matthew 6:9-13). May Your kingdom come, and Your will be done, on earth as it is in heaven. Amen.

Questions for reflection and meditation:

1. Who appointed Paul and gave him the authority to proclaim the Gospel?
2. What is your definition of a saint?
3. Do you see yourself as a saint? If not how would you describe yourself?
4. God has made Paul alive and gave his life meaning and purpose. What gives your life meaning and purpose?

Prayer based on Romans 1:8-12

An example of the life and calling of every saint,
given by God through Paul!

Father, thank You for this long introduction from Paul (Verses 1-6). Open our eyes, ears, and minds so that we may see, hear, and understand Your rightful claim and calling on our lives.

It is paramount for Your Church in Rome and for all of Your saints to know Paul well so that all will take the words of Paul seriously. This introduction is the longest that Paul ever wrote to any Church, for he wrote this letter to Your Church in Rome before he ever visited them. We do not know how Your Church began or could begin in the capital city of a pagan empire. We do know how Your Church in Jerusalem began. (Acts chapter 2) We also know how Churches were planted and established by Paul and his companions through much persecution and sacrifice. (read Acts and the letters to the Churches) Paul is thankful for the Church in Rome. He praises God for them because they live holy lives that put God on display for all the world to see. (Verse 8) They are not just positionally holy (set apart like an inanimate object that is dedicated to Your service), but their holiness is lived out for the world to see. Paul rejoices over them and fervently prays for them without ceasing. (Verses 9-10) Paul loves the saints of God and longs to be with them. Paul prays for God to send him to Rome. You answered his prayer but not the way Paul expected. Paul never imagined that he would come to Rome in chains. (Acts chapter 27) Paul wanted to establish and strengthen the saints in Rome. He also wants to learn from them and be encouraged by their faith. (Verses 11-12)

Father, teach us to love and serve others with the same love and humility on display in the life of Paul. Amen.

Questions for reflection and meditation:

1. What made the Church in Rome so influential?
2. What makes a Church weak and ineffective?
3. Can anyone be saved without living a holy life? (Hebrews 12:14)
4. How did Paul, coming to Rome in chains, serve the purpose of God? (Philippians 1:12-14)

5. How often does God surprise you with His answers to your prayers?
6. How often do you pray, and what do you ask for from God?
7. How many examples of a saint does God give us in this passage?

Prayer based on Romans 1:13-15

A Word about our responsibilities and obligations to live righteously and sacrificially for God and others. (Matthew 25:40)

Father, we thank You for saving Paul and filling him with Your Spirit so that he can love others as You have loved him.

The love of Paul for the saints is clearly on display: Paul strongly desires to come to Rome to preach Your Gospel and to reap a harvest among them, but he must remain where he is, for he can not neglect the great harvest that You have given him. Paul sees himself under obligation, not only to the saints but to all people. Paul is aware of Your great love poured out on him and is compelled to pour himself out for others. (2 Corinthians 5:18)

Father, we praise You for the great example You give us through the apostle Paul. May we become more and more aware of the great love that You have poured out on us and feel the same obligation to pour ourselves out for others. Amen.

Questions for reflection and meditation:

1. Do you have a strong desire to remain where you are? Why or why not?
2. What motivates you to move on or to stay put?
3. Why did Paul feel obligated to everyone? (Verse 14)
4. What obligations are you currently bound to keep?
5. What benefits have you received from humbling yourself, praying, and seeking God for direction? (Psalm 25:9)
6. What losses have you incurred from trusting in your wisdom?
7. What makes it possible for you to rejoice in the trials and obligations that God has given you? (James 1:2)

Prayer based on Romans 1:16-17

A prayer for the righteous to live by faith in the Gospel.

Father, we praise You, for You have given Your children everything they need to live a holy life. (2 Peter 1:3)

Father, give us a fuller understanding of Your Gospel: more desire to proclaim it, more zeal for it, and more joy in living it. Only the Gospel has the power to open blind eyes and save us from Your wrath. May we know the Gospel well and preach it accurately and regularly to others and ourselves. Your kingdom has come! Jesus has defeated Satan – set us free from the power of sin – rose from the dead, and given all authority and power. May we not be rebels, but bow to Jesus – Who is seated at Your right hand and rightfully has all power and given all authority, overall. Lord, we praise You for taking the wrath that we deserve and providing the righteousness that we lack. Jesus made it possible for us to die to sin and live for righteousness. (1 Peter 2:24) May we not be ashamed of the Gospel, for it is the power of God, for those who are being saved. (1 Corinthians 1:18)

Father, may we accept the fact that we have no righteousness of our own and quit making excuses for our sin. First, show us Your holiness. Then we will see the seriousness of our sin and our desperate need for Your righteousness. (Isaiah 6:5) We praise You Father, for sending Your Son and providing the righteousness You require for all those You effectively call. (Isaiah 43:6-7) We praise You Jesus, for sending the Holy Spirit to live and reign in all who believe. (Romans 8:9) You do all this so everyone You declare righteous will live by faith and not by works. May the hearing and proclaiming of Your Gospel have its full effect and cause many to humble themselves under Your mighty hand and be exalted. (1 Peter 5:6) You tell us that the righteous shall live by faith. And so they will, by Your grace – for no one can stay Your hand or thwart Your purposes. (Isaiah 43:11-13) Father, may we trust in You to faithfully give us the grace we need every day to live by faith. Amen.

Questions for reflection and meditation:

1. How has your understanding or misunderstanding of the Gospel affected how you live and pray?

2. What must you do to live a holy life, distinct and separate from the world?
3. On a scale of 1 to 10 (1 being ashamed of the Gospel) and (10 being bold to proclaim it), Where do you stand?
4. What would it take to give you more confidence to proclaim the Gospel and live for God?
5. In who's righteousness are you trusting?
6. How is the righteousness of God on display in your life?

Prayer based on Romans 1:18-23

The just wrath of God poured out on all who dishonored Him.

Father, we thank You for Your kindness in giving such strong warnings to people who rebel against You.

We all have dishonored You by living for our glory. Instead of acknowledging You as our Master and serving You, we all became enslaved to lesser things and served them. We have put so many things before You, and just one single rebellion deserves death. In the light of how we have lived our lives, may we be amazed by Your incredible patience and the great mercy You have shown to rebellious sinners!

You tell us that Your wrath is against all ungodliness. Your righteous character must oppose the unrighteousness and ungodliness of all who suppress Your truth. Every time we fail to speak of Your glory, we suppress Your truth. We either proclaim Your Glory, or we do not. We are either living for You or against You. There is no middle ground. (Matthew 12:30) From the creation of the world, Your invisible attributes can be clearly seen and understood in the things that You have made. We are without excuse because You have spoken to us through Your creation. (Psalm 19:1-4) We all have chosen to rebel, and have rejected Your righteous rule over us – the result is that our foolish hearts are dark. We have become fools, for we choose to live for ourselves and do what is right in our own eyes. We have trusted in our own wisdom and rejected You and Your ways. You will not allow us to continue to worship creative things (idols) and deny Your righteous claims on our lives. We belong to You, for You have created us and redeemed us. (1 Corinthians 6:19-20)

Father, forgive us for having a highly inflated view of ourselves and a small view of You. Grant us repentance so we may die to ourselves and live for righteousness. (1 Peter 2:24) Amen.

Let us read and meditate on (Romans 3:10-18).

Questions for reflection and meditation:

1. In what ways have you suppressed the truth and fallen short of His glory?

2. How does living for our glory instead of His glory suppress His truth?

3. Can you give a testimony where you boldly chose to proclaim His truth when your flesh preferred to ignore it and suppress it?

4. What is your definition of an idol?

5. What idols do you have in your life, and how have you come to recognize them?

6. When you have time to think, where do your thoughts go?

Prayer based on Romans 1:24-32

God's righteously responds when we exchange the truth about Him for a lie.

Father, You are worthy of all honor and glory and praise. Give us a larger and more accurate view of You so we may honor You as we should and not be deceived or discouraged by circumstances. May we never run from You, but be quick to run to You and find grace and mercy in our time of need. (Hebrews 4:16) Teach us, lead us, and grow us up to be mature believers – who believe in Your power and authority over all things. May we live for one purpose, to exalt Your name by bearing witness to Your truth. You are worthy of all praise.

What we believe about God will determine how we interpret Scripture. And therefore, how we will live. Three times in this Scripture, a strong warning is given: to those who reject Your truth and choose to live a lie. You clearly tell us that You will give them up to their dishonorable passions. Does this mean that You are a passive God – who would choose to step out of the way, or are You an active God that is able and determined to bring about Your good purposes at any cost. (Isaiah 46:9-11, 1 Corinthians chapter 5, 1 Timothy 1:15) You continue to give a strong warning to those who create new orders and practices of their own and encourage others to do the same.

Father, forgive us for exchanging the worship of an idol that we have manufactured for the true worship of You. You tell us all idolatry will lead to immorality. Give us more desire to live holy lives before You and others: for the world will never be reached by a people who look more like the unsaved than the saved. (Ephesians 4:22-24) Amen.

Questions for reflection and meditation:

1. How does God respond when we suppress the truth and live a lie?
2. How have your beliefs or misbeliefs about God affected your response to situations?
3. Why does God give people over to their passions?
4. What are some of the ways that you have suppressed the truth about God?
5. What are the clear distinctions between people who belong to God and those who do not?

PRAYER BASED ON ROMANS 2:1-11

*The wrath of God is against all who will not follow Him
and His kindness toward those who do.*

Father, we praise You, for You are holy, righteous, and perfect in all Your ways. (Isaiah 55:8-9)

You warn us that Your righteous wrath will fall upon all who practice ungodliness. You specifically address those who practice self-righteousness and lovingly warn all that none will escape Your judgment. You also warned those who presume on Your riches and kindness and see no need to turn from their wicked ways, for they are confident that You will forgive them, regardless of how they live their lives. May we not forget that Your kindness is Your means to repentance. You clearly warn all those who will not repent. Their hard unrepentant hearts are storing up Your wrath for themselves. Because You are a Holy Righteous God, You will render each one according to their works. (Psalm 62:12, Revelation 20:12) Those who seek to honor You will receive eternal life, but those who are self-seeking and will not obey Your truth will experience Your fury and wrath. You promise tribulation and distress for everyone who does evil. First, the Jews and then the Greeks, for You will show no partiality because You are holy and just in all Your ways.

Father, we thank You for this call to be sober-minded. You know what we need. May we embrace Your word, delight in it, and live. Amen.

QUESTIONS FOR REFLECTION AND MEDITATION:

1. What is self-righteousness, and why will it incur the wrath of God?
2. What is the warning given to those who are self-seeking?
3. What is the reward promised to those who live under the authority of God?
4. Do you see the need for repentance, or are you presuming on the kindness of God?
5. What has led you to repentance?
6. Why does God not show any partiality?

Prayer based on Romans 2:12-24

*The Gentiles will perish without the law. The Jews are under the law.
All who boast about keeping the law will die in their sins.*

Father, We praise You for You are perfect in all Your ways.

You tell us there are two groups of people on the earth. The Gentiles are without the law, and the Jews are under the law. They will both perish because they are fallen, creatures. God has given the Gentiles a moral conscience, but they have failed to do what is right. You have given the Jews Your law, but they did not to keep it. All will die in their sins apart from a Savior. (John 8:24) Hearing is not enough and being sincere is not enough. To be saved we must keep and obey Your law perfectly. Your requirements are given in (Matthew 5:48). You know the secrets of men, and You are the final judge. Your judgment will be perfect. It will be in proportion to our rejection of Your revelation to us. We can never trust our ability to keep Your law or find confidence in our own wisdom. You do not want us to be blind guides or foolish instructors. In (verse 24), You tell us that the Jews dishonored Your name among the Gentiles, for they did not keep the law You gave them.

Father, may we never grieve You or dishonor You in any way. We need You, for only by Your Spirit living and reigning in us will we be able to keep Your law and bring glory to Your name. May we never forget who You are, what You have done for us, and our desperate need for Your sustaining grace. May we always look to You for Your wisdom and never trust in our own. (Proverbs 3:5-7) Amen.

Questions for reflection and meditation:

1. Are the Jews who have been given the law any better off than the Gentiles? Or are they worse off?
2. What was God's purpose for creating us and giving us the law?
3. What does it take to live a life that pleases and honors God?
4. How can anyone be saved from the wrath of God? (Luke 18:27)

Prayer based on Romans 2:25-29

*Circumcision is not outward and physical
but inward, a matter of the heart.*

Father, we thank You for circumcising hearts and giving Your children life in You.

You chose Israel and set them apart from all other nations. You gave them circumcision as a sign and seal of Your covenant with Abraham. (Genesis 17:9-14) Many Jews believed that they were saved from Your wrath because they were circumcised. You make it clear that we can not be saved from the wrath of God by any works of man. (Ephesians 2:8-9) You tell us that a circumcised Jew who does not obey You is unsaved, but an uncircumcised Gentile who is obedient is, saved. You tell us that salvation occurs when a heart is circumcised. A sure sign of salvation is love for You, displayed by obedience to Your Word. (John 10:27)

Father, make us diligent to confirm our calling and election. (2 Peter 1:10.) Amen.

Questions for reflection and meditation:

1. What has kept you from resting in the salvation of God?
2. What evidence do you have that your heart has been circumcised? Is it possible to know for sure? Why or why not? (1 John 5:13)

Let us read and meditate on Hebrews 4:1-13.

Prayer based on Romans 3:1-8

*God chose Abraham, made his descendants into a great nation,
and remained faithful to his people for over 4000 years, even
though they were unfaithful.*

Father, we praise You for choosing Israel. You made them into a great nation, supernaturally kept them, and blessed them to this very day.

You have made Yourself known to the Jews, so all can know You more by studying the history of the Jewish nation that You have preserved for us in the Old Testament. Your dealings with Your people can teach us volumes about Your great character. Paul speaks of the advantages of the Jews. You chose them and gave them Your Word. You delivered them and showed them Your wisdom and power. What a great privilege it was to be a Jew. The Gentiles never had that privilege. Being raised in a Jewish home would have advantages similar to being raised in a Christian home today. Having Christian parents, attending a Christian Church and Christian school, and reading your Bible may give you a great advantage, but none of those advantages can save you. Paul asks the Roman saints three questions. Can the unfaithfulness of man nullify the faithfulness of God? Paul emphatically answers, By no means! God's truth will always prevail, and all lying men will be defeated. If our unrighteousness can not nullify the faithfulness of God but can show God's righteousness, then is God unjust to pour out his wrath on us? Paul's answer is, Certainly Not! God is perfect in all His judgments! How can God punish us if our sin helps to display His righteousness? Paul tells us that to do evil so that grace may abound is foolish and twisted and worthy of condemnation. (Romans 6:1-2)

Father, we need You to keep us from gross errors in our thinking. We are so prone to wander and to think too highly of ourselves. May we grow in our desire to spend more time in Your Word and have our thoughts and ways conformed to Yours. May we be filled with the joy that only comes from knowing You and living for You. Keep us from every evil deed, as You have promised to do, for those who love You. (2 Timothy 4:18) Amen.

Let us meditate on 2 Chronicles 16:9.

QUESTIONS FOR REFLECTION AND MEDITATION:

1. Why is the existence of the Jewish race today so miraculous?
2. How does the study of the Old testament serve us today?
3. What advantages did the Jews have over the Gentiles?
4. If our unrighteousness cannot nullify the faithfulness of God and our sins are forgiven and paid for, then what motivation do you have to mortify sin?
5. What would it take in your life for you to walk in perfect harmony with God and avoid all evil?
6. Have you ever had any thoughts and concerns about avoiding even the appearance of evil?

Prayer based on Romans 3:9-20

*No one is righteous or justified by works. Every mouth stopped,
and the whole world will be held accountable to God.*

Father, thank You for revealing Yourself through Your Son and for giving us the knowledge of sin through the law.

(Verse 9) tells us that the Jews are no better off than the Gentiles, for all are under sin. (Verses 10-18) gives a clear and accurate account of all men and women. (Verse 19) tells us that everyone will be speechless in God's courtroom since all are guilty. (Job 4:4-5) You have revealed Yourself and showed us how we should live. We are without excuse. We will either accept Your Word and live under Your authority or reject Your Word and live as a rebel.

Father, we thank You for giving us Your law through Moses. You also made Yourself known to us through creation. Without knowing Your righteous ways, we would never see our sin and repent. Father, may we not be a people who believe that they are good: trust in their own goodness and wisdom, boldly do what is right in their own eyes, and have no fear of You. Open our eyes and hearts so that we may see our sin and know our total inability to live the life that You have called us to live. (a life that pleases and honors You) May we be a people who see their desperate need and regularly call upon Your name. (Romans 10:13) Thank You for giving life to those who accept Your Word and live under Your authority. Amen.

Questions for reflection and meditation:

1. In (verses 10 18), how does God's assessment of all men and women differ from yours?
2. What is your response to God's Holiness? (Isaiah 6:5)
3. What was God's purpose in giving the law?
4. Can anyone keep the law? Why or why not?
5. Is (Romans 10:13) a one-time act or a way of life?
6. What is the greatest need and hope for all men and women?
7. When you see people struggling, do you give them good advice or Good News?
8. When you encounter a situation, do you lean on your own abilities and understanding, or do you call upon the name of the Lord?

PRAYER BASED ON ROMANS 3:21-26

A holy and righteous God can not overlook sin.
Every sin must be paid in full by someone.

Father, We praise You for sending Your Son to die in our place and take the wrath that we deserve so that all who believe in Your Son can be justified (declared righteous).

You tell us that there is a righteousness, apart from the law: foretold by the Law and Your Prophets, and is now given to all believers through the life, death, and resurrection of Your Son. You tell us that all have sinned and will stand condemned in Your court unless justified by Your grace (unmerited favor). You tell us that it was Your perfect will and plan to crush Your Son. (Isaiah 53:10) (Verses 25 and 26) both tell us that Jesus's death was necessary to demonstrate Your righteousness, for a holy and just God can not allow any sin to go unpunished. All sin must be paid in full by someone. Jesus's death on the cross accomplished what nothing else could. (the complete satisfaction of Your righteous requirements) Jesus, who knew no sin, became sin for us and took the wrath that we deserved so that we may become the righteousness of God (2 Corinthians 5:21)

Father, we praise You, for You are righteous and the justifier of all who You have drawn to faith in Your Son! (John 6:44) Amen.

QUESTIONS FOR REFLECTION AND MEDITATION:

1. How can a holy and righteous God forgive sinners and remain righteous?
2. What attributes of God do you see on display in the crucifixion?
3. Why did Jesus die on the cross and how does His death change the way you live today?

A believer will always rejoice and be affected (cut to the heart) when they hear the preaching of the Gospel. And they will continue to grow into a deeper understanding of what transpired on the cross. (2 Corinthians 3:18)

Prayer based on Romans 3:27-31

*Since we can not keep the law, God took the initiative
to provide the righteousness required.*

Father, we praise You, for You have saved us and justified us by faith alone. Thank You for empower us to keep Your law by Your sustaining grace.

You want us to understand, fully appreciate, and never forget that You have freely justified the guilty, who believe in Your Son. What fellowship can light have with darkness? We all have chosen to live in darkness – we are guilty, without excuse, and deserved Your wrath. Because we have no righteousness of our own, You had to take the initiative to provide what we require through the death of Your Son. You tell us that there is no room for us to boast, for we did not contribute anything to our salvation. You have justified the circumcised by faith and the uncircumcised through faith. No one can be made right with You (saved) by keeping the law, but all believers keep Your law when You save them.

Father, we praise You for Your incredible gift. You have blessed us and equip us for good works. May we never forget that You are the source of everything we receive. May we see ourselves as an instrument in Your hand, set apart for good works, which You have prepared in advance for us to do. (Ephesians 2:10) Since You have called us, equipped us, and prepared the good works for us to do, where is their room for boasting? Father, May all our boasting be in You and not in ourselves so that Your power may be seen in our lives. (2 Corinthians 12:9-10) Amen.

QUESTIONS FOR REFLECTION AND MEDITATION:

1. Was it your decision to be saved, or was it God's?
2. If God choose not to elect you, how would that make Him unrighteous?
3. Can you give a reason for God's decision to save you?
4. When are you tempted to boast and about what?
5. What do you have that you have not received?
6. What is your motivation for keeping the law?
7. How are you serving as an instrument in God's hands?

Prayer based on Romans 4:1-8

God justifies the guilty because they believe.

Father, You are merciful. Although Abraham and David both sinned, You counted them righteous because they believed in You.

You counted Abraham righteous, apart from works. (Genesis 15:6) You tell us that one who works does not regard his wages as a gift but may boast about what they have earned. Your desire is for Your saints to understand Your ways so that they will not boast in their works but in Your work. You also give us an example from David – he describes the blessedness of a man to whom God imputes righteousness apart from works. (Psalm 32:1-2)

Father open our minds and our hearts so that we may receive Your truth and rejoice in who You are and what You have done. May we be a people who do not trust in our works but believes in You who justifies the ungodly. Amen.

Let us meditate on Psalm 32:1-11

Questions for reflection and meditation:

1. What problems will occur if we believe that we are saved by our works?
2. Why does God actively oppose the proud? (1 Peter 5:5b-6)
3. What needs to change in your life in order to experience more of the grace and power of God?

Prayer based on Romans 4:9-12

Abraham was declared righteous before he was circumcised.

Father, thank You for blessing Paul and giving him the strength to stand in the face of opposition and boldly proclaim Your truth.

The Jews believe that Abraham was a paragon of virtue, but Paul declared that he was a sinner saved by grace. You accepted Abraham as righteous, not because of anything he had done but because he believed in Your promise. Paul asks, is the blessedness that David spoke of in (Psalm 32) only for the circumcised Jew, or is it also for the uncircumcised Gentile? Paul tells us that Abraham was not made righteous by circumcision, for he was declared righteous 430 years before circumcision existed. Paul tells us that circumcision is an outward sign of the promise given to Abraham. Abraham was declared (counted)righteous because he believed in God. Abraham was the father of all who would believe in the promise, not only the circumcised Jew but also the uncircumcised Gentiles. All who walk in the faith that Abraham had before he was circumcised are the true descendants of Abraham.

Father, we need the faith that You freely gave to Abraham so that we may also walk in Your ways. May we know the joy that only comes from listening to You and striving to do Your will. May we look confidently to You for the guidance and strength we need to live a life that gives You all the Glory, Honor, and Praise, You so rightfully deserve. Amen.

Questions for reflection and meditation:

1. What motivates you to stand firm and proclaim God's truth?
2. Do you see a saint as a paragon of virtue or as a sinner saved and kept by grace?
3. How is it possible to experience the blessedness that David speaks of in Psalm 32?
4. When have you cried out to the Lord to teach you to pray, delight in His Word, give you more joy, wisdom, guidance, ...?

PRAYER BASED ON ROMANS 4:13-25

Good works done in our own strength will not save us.

Father, thank You for this example of Abraham's faith. You counted Abraham as righteous only because he believed in You. Open our minds and hearts so that we may receive this truth and rejoice more and more in Your salvation.

You tell us, the promise to Abraham did not come through the law but through the righteousness of faith. Your law demanded obedience and performance, impossible for us to do in our own strength. Your law brings wrath, but where there is no law, there is no transgression. So it was for Abraham. The promise given to Abraham transpired 430 years before Moses received the law for the Jews. Thank you for providing the righteousness that You require through Your Son to all who believe. You give life to the dead and calls into existence the things that are not, as though they were! You declare Your children righteous, not because of any works they had done but because they believe. Abraham believed against all hope that he would become the father of many nations, even though he was very old and his wife was barren for ninety years. Because Abraham believed in Your promise, he was counted righteous. The same is true for all who believe in the life, death, and resurrection of Your Son.

Father, may we gratefully and humbly believe that Your Sons finished work is sufficient for our salvation. Amen. (Mathew 5:20)

One wise man once said that an ounce of Faith gives more glory to God than a ton of works.

QUESTIONS FOR REFLECTION AND MEDITATION:

1. What good work can you trust in for salvation?
2. Do you believe and rejoice in the truth of (Romans 8:16-17)?
3. Scripture tell us that we are saved, by faith alone apart from works; then how can God rightly judge us by our works? (Revelation 20:12, Psalm 62:12, 1 Peter 1:17)
4. What circumstances in your life have made it difficult for you to believe in the promises of God?

5. What did Abraham do that caused him to grow strong in his faith. (verse 20)

6. What does it take for someone to be counted as righteous? (Verse 24-25)

Prayer based on Romans 5:1-5

The peace known by a saint is more than an internal feeling.

Father, We thank You for the peace You made through the sacrifice of Your Son.

After four chapters of thoroughly describing the war between God and man, Paul declares a peace that is more than an internal feeling but an external and objective condition that now exists between God and all believers. All hostility removed and peace given to those who believe in the work of Your Son – who became sin – and took the wrath that we deserved. (2 Corinthians 5:21) The curtain in the temple, which separated God from man and protected man from God, was torn in two. (Matthew 27:51, Hebrews 10:19-22)

Father, may all know and rejoice in the peace that came through the shedding of Your Son's blood. May we be confident and trust in Your righteous ways so we can embrace and rejoice in our sufferings, knowing that all things are from Your hand, and designed by You for Your glory and our good. (Romans 8:28) May we rejoice daily, for You have given all believers the light of the knowledge of Your glory through Your Holy Spirit. (2 Corinthians 4:6) We praise You for Your precious gift! Amen.

QUESTIONS FOR REFLECTION AND MEDITATION:

1. Why does Paul spend four chapters describing the problem of the fallen nature of man, before he presents the good news of the Gospel? Should this be the way you present the Gospel?
2. Is internal peace a sure sign of salvation? Why or why not?
3. What are the sure signs of salvation?
4. Why would a Christian rejoice in their sufferings?

Thoughts from a Martin Luther sermon:

It is possible to live in the flesh, experience peace in the world, and have no peace with God. The opposite is ironically true for a believer who lives in the Spirit. The world will persecute a believer, and a believer will have peace with God. (2 Timothy 3:12)

Prayer based on Romans 5:6-11

*God reconciles the ungodly and gives them the
ministry of reconciliation. (2 Corinthians 5:18)*

Father, we praise You and rejoice in who You are and what You have done. You chose to love us while we were Your enemies.

We were all without strength and enemies of You. To lay down Your life for a good man is one thing, but to lay down your life for Your enemy is quite a different thing. Lord, You have done what no other man could do! You took the initiative and reconciled the ungodly! You justified us by Your blood and took the wrath the we deserve! May we tremble as we think about where we would be apart from Your saving and sustaining grace. We are what we are by Your Grace!

Father, As we meditate on how You have shown such great love to such great sinners, may we be overwhelmed by Your grace: conformed to Your image, have a greater appreciation for what You have done, and a greater desire to serve You and the lost. Empower us to be as kind to the wicked as You are. (Luke 6:35-36) May we extend to others the mercy and grace You have extended to us. (2 Corinthians 5:18) And may our kindness be like Yours and lead others to repentance. May we glorify You in all that we do and say for You are Worthy!!! Amen.

QUESTIONS FOR REFLECTION AND MEDITATION:

1. Under what circumstances have you doubted the love of God for you?
2. Are your beliefs shaped by the Word of God or buy something else.
3. Where do you receive good counseling and teaching?
4. How often do you rejoice in and testify to the goodness of God in your life? (Psalm 145:4-6)
5. If someone asks you, what good has God done for you, what would you tell them?
6. When was the last time you showed kindness to an enemy?

Prayer based on Romans 5:12-21

The act of one man brought judgement and death to all.
One righteous act justified and gave life to all who believed.

Father, we praise You, for there is no life apart from You. (Psalm 16:2, Psalm 73:25)

You tell us that sin entered the world through the disobedience of one man, and death spread through sin to all men – for all have sinned and fallen short of the glory of God. (Romans 3:23) The disobedience of one man led to a loss of peace with You. Only through the perfect obedience of one man can peace be restored. (Luke 2:13-14) Your judgment followed the one trespass of Adam and brought condemnation to all but the free gift through the perfect obedience of Your Son followed many trespasses and brought justification and life to all who believe. You gave us the law through Moses to increase our awareness of sins. You knew that giving us the law would not make us righteous but would cause transgressions to increase. You did this so that the increase of disobedience would show the power of Your abounding grace. (Romans 5:6) We are either in Adam or in Christ. We were born in Adam and will die in sin unless we are born again and made alive in Christ for now and forever more. (John 3:3)

Father, We praise You, for You have destroyed the works of the devil. Only You can break the bondage of sin and set us free. The one Your Son sets free is free indeed! (John 8:36) Amen.

Questions for reflection and meditation:

1. In what way were Adam and Jesus the same?
2. What are the differences between Adam and Jesus?
3. What did the giving of the law accomplish?
4. What did Jesus accomplish through his death on the cross?
5. What are the consequences of being born in Adam and the rewards of being born again in Jesus?

PRAYER BASED ON ROMANS 6:1-14

We can be freed from the bondage of sin, and united
with Him in a resurrection like His.

Father, We praise You for Your wisdom and power. You sent Your Son to die the death we deserved so we may be set free to walk in the newness of life in harmony with You.

We need You, for we have a fallen nature; we can be so foolish in our ways, flawed in our reasoning, and so unloving in our actions. You remind us that all who live in union with Christ have died to sin. You baptized them into Christ through Your Spirit. If this is so, how can we continue to live in sin? If we are dead to our sin, how can sin have power over us? You tell us that no one can serve two masters he will love one and hate the other. (Matthew 6:24) If Jesus becomes your Master, you can no longer be in bondage to sin. Sin has no dominion over those who have died to sin and are living for You! (1 Peter 2:24) Believers, become new creatures enslaved to righteousness and no longer enslaved to sin. We are free to walk joyfully in harmony with You in the newness of life! All this is possible because Your Son died in our place – You raised Him from the dead – and gave Him dominion over all things! (Ephesians 1:19-23) Therefore, we can consider ourselves dead to sin and alive to You. (Verse 11) You have delivered us from death to life and made us instruments of righteousness! Even when we fall, we can rejoice in knowing this truth. Those who belong to You will struggle with sin. There is a greater struggle for a believer than an unbeliever, for an unbeliever does not struggle with something they love. You may rightly see that you are tightly held captive by sin, and are too weak to break free, for you have tried and failed to escape many times. The harder you struggle, the more you will weaken, until all hope of victory is lost. We need our downtrodden eyes lifted to see You and Your great love for us – no matter how far we have fallen. (Romans 5:6-8, Psalm 34:18) You have the power to break the bondage of sin. (John 10:10) Life with You is possible and far better than any life with sin. (Psalm 63:3, Psalm 84:10) Mortifying sin is well worth the effort, for no pleasure on this earth can compare with the joy of knowing You. As we grow in our love for You, we will grow in our hatred for sin – for all sin separates us from the One we love.

Father, give us the faith to believe that You have the power and the desire to deliver all who cry out to You. (Luke 12:32) You have promised that sin will no longer have dominion over those who have died to it. May we be quick to believe Your promise and run to You and receive Your amazing grace. Amen.

QUESTIONS FOR REFLECTION AND MEDITATION:

1. Why is it impossible for a believer to continue to live in unrepentant sin? (1 John 3:8-9)
2. How do you respond to sin in your life?
3. What does it mean, in (verse 11), to consider yourself dead to sin and alive to God? (Romans 14:7-8)
4. What makes the struggle with sin greater for a believer than an unbeliever?
5. Compare the consequences of living for sin, with the benefits of living for God? (Romans 8:5-6)
6. Are you overwhelmed by sin or are you overwhelmed by the grace of God? (1 John 4:4)

Prayer based on Romans 6:15-23

*To be enslaved to sin is foolish when you could give up
and live enslaved to righteousness.*

Father, we praise You, for we see, through the example of Your servant Paul, that You are a thorough and patient teacher.

You know we are weak and easily blinded by sin. We are slow to understand, and therefore we improperly apply Your truth. In (verses 1-14), You teach us good theology. You tell us, who You are, what You have done, and how we should respond to Your grace. In (verses 15-23), You repeat Your teaching to the Romans, using the very appropriate illustration of slavery. The Romans could easily understand this illustration because the majority of them lived under a master. Father, give us ears and humble, teachable hearts, open to receive Your teachings. Once again, You tell us If we surrender to anything, we will become enslaved to the thing we obey. Obeying sin will lead to death, but obedience to You will always lead to righteousness. A believer is enslaved to Your righteousness and set free from the bondage of sin. Any unrepentant sinner who continues to sin is deceived and will become enslaved to sin.

Father, keep us from all deception. May we never forget that the wage of sin is death, but Your free gift is eternal life in Christ. Amen.

QUESTIONS FOR REFLECTION AND MEDITATION:

1.   What does chapter 6 tell you about the attributes of God?
2.   What does it mean to be enslaved to sin or God?
3.   How is the grace of God working and on display in your life?
4.   What makes a believer distinctly different from an unbeliever?
5.   Why is surrender so hard and an absolute requirement for us to live for God?
6.   What is so wrong and dangerous about believing that the grace of God gives us the freedom to sin?

Prayer based on Romans 7:1-6

Freedom comes from knowing God through death.

Father, We praise You, for You are good in all that You do. All of Your ways are perfect. Everything You give is for our good and equips us to live for Your Glory. (Psalm 84:11) We need You to open our minds and hearts so our fallen intellects can understand Your ways.

You tell us that the law has dominion over a man only as long as he lives. We can not be righteous by keeping the law – the law can only make us aware of our sins and will bring us into bondage if we try to keep the law in our own strength. Our only escape is death. We must die, to the law, if we are to be free of its bondage and be able to give ourselves to another. You give us the analogy of marriage to illustrate this principle. A man is bound to his wife as long as she lives, but when she dies, he is free to give himself to another – so it is with us. We must die, to the law, if we are to be free from its bondage and live for another. How can we be free from the things that hold us in captivity? We need an almighty deliverer to save us and to keep us from all evil.

Father, we must cry out to You for the strength we need to live the life that You have called us to live. May we call upon Your name and experience the joy and the victory that comes from knowing You through death. Amen.

Let us read and meditate on Romans 6:5-11.

Questions for reflection and meditation:

1. Why do we have to be continually reminded that only God is good?
2. How are you tempted to wander from God?
3. Where is your greatest joy found?
4. What have you died to so you could live for something else?
5. Can you give a testimony of how you experience joy through death?

Prayer based on Romans 7:7-13

The law which promises life is good and brings death to all.

Father, we praise You for making us aware of the law and then providing the righteousness we need to keep the law!

You have told us, through the apostle Paul, that sin increased through the giving of the law. The law can not bring life but will bring death and condemnation for those who strive to be made righteous by keeping the law. Paul then ask the question, Is the law sin? And then quickly answers, By no means! He tells us that the law is good, and the problem is not with the law but with us. The law is good because it reveals our sin. Without seeing our disobedience, we would never see our desperate need for repentance, and without repentance, we will all die in our sins, without ever knowing You and Your salvation. (Matthew 7:23) We thank You for giving us the law and sending Your Son who willingly took the wrath that we deserved so we may die to ourselves and live for righteousness. (2 Corinthians 5:21)

Father, may we not be deceived and held captive by sin. May we be captivated by Your love for us and be set free to live for Your pleasure and purpose. Amen.

QUESTIONS FOR REFLECTION AND MEDITATION:

1. What was the purpose of God in giving us the law?
2. Why will all who strive to be righteous by keeping the law fail?
3. What is your biggest problem? And your greatest need?
4. Why is humility necessary for salvation? (Matthew 5:3, Luke 18:11-14)
5. How has sin deceived You?
6. How have you been delivered from sin?

PRAYER BASED ON ROMANS 7:14-25

The struggles and cries of every true believer:

Father, You know our struggles will increase when we have a small view of You and a highly inflated view of ourselves. We praise You and thank You for Your kindness in giving us this description of a saint through the testimony of Paul.

First and foremost, Paul tells us that a saint must be aware of their sinful nature. (Verse 14) Paul saw himself correctly and never forgot that he is the chief of all sinners. (1 Timothy 1:15) Paul then describes the war that goes on in the life of every believer. There is a war between the flesh and the Spirit. This war begins when the Holy Spirit takes up residence in a believer. Since every believer has the Holy Spirit living in them (Romans 8:9), all believers will be aware of their sinful nature. (Verse 18) Like Isaiah, we will all become aware of our sin in the light of God's presence. (Isaiah 6:5, Romans 4:6) Paul knows the life he is called to live and is aware of his total inability to live it. (Verse 19) Paul, just like all believers, will delight in Your law. (Verse 22, Psalm 119:47-48) Paul, like all believers, will always cry out for deliverance when tempted. (Verses 24-25, Romans 10:13)

Father give us a mind and a heart that is open to Your teaching and guidance? Amen

QUESTIONS FOR REFLECTION AND MEDITATION:

1. Why is a big picture of God and an accurate view of self necessary for fruitful ministry?
2. Who is the greatest sinner that you know?
3. How many descriptions of a saint does God give us in this passage?
4. How do you relate to the struggles Paul had as a believer?
5. What does it take to be an effective servant of God?
6. What drives you to your knees in prayer?
7. How often do you cry out for deliverance when you are tempted or for forgiveness when you sin?
8. Is there a war going on in your life? If so, How would you describe it? When did the struggle begin?
9. Are you growing in your prayer life and your love for God? Why or why not? (Proverbs 4:18)

Prayer based on Romans 8:1-11

*The believer's glorious state is proclaimed and contrasted
with the unbeliever's dangerous and pitiful state.*

Father, we praise You for You have done what the law, weakened by our flesh, could never do. You sent Your Son to live the life we could never live and to die the death that we deserved to die in order to fulfill the righteous requirements of Your law. We praise and thank You, for You have freed us from the law of sin and death. There is no condemnation for those redeemed by Your blood. Your Son offered a complete atonement, and Your Justice does not require a second punishment. We are free to walk in harmony with You through the power of Your Holy Spirit that lives and reigns in all who believe. For all this we praise You!

You contrast the difference between following the flesh and following the Spirit. You tell us that following the desires of the flesh will lead to death, but following the Spirit will lead to life and peace. Those who set their minds on the flesh will live a life driven by their passions and desires. You tell us that a mind fixed on the flesh is hostile to You, will not submit to You, and can not please You. All who call upon Your name will receive Your Holy Spirit, who will convict them, and guide them into Your Truth. (John 16:8-15) You give Your children new desires and cause them to turn from evil and walk in Your ways. (Ezekiel 36 25-27) Everyday we will make hundreds of decisions. We will either follow our flesh or follow Your Spirit. What we experience in the future will depend upon what we fix our minds and affections on today.

Father give us the wisdom and the power we need to make good choices. May we end all our days rejoicing in serving You and praising You for the glorious freedom made possible through Your Son. (John 8:36) Amen.

Questions for reflection and meditation:

1. Why did Jesus have to die on the cross?
2. What is the difference between conviction and condemnation?
3. How do you set your daily priorities?
4. What does it require for you to walk in harmony with God?

5. Are your days filled more with sowing to the Spirit or sowing to the flesh?

6. Describe your most joy-filled days? What would have to change for you to have more of them?

Prayer based on Romans 8:12-18

The life of a new creature in Christ compared with the old life in Adam.

Father, we praise You for the order, clarity, consistency, and the sufficiency of Your Word.

You remind us again that the pursuit of our fleshly desires leads to death, and that the pursuit of holiness will lead to life. Those who are led by the Spirit are new creatures with new desires. They love the things You love, and they hate the things You hate. Saints are aware of their sinful nature, which wars against Your Spirit that lives in them. They will choose to die to their sinful passions in order to live for Your pleasure and glory. You tell us those born again are no longer held in bondage to the devil but have a new Master. They will be joyful bondservants, for they love You more than life itself. (Psalm 63:3) You have adopted them, and they are Your children through a new birth. As Your children, they rest secure in You and know they are heirs of their Father and fellow heirs with Your Son. They desire to be united with Your Son in His suffering and raised with Him in glory (Romans 8:17)

Father, You offer us a new identity in You, free of all anxiety and bondage. May we, by the power of Your Spirit living in us, no longer live in fear but rejoice in a new relationship with You. You tell us through the apostle Paul that the sufferings of this present time can not compare to the glory revealed to those who believe. (Verse 18)

Father, we confess that our thoughts are often too small and self-centered. Give us an eternal perspective so we may embrace our sufferings, knowing that all things are from Your hand and for Your glory. May we never forget that only those who suffer for Your glory will reign with You forever. (Revelation 3:21, Hebrews 10:39) Amen.

Not grace to bar what is not bliss, nor flight from all distress, but this: It's Grace that orders are trouble and pain, and then, in the darkness, is there to sustain. John Piper 1966.

Questions for reflection and meditation:

1. How has the pursuit of fleshly desires led you to death?

2. How have you been convinced that the pursuit of holiness is worth it?

3. When it comes to living the Christian life, Why is it necessary to suffer? (2 Timothy 3:2)

4. How many characteristics of a saint are given here in this passage?

5. What did you need to lose to gain Christ? (Luke 14:33)

6. Is it possible to give up everything for Christ and not gain more than you have given up. Why or why not? (Luke 18 28-30, 1 Corinthians 13:3)

7. What are the benefits of having an eternal perspective?

8. Why is it necessary to suffer with Him to be glorified with Him? (Verse 17b)

9. Which fruits of the Spirit, given in (Galatians 5:22-23), do you need to grow in the most?

PRAYER BASED ON ROMANS 8:19-25

Considering the weight of our sin and the glory of God.

Father, we praise You for all Your great and glorious promises. You will liberate all creation from its bondage to decay. You will lift the curse and reveal Your children in glory on that final DAY. All will stand before Your judgment and receive what they are due. (2 Corinthians 5:10) At that time, You will remove all sin from those who have lived for You, and they will be spotless and blameless when they see You face to face. They will all dwell with You forever in a new heaven and a new earth. (Revelation 21:1-4) For all this we praise You!

Father, we are such a needy people. We have a shallow understanding of our current condition and little faith and hope in Your future promises. Forgive us, Lord, when our eyes are fixed on the world and not on You. Have mercy on us and give us open ears and minds so we may hear, understand, and conform to Your ways. Help us to grasp the disastrous consequences of the fall of Adam and the reasons for our groaning. When Adam sinned, You rightfully subjected all creation to frustration and futility. May we see how and why the world has fallen into disorder. You tell us that all creation waits with eager longing for the revealing of the sons of God (all who are led, by Your Spirit), (Verse 19) May we come to understand and embrace the fact that we are pilgrims and aliens in this world. (1 Peter 2:11) All believers, since the fall of Adam, have been groaning. (Verses 23-24) May we know that we were made for something greater than this world and look forward to a permanent home with You. (Hebrews 11:13-16) May we groan and long for the DAY when our flesh will no longer war against Your Spirit, and we stand in Your presence face to face without sin. (1 John 3:2)

Father, we pray for all who live apart from You, without hope. We thank You for giving hope to Your children as they eagerly await the redemption of their bodies. You have given them the first fruits of the Spirit as a deposit and guarantee of what is to come. (2 Corinthians 1:21-22) May are eyes not be fixed on this world but fixed on You. Give us the wisdom and strength we need to stand confident in You for You will do all that You say You will do. (Isaiah 46:9-10) May Your kingdom come, and Your will be done on Earth as it is in heaven! Amen.

The Bible divides people into two groups. (sheep and goats, wheat and tares, those who are for him and those who are against him) There is no middle, apathetic group. There are those who love God and live to proclaim His truth and those who hate God and suppress His truth.

Questions for reflection and meditation:

1. Are you a sheep or a goat?
2. In what ways have you been conformed to the Word of God or to the ways of the world?
3. Are you at home in this world, or do you long for another?
4. Are you longing to see Jesus face to face? Why or why not?
5. How often do you pray for His kingdom to come? His will to be done in your life, your Church, and in His world?

PRAYER BASED ON ROMANS 8:26-30

*An array of benefits for those who love God
and are called, justified, and glorified.*

Father, we praise You for You know all things, including all our weaknesses – and yet You love us and desire to enable us to live a holy life through the power of Your Holy Spirit.

Apart from You, we can not love You as we should: we can not worship You as we should, and we can not pray as we should. (John 15.5) You hear all the prayers and groans of Your children. When they are confused and broken and do not understand Your will, Your Spirit will intercede for them with groans that are too deep for words! Father, we thank You for giving us an advocate who lives forever and will faithfully intercede for Your children! (Hebrews 7:25, 1 John 2:1) Therefore, You tell us to draw near to the throne of grace and receive mercy in our time of need. (Hebrews 4:14-16) You tell us that You work all things to the good, for those You called according to Your purpose. You call us to conform to the image of Your Son, who was the firstborn of many brethren. It is Your will to do so. (1 Thessalonians 4:3), You call Your children, justify them (declare them not guilty), and glorify them! (Verse 30)

Father, we praise You, for all things are possible for You. (Mark 10:27, Luke 1:37) You will do all You purpose to do! (Isaiah 46:9-11, Job 42:2)

Father, may we all believe that You are who You say You are so that we may trust and rest in Your absolute power and goodness. Amen.

QUESTIONS FOR REFLECTION AND MEDITATION:

1. Is there anything that God does not know about you? (Psalm 139:1-6)
2. Do you find it astonishing that God knows so much about you and yet still loves you?
3. What things have you done that are impossible to do in your own strength?
4. Does God hear all of your prayers? Why or why not?

5. Do you believe that God is interceding for you, even when you are unfaithful, confused, broken, and do not know how to pray? Why or why not?
6. Are you quick to run to the throne of grace in your time of need, or do you run to something else?
7. How are you being spent for Him, and how is He conforming you to His image?
8. How are you more like Him today than you were last week, last month, or last year? (Proverbs 4:18)
9. How is your faith in God on display in your life?

PRAYER BASED ON ROMANS 8:31-37

Confident in the love of God and His faithful provisions.

Father, we praise You and thank You for all You have done and all You will do for Your children.

You tell us that those You called You also justified, and those You justified You also glorified. (Verse 30) You did not spare Your own Son but gave Him up for us all. What can we say in response to Your actions? If You have given up Your Son for Your children, You surely, will not withhold any good thing from them! (Psalm 84:11) Father, may we never doubt Your love and power. Your powerful love for us should compel us to love our enemies so that we can be more than conquerors. A conqueror only defeats their enemy, but the power of Your love can overcome our enemies and cause them to join us in Your mission.

Father may we stand with confidence in You – knowing that nothing can separate us from Your love. (Verses 38-39) Amen.

QUESTIONS FOR REFLECTION AND MEDITATION:

1. If someone were to ask you how do you know that God loves you, what would you tell them?
2. How have you responded when God has withheld something from you? (Psalm 84:11)
3. How do you respond to those who oppose you?
4. How can you be more than a conqueror through God who loves you? (Verse 37)
5. Do you believe that God is for you and that nothing can separate you from the love of God in Christ Jesus? Why or why not?

PRAYER BASED ON ROMANS 9:1-6

God faithfully pursues rebels who insist on doing
evil and delights when we do the same.

Father, You tell us that You take no pleasure in the death of a wicked. Your desire is for the wicked to turn from evil and have life in You. (Ezekiel 33:11) We praise You for Your great love for Your enemies. Thank You for giving us this example of the love of Paul for the lost.

In (verses 2-3), You show us the heart of Paul. He had great sorrow and unceasing anguish over his Jewish kinsman who had rejected Your salvation. Paul saw himself as the least of the apostles and the foremost of all sinners. (1 Corinthians 15:9, 1 Timothy 1:15-16) Because Paul knew that he was a great sinner, he was aware of Your great power and love. Therefore, he had a strong desire for his kinsman to know You as he does. Paul was willing to pay any price to see his kinsmen saved from Your wrath. Paul, because of his union, with Christ, was a man of sorrows and acquainted with grief. When Your Son was on this earth, He was known as a Man of Sorrows and acquainted with grief. (Isaiah 53:3) He wept over Jerusalem. (Matthew 23:37) He also wept over the Jews for their lack of faith at the death of Lazarus. (John 11:35-37) Paul goes on to tell us of the glorious inheritance of the Jews. You chose them and gave them the covenants, the Books of the Law, the Prophets, the worship, and the promises. Lastly, You chose to reveal Yourself, through the incarnation of Your Son, in Jewish flesh. Jesus would come and be the promise Messiah (the Son of David) – who would be King overall and would reign forever and ever – as foretold by the profit Isaiah over 600 years before the birth of Christ. (Isaiah 9:6-7) Paul proclaims the majority of Israel (the descendants of Jacob) rejected Christ. (Genesis 32:28) Paul then assures us that the Word of God did not fail, for all who descended from Israel (Jacob) do not belong to Israel. No one will be saved from Your wrath by their heritage or any work of man.

Father, Keep us from downplaying the miracle You do in the conversion of every believer. Make us see how unlovable we are so that we may experience more of Your love and know Your power to save even the most unregenerate sinner. (Romans 5:8) You remind us that those who know how much they are loved and forgiven will love and forgive much. (Luke 7:47) Open our eyes to see how much we are loved and forgiven: so we may have more compassion for those who are perishing, more desire to see them saved, and more faith to believe in the power of the Gospel to change lives. May we never forget that Satan has blinded the eyes of all who are perishing. (2 Corinthians 4:3-4) Father, give us more insight and compassion for the lost and make us fishers of men. (Matthew 4:19) Amen.

QUESTIONS FOR REFLECTION AND MEDITATION:

1. Why did Paul have great sorrow and unceasing anguish for unbelievers? (Verse 1)
2. Why is your burden for the lost so great or so small?
3. What advantages did the Jews have over the Gentiles?
4. How have you come to salvation, or what keeps you from being saved?
5. How can sinful man be made right with a Righteous God?
6. How can one become sorrowful, aquatinted with grief, and filled with joy?

Prayer based on Romans 9:7-13

God is independent, powerful, wise, and perfect in all his ways. He has the right and the power to carry out all of His plans in whatever way He chooses. His ways and timing are perfect!

Father, we praise You and thank You for who You are and what You have done. Open our minds and hearts and give us a bigger more accurate picture of You.

You tell us that not every descendant of Abraham is a child of the are promise and counted as offspring. In (Verse 8), You speak of children of the flesh and children of the promise. The only children counted as offspring are the children of the promised. You promised Abraham that his heir would be his very own son. (Genesis 15:4) Abraham and Sarah did not wait on Your promise. (Genesis Chapter 16) Therefore, Abraham had two sons, one born to Hagar (Ishmael) and the promised child born to Sarah (Isaac). Abraham loved Ishmael and wanted him to live before You, but You said No to Abraham. You told him that Sarah, your wife, will bear you a son, and you shall call him Isaac. You then proclaimed that You would establish Your covenant with Isaac. (Genesis 17:18-19,21) You answered the prayer of Abraham to bless Ishmael and promised Abraham that You would make the descendants of Ishmael into a great nation. (Genesis 17:20) You tells us more about the birth of Isaac and Your dealings with Hagar and Ishmael in (Genesis 21:1-21) Isaac was 40 years old when he married Rebecca. You opened her womb, and she conceived and bore two sons, Esau and Jacob. You told Rebecca there were two nations in her womb, they would be divided people, and the older would serve the younger. (Genesis 25:19-23. You chose Jacob over Esau before they were born to show that Your choice was not because of any works done in the flesh. Jacob lived a life of deception until You changed him and his name, from Jacob the deceiver to Israel Your servant. (Genesis 32:22-30, 35:1-15) You exercised Your freedom, wisdom, and power to do all You please. Your desire is to show Yourself to all nations. Therefore, You elected Jacob and then fulfilled Your purpose through him even though Jacob was a deceiver. Your ways are great and deserve all our praise!

Father nothing is too hard for You! Only You can lead us out of death and into new life. We need You! We are lost unless You reveal Yourself to us. Show us Your great ways so we may live all our days in humble adoration of You. Amen.

QUESTIONS FOR REFLECTION AND MEDITATION:

1. What does (verse 6) mean when it says not all who are descended from Israel belong to Israel?
2. What is required for someone to become a child of the promise?
3. What blessings come from praying and waiting on God the Father overall?
4. What consequences come when we foolishly fail to pray and act in our own wisdom?
5. How can God know and be sure of the outcome of every event?
6. How does the dramatic conversion of Jacob give you hope?

Prayer based on Romans 9:14-18

God is independent – He will carry out his plans according to
His perfect will – He can not be swayed or stopped.

Father, we praise You for You are perfect in all of Your ways. You have never done anything wrong. You are good and just in all You decree.

You told Moses that You show mercy on whom You choose and compassion on whom You choose. (Exodus 33:19) You have the freedom and power to do whatever You decide to do. Your actions can not be controlled by anyone or anything for You act for Your pleasure and Your glory. (Isaiah 46:9-11, Ephesians 1:3-10) Help us to understand that everything You do is for Your glory and our good. You raised Pharaoh up and hardened his heart so that Your power may be seen and proclaimed. Through the 10 plagues You showed Your power over every god the Egyptians worshiped. Egypt was in ruin, and You delivered Your people out of the hand of Pharaoh. In (Verse 14), Paul asks is God unjust? Paul answers, By no means! Exodus 8:32 and six other verses tell us that Pharaoh hardened his own heart. You did not cause Pharaoh to do anything that his heart did not desire to do. It was amazing how hard the heart of Pharaoh was, for even after the 10 plagues which left Egypt in ruin, he would not repent. He decided to set out after the Israelites and recapture them. You parted the Red Sea, deliver Your people, and then utterly destroy Pharaoh and his army. We praise You, for You are just in all Your ways! You show Your mercy on whomever You will and You hardened whomever You will. May we never call You unjust and foolishly oppose You in any way. Some say You are unjust to condemn sinners and others say You are unjust when You choose to save sinners. Have mercy on us, Lord, and be patient with us, for we are so slow to comprehend and accept Your independence and great worth. You have told us that You have come so that we may have life and have it abundantly.

Father, show us how to live the abundant life You generously give to all those who belong to You. (John 10:10) Keep us from chasing after the world which will never satisfy. Show us the true joy that can only be known when we live for You. Come Holy Spirit, convict us, empty us, and fill us, so that our lives may be a passionate pursuit of Your glory, and be filled with everlasting joy and lacking no good thing! Amen.

QUESTIONS FOR REFLECTION AND MEDITATION:

1. When have you been tempted to question God's ways or His commandments?
2. Why is it so difficult for us to comprehend God's independence and His self exaltation?
3. Why is it good for the Holy One to act for his pleasure and Glory And so wrong for us to do so?
4. Why does God want His glory seen and his people to worship him?
5. What is the best gift that God can give you?
6. How would you describe the abundant Life in Christ? Why do you want it? What must you give up to have it? (Luke 14:33)

PRAYER BASED ON ROMANS 9:19-29

God is sovereign over ALL and knows every creature and every event.
God is independent and free to act according to His purpose and pleasure.
(Ephesians 1:5-6)

Father, You are Lord over All. May we rest in Your Lordship?

You teach us that You are Lord over all. You are aware and take full responsibility for everything that happens. You made the deaf and the blind. (Exodus 4:11) You form the light and create darkness. You make well-being and create calamity. (Isaiah 45:7) Does disaster come unless the Lord has done it? (Amos 3:6) You tell us that not even a sparrow falls from a tree apart from You. (Matthew 10:29) You know every event and every creature, past, present, and future. You hem us in, are acquainted with all our ways, and even know what we will speak before it is on tongue. (Psalm 139:3-6) Your Word clearly teaches Your absolute sovereignty over all things. It also teaches that we are responsible and accountable for our actions. We are to lay aside every sin and run a good race. (Hebrews 12:1-2) We are to strive to make our calling an election sure. (2 Peter 1:10) We are to train ourselves for godliness. (1 Timothy 4:7) We are to walk in a manner that is worthy of Your calling. (Ephesians 4:1) We are to choose this day whom we will serve. (Joshua 24:15) We are to test and discern the will of the Father, and we are not to conform to this world. (Romans 12:2) Your absolute sovereignty and our responsibility to live a holy life (distinct and separate) are both clearly taught in Your Word. May we rest in Your sovereignty and accept our responsibilities. In (verse 19), Paul anticipates a question that his readers could ask. If the Father failed to draw us to Himself (John 6:44), How can He hold us responsible? Paul answers the objection by reminding us of the sovereignty of God. Does not the Potter have the right to do whatever he wishes with the clay that belongs to Him? Paul asks them, What if God chooses to endured with much patience the dishonorable vessels (His vessels of wrath) so that the riches of His glory might be made known to His vessels of Mercy. Would that make God unjust? (versus 22-23) In (Verse 24), Paul proclaims that You have not only called the Jews but also the Gentiles to be Your people. Paul then gives us an example from the prophet Hosea. Paul tells us that although the number of the sons of Israel will be vast, only a remnant will call upon His name and believe. (Isaiah 10:21-22)

Paul then proclaims if God did not choose some, we would all be like Sodom and Gomorrah.

Father, we have all rebelled against You and have been objects of Your wrath. We praise You for Your kindness, patience, and mercy. We need You Lord, to draw us to Yourself so that we may come to rejoice in Your redemption. No one can come to me unless the Father draws them. (John 6:44) May we strive with all the strength that You provide so that we may live the life of holiness that You have called us to live. (Colossians 1:29) Amen.

QUESTIONS FOR REFLECTION AND MEDITATION:

1.   God can and will carry out His purposes, with or without us. Who does God want to include in what He is doing and Why?
2.   Why will God hold us accountable if we do not participate in His work?
3.   What does it take to grow in holiness?
4.   Do you prefer to be left alone to make your own choices? Why or why not?
5.   What does God owe you? What do you owe Him?
6.   Is God unjust when He opposes some and gives grace to others?
7.   Why does God resist the works of the proud and give grace to the humble?
8.   Have you ever been thankful to God for keeping you from your ways and showing you His ways?

PRAYER BASED ON ROMANS 9:30-10:4

*The Jews who pursued righteousness through keeping the law did not
obtain it – the Gentiles who were apart from the law did obtain it.*

Father, we thank You for the gift of Your righteousness through Your
Son to all who believe.

In Romans chapter 9, You tell us how You worked in the past. We praise
You for You were faithful to Abraham and the descendants of Jacob,
even though the vast majority rejected Your righteousness and pursued
their own through the works of the law. Starting in (verse 9:30) and
continuing through (chapter 10), You tell us about Your work and the
response of Your people in the first century. The Gentiles, who did not
have the law, received the righteousness provided by Your Son through
Faith. The descendants of Jacob who pursued righteousness through
keeping the law never attained it. Jesus became a stumbling stone and a
rock of offense to them. The Jews had a zeal for God but were ignorant
of Your righteousness and sought to establish their own. They did not
realize that Your Son was the fulfillment of the law. (Matthew 5:17-20)

Father, may we have ears to hear, eyes to see, and minds that will admit
our need for a righteousness that is not our own. May we respond by
submitting to You and receiving Your imputed righteousness provided
through Your Son. Amen.

QUESTIONS FOR REFLECTION AND MEDITATION:

1. How did the Gentiles receive Your righteousness, and why did
    the Jews fail to receive it?
2. Why is Jesus a stumbling stone and an offence to those who
    pursue their own righteousness?
3. Although Paul believed in the absolute sovereignty of God, it
    did not inhibit him from praying fervently for the salvation of
    the Jews. (Romans 10:1) How is that possible?
4. What does Paul mean when he says that the Jews have a zeal
    for God, but not according to knowledge?
5. What does it mean for Jesus to be the end of the Law for
    everyone who believes?

PRAYER BASED ON ROMANS 10:5-13

*Righteousness, based on faith, is available to
all who believe and call upon the Lord.*

Father, we praise You for making it possible for us to have life in You, both now and for all eternity.

You have made Your will perfectly clear and accessible to the Jews; through the book of the law written by Moses. (Deuteronomy 30:10-11) Paul contrast the difference between gaining righteousness by works and gaining imputed righteousness through faith. Paul quotes (Leviticus 18:5), If a man keeps the law, he shall live was never disputed even by Your Son. (Luke 10:25-38) Paul has already taught that keeping the law is impossible due to the fallen nature of man. Paul then quotes (Deuteronomy 30:12-14). We can not ascend into heaven or descend into the abyss. There is no place for us to go and nothing we can do to receive Your favor and the imputed righteousness we need to live for You. You tell us that Your Word is near. You must come to us and impute Your righteousness to us. All who believe in You will not be put to shame, for You will bestow Your riches on all who call upon Your name, both Jews and Gentiles. We praise You, Lord, for You have paid for our sin and endured the full wrath of Your Father so that we may die to sin and live for righteousness. (1 Peter 2:24) What an exchange! You take our sins, and we receive Your imputed righteousness.

Father, may we accept our condition and bow before You. We are lost and needy and can not save ourselves through any works of our own. (Ephesians 2:8) Do whatever You must do to humble us, so that we will call upon Your name and live. (Romans 10:8) Amen.

Quote from Charles Spurgeon: We must be willing to lay aside our righteousness, for it is a mass of filthy rags, fit only to be burned. (Isaiah 64:6)

QUESTIONS FOR REFLECTION AND MEDITATION:

1. Scripture only speaks of two types of people and two ways to live. How does this Scripture contrast the difference between the saved and the lost?

2. What does it mean to confess that Jesus is Lord and why was it so difficult for the Jews to do that?
3. Is calling on the name of the Lord a one-time act or a way of life?

Prayer based on Romans 10:14-21

The Gospel is the power of God that changes lives.

Father, we thank You for the preaching of Your Gospel which opens the ears to all who will hear.

(Verses 14-15) describe the sequence of events that must occur to bring someone to faith in Christ. The process begins with God and ends with people who believe and call upon the name of the Lord, and then they go forth and tell others. Although Your word is powerful and can change lives, many do not obey, for they refuse to hear. The heart of Paul is broken, for his Jewish brothers, for they have been given Your Word but choose not to obey. Paul quotes (Psalm 19:4): Your voice has gone out to all the earth. God's creation and revelation speak clearly and all are without excuse. (Romans 1:20) Paul goes on to quote (Deuteronomy 32:21) I will make you jealous of those (the Gentiles) who are not a nation. Then he quotes (Isaiah 65:1) I have been found by those (the Gentiles) who did not seek me. Paul then closes with (Isaiah 65-2) I stretched out My hands all day long to a rebellious people, who walk in a way that is not good, following their own desires.

Father, may we hear Your Gospel, be changed by its power, and then proclaim it to a lost and dying world. Make us a people who quickly call upon Your name daily and regularly tell of Your wonderful works. (Psalm 40:5) You tell us that those who do not call upon Your name do not believe, for they have not heard. Lord, give us ears to hear, and preachers who preach Your Gospel. May the hearing and the spreading of Your Word be our greatest passion and joy. Amen.

Let us study and meditate on Luke 15:11-32

QUESTIONS FOR REFLECTION AND MEDITATION:

1. Why is it necessary for God to draw someone to salvation? (John 6:44)
2. What is the posture of God toward obstinate and stiff neck people?
3. What is your posture toward obstinate and stiff neck people?

PRAYER BASED ON ROMANS 11:1-10.

God's future plans for His Church revealed – He is faithful
and will not reject His people whom He chose by grace.

Father, we praise You, for You are absolutely perfect in all Your ways. Nothing can stop You from doing all that You purpose to do, and all You purpose to do is good. May You impress these absolute Truths on our minds as we seek to interpret life through the lens of Scripture. May our beliefs not be shaped by our experiences or circumstances, but firmly established on the solid foundation of Your Word. We praise You for Your Word and Your glorious work!

Chapter 11 opens with the question, Has God rejected His people? The question is legitimate since the vast majority of Jacob's descendants have rejected God. Paul answers emphatically, By no means! Paul does not look at the circumstances, but stands on Your Word. You will not cast off the people You have chosen. (Jeremiah 31:35-37) Paul then uses himself as an example. The life of Paul is living proof that You are faithful. Since You are faithful, You will never reject those You elect. Paul then reminds the Romans when Elijah was Your only prophet left in Israel. Although Israel had forsaken Your covenant, thrown down Your altars, and killed Your prophets, You raised up Elijah to oppose the 450 profits of Baal. (1 Kings 19:14) Although millions rejected You and worshiped other gods, You still preserved a remnant. You told Elijah that You had over 7,000 that did not bow their knee to Baal. (1 Kings 19:18) Israel and the Church exists today only because of Your mighty interventions! May we never forget that You will do all that You purpose to do – You will have a people of Your own. In (verse 5), Paul proclaims to the Romans that God will always have a remnant, chosen by His grace and not by works. The elect will have a righteousness apart from themselves through faith, and the rest will all be blind to the Gospel. (Verse 7) All this is according to Your good purpose. You gave them a spirit of stupor so that their eyes would not see and their ears would not hear. (Verse 8)

Father, may we not grow dull. We are prone to reject Your ways and foolishly trust in our own wisdom. Forgive us Lord, and give us the grace we need to turn from our foolish ways. Remove our heart of stone, and give us humble hearts that follow hard after You, regardless of the cost. Amen.

Let us read and meditate on (Ezekiel 36:25-27)

QUESTIONS FOR REFLECTION AND MEDITATION:

1. How does your confidence in God, or lack of it, affect how you live?
2. Will you ever be abandoned by God? Why or why not?
3. Why does unfaithful Israel still exist today?
4. Why does the Church still exist *today*? (Matthew 16:18)
5. Do you believe that God has a remnant today? Why or why not?

Prayer based on Romans 11:11-24.

God fulfills His purposes through the blindness of the Jews.

Father, we praise You, for You will bring about the salvation of Your chosen people.

Out of Your extreme love for Your people will come and have come extreme measures to bring them to salvation. You sent Your Son to be a stumbling block and a rock of offense to the Jews so that Your Gospel would go forth to all Nations (the Gentiles). At Antioch, the Jews would not accept Your Gospel and drove Paul and Barnabas out of the city. (Acts 13:46-47) Paul loved his kinsman and spoke Your Gospel to them first. When they rejected Your Word, he obediently followed his calling to the Gentiles. It was the blindness of the Jews that served Your purpose, to bring salvation to the Gentiles. Paul says he magnifies his ministry in order to make his fellow Jews jealous so they may come to salvation (Verses 13-14) Paul was a man of faith and had confidence in Your saving work even in the hardest of hearts. He looks forward to see Your glory mightily displayed by the salvation of the Jews. Paul goes on to elaborate on Your work. You have broken off some of the natural branches (the Jews) so that the Gentiles could be grafted in and share in the nourishing root of the olive tree. (Verse 17) Paul warns the Gentiles not to be arrogant toward the natural branches. He tells the Gentiles that they do not support the root, but it is the root that supports them. The Jews were broken off because of their unbelief so that the Gentiles could be grafted in. Paul then issues a strong warning to the Gentiles. He calls them not to be proud, but to fear, for the same God that broke off the natural branches will break off every branch that does not bear fruit. (John 15:6) You remind us that You are kind to those who abide in You, and severe with those who reject You and live for themselves. (Verse 22) If You have the power to graft the Gentiles into the vine, then surely You can take the natural branches that have been broken off and graft them back into the vine. (Verses 23-24)

Father, may we be amazed and rejoice in Your ways. May we remember Your steadfast love and just how far You will go to save everyone that You have chosen. You love us so much that You will pursue us until our last breath. You are more interested in our sanctification than You are with our comfort. (1 Thessalonians 4:3)

Father, give us this kind of love for others and bring us to Yourself, so that we may find joy, rest, and security in You. Amen.

Quote from Charles Spurgeon:

If sinners be damned, at least let them leap to hell over our dead bodies. And if they perish, let them perish with our arms wrapped around their knees, imploring them to stay. If hell must be filled, let it be filled in the teeth of our exertions, and let no one go unwarned and unprayed for.

Let us read and meditate on John 15:1-8

QUESTIONS FOR REFLECTION AND MEDITATION:

1. What extreme measures has God taken to bring His people to salvation?
2. What did it take to bring you to salvation?
3. Why will God break off every branch that does not bear fruit?
4. Why must God be both kind and severe? (Verse 22)
5. How often do you ask God to show you His ways?
6. Do you spend your days joyfully doing what God calls you to do, or do you live for another purpose?

Prayer based on Romans 11:25-36

The mystery of the salvation of Israel.

Father, we praise You, for Your gifts and calling are irrevocable. Because You are faithful to Your promises, we can stand firm. You are our Rock and our fortress. (Psalm 18:2) For all You are, and all You do, we praise You!

You do not want us to trust our own ways or remain ignorant of Your ways. You have caused the partial blindness of Israel, which will last until the full number of the Gentiles come to salvation. The deliverer will come from Zion and will banish all ungodliness from Jacob. (Isaiah 59:20, Isaiah 27:9) Although Israel is Your enemy, for they opposed Your Gospel, You still love them, because You have chosen to do so. Your promises to Abraham and his descendants still stand today, for You tell us that Your gifts and Your calling are irrevocable! You then remind the Gentiles that they were once disobedient and received mercy through the disobedience of Israel.

Father, in the light of Your glorious ways, may we break out in glorious praise, as Paul did in (verses 33-36). Amen.

Let us read and meditate on Romans 11:33-36.

Questions for reflection and meditation:

1. What is the mystery that Paul wants the Romans to be aware of?
2. What does God promise to do in (Verses 26-27)?
3. How Is God fulfilling His purposes in you? (sanctifying you)
4. How do you respond when you realize that God is infinitely complex and unfathomable?

PRAYER BASED ON ROMANS 12:1-2

A living, holy, and acceptable sacrifice to God.

Father, we praise You for Your mercy and kindness toward us!

You have been merciful to us. You have not given us what we deserved. We rebelled against You, suppressed Your truth, and lived for our own glory. We have been fools and exchanged Your glory for idols. (Romans 1:18-23) You describe our condition in (Romans 1:29-31). Since we have disobeyed You, we deserve Your wrath and fury. (Romans 2:8) We have sought our own righteousness and rejected Yours. (Romans 3:10-18, Romans 10:3.) We have all sinned and fallen short of Your glory. (Romans 3:23). You have shown mercy to us and have done what no man could ever do. You died for Your enemies to fulfill the righteous requirement of the law. (Romans 5:6-8) Your desire is for Your enemies to live and become new creatures who walk according to the Spirit and not the flesh. (Romans 8:4) In the light of all this, how should we respond? Under Your old covenant, the Jews presented dead sacrifices to atone for their sins. Under Your new covenant, You call us to present our bodies as a living sacrifice in service to You. (Romans 6:13, 1 Peter 2:5) A living sacrifice is the only acceptable, reasonable, rational, and intelligent response, in the light of Your mercy. You call us not to be conformed to this culture but to be transformed by the renewal of our minds so that we will have the ability and the desire to test and discern Your good, acceptable, and perfect will.

Father, keep us from pursuing our own ways. Humble us under Your mighty hand and direct us so we may see Your good, acceptable, and perfect will for our lives and live for Your glory and Yours alone! Amen.

QUESTIONS FOR REFLECTION AND MEDITATION:

1. How often are you aware and overwhelmed by the grace and mercy of God?
2. Do you dwell on what you do not have more than you rejoice in what you have received from God?
3. What fruit is seen in your life since you have become a living sacrifice (holy and acceptable to God)? (Galatians 5:22-23)

Prayer based on Romans 12:3-8

*The grace of God is known to those who believe
and their response is worship.*

Father, You are good, and everything You call us to do is good.

You have called us to be a living sacrifice. May we joyfully lay down our lives to know You, serve You, and make known Your good, acceptable, and perfect will. You must reveal Yourself to us, and we must be overwhelmed by all that You have done for us before we can joyfully live sacrificially for others. You tell us through the apostle Paul what a living sacrifice requires. We are not to think more highly of ourselves than we ought. We are to remember the measure of faith that You have given to us and be sober in our judgments. We must know that we are one body, dependent on one another, responsible for one another, and accountable to You and each other. You encourage us to sacrificially care for one another by sharing the gifts that You have given to us with zeal.

Father, may we recognize and rejoice in the measure of Faith that You have given to every believer. May we respond to Your call to sacrificially serve one another as good stewards of the gifts of grace that You have given us. (1 Peter 4:10) Amen.

Questions for reflection and meditation:

1. What makes it possible for someone to live sacrificially for others?
2. What is God's purpose for the local church?
3. Where and how do you practice living sacrificially?
4. What makes God's Church different from any other organization?
5. Is the gathering of local believes an option or a necessity? Why or why not?

Prayer based on Romans 12:9-21

Many mandates and identifying marks of a Christian:

Father, we thank You, for every mandate and exhortation that You give in these 13 verses. Give us ears to hear and hearts that desire to live sacrificially for You and others. May we rejoice in Your Word and be appropriately humbled, convicted, and changed as we read and meditate on (Romans 12:9-21).

Note: (Verse 9) tells us to hate what is evil and to hold fast to the good. (Verse 21) concludes by telling us not to be overcome by evil but to overcome evil with good. The verses in between describe a sacrificial life lived for God and for the benefit of others!

Questions for reflection and meditation:

1. How many marks of a Christian, described in this passage, are on display in your life?
2. If you were under arrest for being a Christian, would there be enough evidence to convict you?
3. What does it look like to overcome evil with good?
4. Is overcoming evil with good a significant part of your daily life?

A wise man once said that if somebody is working to fill a barrel with tares, I will overcome his efforts by filling the barrel with wheat.

Prayer based on Romans 13:1-7

Genuine love is on display through submission.

Father, we praise You for You are perfect in all Your ways.

In Romans 12, You call us to present our bodies as a living sacrifice, holy and acceptable to You. You told us what our worship should be like in Your Church, what our relationships should be like with other saints, and finally, what our relationships should be like with unbelievers, even those who oppose and persecute us. Your call is good, perfect, and far beyond our ability to comply. Your call will never be fulfilled by those who live for themselves and trust in there own strength. You not only show us the righteousness that You require, but You have chosen to give the righteousness You require to all Your children so they may live for Your glory. All this is according to Your good and glorious plan! (Isaiah 43:3-7) For all of this, we praise You!

You continue in Romans 13 to teach Your saints how they should respond to government authorities. You are perfect and consistent in all Your ways. Since You call us to submit to You and others, it should come as no surprise when You call us to submit to government authorities. First, You tell us that You have established every authority by Your command, and none exist apart from You. (John 19:11) Therefore to rebel against authority is to rebel against You. Second, You tell us to fear doing evil, for You will pour out Your wrath on all ungodliness. (Romans 1:18) You will use the authorities to carry out Your righteous purpose. Third, You tell us not to fear anything if we do good because You are overall and the one who ultimately rewards and punishes. The one who fears You will be wise (Proverbs 9:10) and fear nothing else. (Isaiah 8:13) Your perfect love casts out all fear. (1 John 4:18) You also promise that all who come to You will find rest. (Matthew 11:28-30) You conclude by commanding us to pay our taxes and show respect and honor to all people.

Father, You call us to live a holy life that is acceptable to You. May we live free from all bondage to sin so that we may please and honor You in everything we do and say. We need You Lord, for our lives will be ruined and lost if we follow our worldly desires. May we trust in Your absolute reign over all things and live under all authority in a manner that pleases and honors You. Amen.

Let us read and meditate on 1 Peter 2:13-24 and Deuteronomy 10:12-17.

QUESTIONS FOR REFLECTION AND MEDITATION:

1. How is your love for God on display in your life?
2. Why do you submit or not submit to the authorities in your life?
3. Is showing honor and respect for others easy or difficult for you? Why or why not?
4. How do you love and care for those who hurt you. What makes it possible or impossible for you to do so?
5. How have you come to trust and rest in God's righteousness?

Prayer based on Romans 13:8-10

Perfectly loving one another is the fulfillment of the law.

Father, we praise You for shining the light of Your glory into our hearts. Apart from knowing You, we can not love others as we should.

You tell us that if we perfectly love one another, we will do no harm to another and fulfill Your law and live. Lord we need You. It is not enough to know how to behave, for apart from You, we lack the power to live righteously. We thank You for sending Your Son who fulfilled the righteous requirements of Your law (Matthew 5:17) so we could die to ourselves and live for righteousness. (1 Peter 2:24). We must respond in humble submission and seek first Your kingdom and righteousness. (Matthew 22:36 40)

Father, conform us to Your image so that our chief desire will be to do Your will and accomplish Your work. (John 4:34) Teach us, guide us, and direct us in Your ways so our joy will be found in You alone. Amen.

Let read and meditate on Psalm 119:33-37

Questions for reflection and meditation:

1. How has your life fallen short of the glory of God? (Romans 3:23, 1 John 1:8)
2. When was the last time you did harm and repented?
3. What actions, words, or deeds have you done that displeased God and harmed others?
4. What is the result of genuine repentance? (1 John 1:9)
5. What is the result of not repenting? (Proverbs 28:13-14)
6. How is the love of God at work in your life?
7. What is your chief desire? And how does it set your priorities and direct your days?
8. Do you hunger for God or are you filled with something else? (Matthew 5:6)

PRAYER BASED ON ROMANS 13:11-14

*A call to wake up, turn from sin, make no provisions
for the flesh, and live for the exaltation of God.*

Father, we praise You, for who You are and for all You have done. You
alone give life meaning, purpose, and joy.

Your Son has destroyed the works of the devil, rose victorious over sin
and death, and sits at Your right hand. You call us to wake up from our
sleep, for salvation has come, and the return of Your Son is imminent.
The night is far gone (the power of sin broken), the day is at hand (Your
righteousness is available for all who will humble themselves and call
upon Your name). You call us to cast off all the works of darkness and
to walk in Your light.

Father, may we look to You and receive Your righteousness and make
no provisions for the flesh. Give us a fresh desire to live for You and
not for our sinful passions and pleasures. Amen.

QUESTIONS FOR REFLECTION AND MEDITATION:

1. What does it look like to be sleeping? What does it look like
   to be awake?
2. Are you living in the light of day, or are you stumbling in
   the darkness?
3. What are the distinct differences between a saved person and
   an unsaved person?
4. In what ways are you growing in your love for God?
5. In what ways are you stumbling in darkness?

Prayer based on Romans 14:1-12

A description of weak and strong believers And warnings for both.

Father, we praise You, for You are the one true Judge; who abhors self righteous judgments and teaches us to judge righteously and not by outward appearances.

You tell us to receive those who are weak in faith and not quarrel with them. You command us not to quarrel over opinions, either ours or theirs. Instead, may we share the Gospel with our brothers and sisters with grace and respect. (Colossians 4:6, Romans 12:10-13) Paul describes the difference between those who are strong in faith and those who are weak in faith. Those who are strong in faith can eat all things with a clear conscience, but those who are weak can not. In (verse 3), Paul warns strong and weak believers. Paul tells the strong believers not to despise the weak believers and tells the weak believers not to judge the strong believers. Weak believers must not consider themselves better than the strong believers because they honor special days or refuse to eat meat sacrifice to idols.

Father, keep us from considering ourselves better than others, for that will always lead us to self-righteous judgments and divisions which You abhor. You command us to judge righteously and not by outward appearances. (John 7:24) Lord, help us to get beyond outward appearances so that we may live and judge righteously. May we strive for Your righteousness in everything we do and say – knowing we all will stand before Your judgment seat and give an account to You. (Hebrews 4:13) Amen.

Questions for reflection and meditation:

1. Do you speak more about your opinions or more about the Gospel?
2. What is the difference between those who are weak in faith and those who are strong in faith?
3. How do you relate to your brothers and sisters who are weak in the faith?
4. What kind of judgment pleases God and what kind of judgment does God hate?
5. When was the last time you judged someone by appearance?
6. Why is judging by appearance such a big issue?
7. How has your knowledge of God changed your behavior?

PRAYER BASED ON ROMANS 14:13-23

*You give us instructions and warnings necessary for
living in harmony with You and others.*

Father, we praise You for Your Word and Your sustaining Grace. Apart from You, we will not keep Your Word and apply it rightly.

You tell us to put aside all self-righteous judgment and resolve not to be a hindrance to the Gospel in any way. In (verse 14), Paul firmly affirms the beliefs of the stronger believers – stating that they are free to eat whatever they want. Paul then asks them to restrain their freedom for the sake of their weaker brothers. Paul tells us if we offend our weak brother by what we eat, we are not walking in love. Paul gives the stronger believers a strong rebuke. He tells them not to destroy the one for whom Christ died. In (verse 17), Paul tell us that Your Kingdom is not a matter of eating and drinking but of righteousness, peace, and joy, in the Holy Spirit. You call us to pursue peace and the mutual building up of believers. (Matthew 5:9, Hebrews 12:14) In (verse 22), You want all believers to realize the importance of being true to their convictions. You tell us that whatever we do must proceed from faith, for whatever does not proceed from faith is sinful.

Father, may we be willing to surrender our rights for the benefit of others. May we care for weak believers who are overly conscience in some matters. May we love them and never encourage them to go against their convictions. Help us see clearly, so we know that being a stumbling block is a terrible sin that You hate. May we never hurt our brothers, by majoring on minors. Make us more aware of Your patience and love for us so that we may be more patient with others and more committed to helping other Christians grow and flourish. Lord, Conform us to Your image so that we will live a sacrificial life for Your glory and for the benefit of others. Amen.

QUESTIONS FOR REFLECTION AND MEDITATION:

1. How have you been a hindrance to the Gospel?
2. Have you ever debated with someone instead of loving them?
3. What rights have you surrendered for the benefit of others?
4. How often do you rejoice in God's patience and love for you?

5. How does your experience of God's patience and love affect your care for others?

6. Why must every act of a Christian proceed from faith?

Prayer based on Romans 15:1-7

Our obligations and calling.

Father, we praise You, for You alone can open blind eyes and allow us to see Your glory and Your calling on our lives.

In (verse 1), You tell us that we have an obligation to bear with the failings of the weak and should not live to please ourselves. You remind us all the reproaches that fall on us fall on Your Son. You Son bore the failings of the weak and works for the good of others. We must also have a high regard for one another and seek after their good and Your glory.

Father, conform us to the image of Your Son – who did not live for His own pleasure but sacrificially laid down His life for the benefit of others. We thank You for Your Word, which You have given to us for instruction so that we may be encouraged and built up. May we do the same for others. Lord, Your desire for us is to be one with You. (John 17:20-21) Give us more desire to live in harmony with You and others so that we may all glorify You with one unified voice! May we remember how You welcomed us and do the same for others. We praise You for reconciling us to Yourself and giving us the ministry of reconciliation. (2 Corinthians 5:18) Fill us with love and gratitude for all You have done, and cause us to respond in love for our brothers and sisters in the faith. Amen.

Let us read and meditate on 2 Corinthians 5:14-6:2

QUESTIONS FOR REFLECTION AND MEDITATION:

1. What is God's calling on your life? How did you come to know it? What does it require of you?
2. What role does the Word of God play in your life?
3. How has God richly blessed you this week?
4. How will you bless another today?

Prayer based on Romans 15:8-13

God's plan to reveal Himself and fulfill His promises to unfaithful Israel – the Gentiles see Your mercy and come to You through the disobedience of the Jews.

Father, You are great and greatly praised for Your wisdom and faithfulness!

You tell us that Your Son left heaven to become a servant to reveal Your truthfulness and confirm Your promises, which You made to the patriarchs. Your Son, the King of the universe, came as a servant and gave Himself up for those who rejected You and killed the prophets You had sent. (Mark 12:1-11) Through this, the Gentiles would come to You and exalt You for the mercy You have shown. You made this promise 600 years before Christ came through the prophet Isaiah. You said the Messiah would come through the root of Jesse, and the Gentiles would seek Him and find hope. (Isaiah 11:10)

Father, draw us to Yourself and fill us with Your Spirit so that we may abound in the love, hope, and joy, that is found only in a life surrendered to You. Amen.

Questions for reflection and meditation:

1. How has God been faithful to keep His promise to Abraham? (Genesis 17:3-4)
2. Why did the Jews despise and reject Jesus? What was the result of their rejection?
3. Have you given up your rights, and do you live to serve your enemies? How can anyone do that? (Philippians 2:5)
4. What must you do to abound in love, hope and joy? (Luke 17:33)

PRAYER BASED ON ROMANS 15:14-21

Being conformed to His image. And boasting in the work of Christ alone for the glory of God and the evangelism of others.

Father, we thank You for revealing Your Gospel to us. You call us, equipped us, and give us the privilege of sharing Your Gospel with others. We praise You, for You save sinners through the hearing of Your Gospel, and You bless the saints who proclaim Your Gospel. We praise You, for only by Your grace can anyone be faithful to Your calling.

You have blessed Your Church in Rome. Although there were relational struggles between the Jews and the Gentiles, Paul believed they had received the Gospel. Paul calls them brothers because he sees strong evidence of faith in them. They are full of goodness, knowledge, and the wisdom to instruct one another in the Lord. These are fruits of the Spirit that can only be present in the lives of true believers. (Galatians 5:23-24)

You directed Paul to write this letter to Rome, because the Roman believers, like us, need to be reminded of Your truth in order to be spurred on to grow in godliness. (1 Timothy 4:7) You called Paul and gave him the grace he needed to share Your Gospel with the Gentiles. Paul served in the priestly service of the Gospel so that the Gentiles would be a living sacrifice acceptable to You. (1 Peter 2:5) Paul says he has reasons to boast in the work he has done for You. (Verse 17) He is resolved not to speak of anything, except what Your Son has accomplished in and through him. Paul knows that he must decrease, and You must increase. (John 3:30) Paul claims that he has fulfilled the ministry that You have given him by preaching the Gospel of Your Son. Paul boldly proclaims Your Gospel because he believes that only through the proclamation of Your Gospel will people see, understand, and be conformed to Your ways.

Father, conform us to Yourself, so we may boldly proclaim Your Gospel, for it is the proclamation of Your Gospel that changes lives. Give us a zeal for Your Gospel, so our passion for the Gospel will exceed all other passions. (Exodus 20:3) Amen.

Questions for reflection and meditation:

1. Are you proud of your work for God as Paul was? (Verse 17) Why or why not?
2. When you evangelize (both to believers and unbelievers) are you resolved to speak of nothing except what Christ has accomplished? Why or why not? (Verse 18)
3. At the end of your day, can you rejoice and say, that you have fulfilled the ministry of the Gospel of Christ. (Verse 19) Why or why not?
4. Does (1 Peter 2:9) describe you?
5. What fruits of the Spirit do you see in your life? (Galatians 5:23-24) Which ones do you need to grow in the most?
6. How is God conforming you to His image?

Let us study and meditate on 2 Timothy 4:5-8

A god-centered life is full of god-centered days.

Prayer based on Romans 15:22-33

*A great example of a life lived under the authority of
God and in relationship with other saints.*

Father, we thank You for the glorious work You have done in and
through Paul.

Paul longed to see the saints in Rome, but he remained where You placed
him. He was faithful to complete the work, You gave him, regardless
of the difficult circumstances. Paul tells the Roman Church about the
Gentile Churches in Macedonia – how they eagerly and rightly gave
to the poor saints in Jerusalem. Paul share his plans with the saints in
Rome and asks them to strive together in prayer with him. Paul asks
them to pray for his deliverance from those in Judea that do not believe:
his service for Jerusalem would be acceptable to the saints and that he
may come to them with joy, and find refreshment in their company.

Father, we thank You for this example of the life of Paul, which You
have preserved for us in Your Word. May we learn from Paul and experience the joy that he had. Show us how to live the abundant life that
You have freely given us through Your Son. Amen.

Questions for reflection and meditation:

1. Why was the life of Paul filled with joy and his ministry
   so powerful?
2. What limits your joy and ministry?
3. How have you benefited from being open, honest, and accountable to other saints?

Prayer based on Romans 15:30-16.2

Making decisions and prayerfully setting priorities.

Father, Paul was Your bondservant. We thank You for showing us how Your bondservants make decisions.

Paul is in Corinth. Rome is about 800 miles to the west, and Jerusalem is about 750 miles to the east. Paul has a strong desire to go to Rome, where he would be refreshed by the saints and receive support for his missionary journey to Spain. What a great, godly desire! Paul looks east to Jerusalem, where his Jewish kinsman oppose him. You have called him to travel to Jerusalem with those who are delivering the offering from the Gentile Churches. Paul believed his presence in Jerusalem would serve to unite the Gentile and Jewish Churches. Paul decides to go to Jerusalem despite all the warnings, opposition, and hardships. Paul loves You and his kinsman and is ready to die for the sake of the Gospel. (Acts 21:10-14) You will answer Paul's prayer and bring him to Rome, but it will be in Your way and in Your time. (Acts chapters 21-28) Paul would have it no other way. Paul joyfully submits to Your ways because he knows that Your ways are higher than his ways. (Isaiah 55:8-9) Paul decides to send Phoebe to Rome to bless her and the Romans with his letter.

Father, You have set a high bar for Your bondservants. Fill us with Your Holy Spirit so we may live for You alone and not for anything else regardless of the cost. Amen.

QUESTIONS FOR REFLECTION AND MEDITATION:

1. How do you set your priorities and make your daily decisions?
2. What was the most difficult decision you ever had to make? How long did it take? How much did you pray over it?
3. Can you recall a time when you said, not my will, but Yours be done?
4. Have you ever experienced a delayed answer to your prayer and then rejoiced over His ways?
5. How have you become convinced that His ways are better than your ways?

Prayer based on Romans 16:3-27

Examples of saints who love the Gospel and are committed to it. A call for Christians to hold fast and watch out for those who do not serve the Lord.

Father, we thank You for showing us how Your Gospel is spread through Your faithful disciples. May it be so with us today.

In (Verses 1-15), You give us an impressive list of people, who belonged to Your Church in Rome. Paul knew them, loved them, consistently prayed, and thanked God for them. They were a diverse group: committed and involved with Paul in spreading the Gospel. (Romans 16:4-5) Some have even risked their lives and reputations for the sake of the Gospel. In (Verse 17), Paul appeals to those in Christ to hold fast to what they have learned and to watch out for those who cause divisions. Such persons do not serve the Lord but their own appetites and will deceive the hearts of the naive. In (Verses 19-20), Paul rejoices over the obedience of the Roman saints and calls them to be diligent in their battle against Satan. Paul assures them that God will crush Satan under their feet. (Genesis 3:15) Paul then honors those in his inner circle who work diligently with him and then breaks out in a wonderful doxology!

Father, we praise You and thank You for You have revealed a mystery, which has been kept secret for ages. You have chosen to bring about the obedience of faith through the preaching of the Gospel of Your Son. Lord, may we hear Your Word, rejoice in it, and live under its authority. Amen.

Questions for reflection and meditation:

1. How did the Gospel spread 1500 miles from Jerusalem to Rome?
2. What hinders the spread of the Gospel today?
3. Who, in your life, do you honor, rejoice over, and disciple?
4. Are you thankful for those who are discipleing you?
5. What causes you to be, or hinders you from, rejoicing in the Gospel and praising God for it?

1 Corinthians

Prayer based on 1 Corinthians 1:1-9

God is faithful and is calling His people into fellowship with His Son.

Father, we praise You for all the work You have faithfully done in Your people!

In (Verse 1), You tell us that You have called and appointed Paul; to be an apostle. May we receive his words and give them the authority and respect they deserve. (Mathew 10:40, 1 Corinthians 14:37) In (verse 2), You give us two facts about a believer: we are saints (those You have set apart), and we are people who choose to call upon Your name daily instead of trusting in our own wisdom. You tell us that believers are enriched in every way and have a testimony about Your work in their lives. We thank You for the grace and peace, You have given to Your children through Your Son. They are not lacking in any gifts. You have called them into fellowship with Your Son and with Your saints. You have given Your children the resources for spiritual growth and transformation. Their lives confirm the work of the Holy Spirit in them. They desire to grow in holiness and are eagerly waiting for the return of Your Son. In (versus 8 and 9) You promise that You will sustain them to the end.

Father, give us eyes to see as You do so that we may be able to see and rejoice in the grace that You have poured out on us and others. May we learn to trust and rejoice more in Your sustaining Grace as we look to You first instead of last. Amen.

Questions for reflection and meditation:

1. What is Paul declaring when he proclaims that he is an apostle?
2. Why is it important for the Corinthians and us to accept Paul as an apostle?
3. What sets a believer apart from an unbeliever?
4. How is God sustaining you and preparing you for the DAY of His return?
5. What testimonies do you have of the faithfulness of God, and do you regularly and eagerly share them?

Prayer based on 1 Corinthians 1:10-16

God is pleased with unity and diversity in His
church and displeased with division.

Father, We praise You, for You are perfect in all Your ways. You show us true unity and harmony within the Trinity. (John 17:21)

You clearly tell us, through the apostle Paul, that You want Your Church to be in complete agreement and have no divisions. (Verse 10) You give examples of factions in Your Church that greatly displeases You. You warned us that if we follow a particular teacher or teaching, we can think more highly of ourselves than we should and then look down on others who do not have our superior knowledge. This pride will cause divisions that will greatly displease You and destroy the witness of Your Church.

Father, have mercy on us, for we often look too much like the world. May we be a light – a city on a hill not hidden. (Matthew 5:14) Make us like Paul. He saw many problems in the Corinthian Church and still loved the Church, was thankful for the Church and rejoice over the Church. May our love for Your bride reflect Your love for us. Lord make us of one mind, one body, one spirit, and one faith so that we may walk worthy of the calling to which You have called us. (Ephesians 4:1-7) May the diversity and unity in our local churches bring You glory, and may there be no divisions among us. Amen.

Questions for reflection and meditation:

1. Is it possible to love Christ and not love His bride? Why or Why not?
2. What are the marks of a healthy Church given to us in this Scripture?
3. What was the chief goal Paul had for the Corinthian Church?
4. How does diversity and unity in a local church please and honor God and bring glory to Him?

Prayer based on 1 Corinthians 1:17-31

The wisdom and power of God and the foolishness of man are on display.

Father, We praise You for the depths of Your wisdom and knowledge. To You belongs all wisdom and power.

Paul knew he was appointed, by You, to preach the Gospel. He was not to make converts through persuasive arguments, for only the preaching of the Gospel will save the proud Corinthians from Your wrath. Paul was willing to preach, what he knew would be foolishness to the Corinthians, for he desired their salvation more than he cared about looking like a fool. Paul lived to exalt You and was deeply concerned about people thinking too highly about him and too little about You. (2 Corinthians 12:6) You tell us that the cross divides the human race into two groups: some are perishing, for they see the cross as foolishness and not worthy of consideration, and others see Your wisdom, power, and righteousness clearly on display in the cross and rejoice. What looks like defeat to one is seen as a great victory to others. You tell us that the wisdom of this world is foolish and is powerless to save anyone. It was Your pleasure to choose something that the wise of this world would consider foolishness to save those who would believe. You used the foolish and weak things of the world to shame the wise; and the mighty. May we exalt Your wisdom and the saving work of Your Son above all things.

Father, May we understand that we have nothing apart from You to boast in. Let our boast be in You, for all other boasting will lead to divisions and quarrels. Lord, show us the way of the righteous and the way of the wicked and give us Your wisdom to choose wisely. Amen.

May we take time to study and meditate on Psalm 1.

QUESTIONS FOR REFLECTION AND MEDITATION:

1. Scripture always divides people into two groups: sheep and goats, wheat and tares, for and against; How does this Scripture contrast the difference between the two?
2. Why does God destroy the wisdom of the wise and oppose and defeat their plans.

3. Why is Paul so concerned about people thinking to highly of him? Have you ever had this concern?
4. What boasting pleases the Lord?
5. What hinders you from preaching the Gospel?

Prayer based on 1 Corinthians 2:1-5

The characteristics of a life live for God.

Father, we praise You, for You send Your servants to accomplish Your mission in Your way and in Your time.

You sent Paul to the Corinthians in weakness and humility to preach Christ and Him crucified. You knew the proud Corinthians and what they needed at this time. You want the Corinthians faith to rest and trust in Your power; and not in any man.

Paul was a man who lived under Your authority and followed Your leading. He preached Christ and Him crucified, even though he knew the Corinthians would see the cross as foolishness and him as a fool. We praise You, for only You can do such work in a man! Paul lives to please You and to do Your will. There would come a time when You call Paul to be bold, and he will be bold and will present strong arguments to the Corinthians. (2 Corinthians 10:4-5) Paul was committed to doing Your work, in Your way, and in Your time, regardless of the cost. He learned how to trust in Your wisdom in everything.

Father, Conform us to Your image. May we be more humble, more obedient, more sensitive to what people need to hear, and more confident in the power of Your Gospel to change lives. Make us more open and submissive to Your guidance and more effective ministers of Your Gospel. Teach us how to follow You so that we can lead others well. Make us willing to be weak when we need to be and to be bold when we need to be so that Your power would be on display in our lives. Amen.

QUESTIONS FOR REFLECTION AND MEDITATION:

1. According to this Scripture, what does it take to be a good minister of the Gospel?
2. Why are we guaranteed to fail, when we do not call upon the name of the Lord?
3. Does God want you to be weak or strong?
4. What makes God delight in His saints? (Isaiah 66:2)

Let us read and meditate on Psalm 16

Prayer based on 1 Corinthians 2:6-16

The wisdom of this world is foolish and will pass away. Wisdom from God is unknown to the world, eternal, and freely given to all believers who ask for it through the Holy Spirit.

Father, You are all-wise. The wisdom of the world is foolishness and will pass away. We praise You, for Your wisdom will never pass away. Thank You for making Your wisdom known to all who will humble themselves, and ask for it. (James 4:2-3)

You want us to know the difference between the wisdom of the Gospel and the wisdom of the world. You tell us that the wisdom of the world is earthly, temporal, and brings destruction, but the wisdom of the Gospel is divine, eternal, and brings the glory of eternal life to all who believe. None of the rulers in the days when Your Son walked the Earth understood Your wisdom, for if they did, they would not have crucified Your Son. (Verse 8) You revealed the wisdom of Your Gospel through Your Son – and then sent Your Holy Spirit to live in all who believe. (Romans 8:9) You tell us that no one comprehends Your thoughts except the Holy Spirit. Only those who receive Your Holy Spirit can understand Your thoughts. (Verses 10-12) You tell us that Your Word is not taught by human wisdom but by Your Spirit. (Verse 13, John 14:26) Your Word is perfect and will interpret spiritual truths to all who belong to You. Those who do not belong to You can not understand the wisdom of the Gospel, because it is foolishness; to them. Your wise plan remains hidden from all except those who love You. True wisdom only comes through humble submission to You. You command the spiritual person to judge all things, for they have the Holy Spirit, whose judgment is perfect, living in them. The unspiritual person does not have the Holy Spirit and can only judge with worldly wisdom. (Verse 15) Those who abide in You will seek Your ways, delight in You, and follow the teachings of Your Word. (Psalm 119:33-35) You conclude by telling us that all who belong to You have the mind of Your Son. (Verse 16)

Father, may we be enlightened by Your Spirit as we diligently study and meditate on Your Word. Give us a mind, a heart, and a will that delights in knowing and following You. You have promised to lead the humble in ways of righteousness. (Psalm 25:9) Amen.

Let us read and meditate on John 14:15-31

Questions for Reflection and Meditation:

1. What is the difference between the wisdom of the world and the wisdom of the Gospel?
2. How and to whom is the wisdom of the Gospel revealed?
3. Can anyone comprehend the thoughts of God? Why or why not?
4. How can one be enlightened and have the mind of Christ?
5. What are the defining characteristics of a child of God?

Prayer based on 1 Corinthians 3:1-8

Planting, watering, and growing up in the faith.

Father, we praise You and thank You for Your righteous ways. You oppose the proud and bring them low, and You give grace to the humble and raise them up. You will reward and discipline Your children according to Your righteous ways. We praise You, for You are good and perfect in all that You do.

You tell us that You cannot speak to us as spiritual people if we are immature and living according to the flesh. You tell us envy, strife, and divisions are signs of immaturity in Christians. They are like babes that can only be fed milk and not solid food. You tell us that proud, immature people boast about who they follow: what teachings they follow, their knowledge, and what they have done. Proud people are ineffective in ministry and cause divisions. You justly oppose the proud because proud people will not learn and grow in godliness. (1 Peter 5:5-6) You tell us not to boast in what we have planted or watered but to boast in You, because it is You who gives the increase.

Father, May we be grateful, humble servants that live for You and continue to grow and rejoice in doing Your work. (Ephesians 2:10) Amen.

Questions for reflection and meditation:

1. What causes envy, strife, and divisions in a Church?
2. What makes it impossible for a proud person to learn and grow in godliness?
3. Some people see God working in their lives everyday and respond with repentance and gratitude and some people do not. What makes the difference?

Prayer based on 1 Corinthians 3:9-15

*The Church's One foundation is Jesus Christ our Lord –
no other foundation will stand.*

Father, we praise You for Your power and wisdom. You have established Your church and sustained it over the centuries. You have built Your Church on a solid foundation. We thank You for Your Word, which gives us wise instructions on how to build on Your foundation.

You call us to be servants of one Master, united together in one body. You give us an example of Your work in the Corinthian Church through Paul. You tell us that Paul and Apollos are fellow workers – who strive together to plant a seed in Your field. You also tell us that the Corinthian Church is Your Building. Since Paul, every church planter has laid a foundation. You tell us that Your Son must be the corner-stone of every foundation laid and central to all the work done by Your Church. (Isaiah 28:16, Ephesians 2:20-22) You warned us that all other foundations will crumble and call us to be very careful how we build upon Your foundation. (Matthew 7:24-27) We should build with gold, silver, and precious stones (eternal and unchanging) and not with wood, hay, and straw (temporary and perishable). You tell us that on the DAY Your Son returns, our work will be tested by fire, and only the work that does not burn will remain. On that DAY, some will receive rewards, and some will experience loss. Although we were mistaken about many things, and who has not, You tell us that we will be saved even if all our works burn, but only by fire. You are so gracious! Only Your work done in Your name will last for eternity; everything else will burn.

Father, may we prayerfully consider our ways and humbly submit to Yours. May we only participate in work that please and honors You. May we work with our eyes on You and eternity. Give us an eternal perspective that will make us good and faithful servants who always listen to You and follow Your leading. Amen.

Charles Spurgeon quote:

It is easy building with wood, and easier still with hay and straw, but then there will be only a handful of ashes left of a whole lifework, if we build with these.

Questions for reflection and meditation:

1. What are the benefits to being united with other believers in one body?
2. What fellow workers are you striving with to plant seeds for the Kingdom of God?
3. How will focusing on eternity made a difference in your life today?
4. What will be the difference between the first coming of Jesus and his second?

Is it possible to be so heavenly-minded that we are no earthly good, or is it more likely that we are to earthly-minded to be any heavenly good?

Prayer based on 1 Corinthians 3:16-17

The love of God is intense, and He will take extreme measures for His glory and for the good of His people.

Father, we praise You for saving us and filling us with Your Holy Spirit.

You tell us that those who You save have Your Holy Spirit living in them, and they become Your Holy Temple. You want all of Your children to live holy (distinct and separate) lives so that the miraculous work You have done in them is on display for all to see. You tell us that Your temple is sacred, and You have promised to destroy anyone who would corrupt Your Church. May we see how much You are one with Your Church and stand amazed. (John 17:22-23) You tell us that You are so united with Your Church that any wrong done against Your Church is against You. (Acts 9:4-5, Matthew 25:40)

Father, give us more love for Your Son and His bride so that all may see the glory You have given to Your Church. Sustain us by Your grace so we may serve You and Your Church faithfully. Amen.

Questions for reflection and meditation:

1. How would you describe the relationship between Christ and His Church?
2. How could someone destroy the temple of God?
3. Why does Jesus consider an attack against the Church an attack against Himself?

PRAYER BASED ON 1 CORINTHIANS 3:18-23

We must become fools if we are to become wise.

Father, we praise You for Your wisdom, grace, and mercy. You willingly give all Your children all things through Your Son. You are a generous King!

You clearly tell us that the wisdom of the world is foolishness. (Verse 19) May we be done with worldly wisdom and all boasting apart from You and foolishly relying on and trusting in human strength. (Psalm 20:7) May we always call on Your name instead of trusting in our own wisdom. (Romans 10:13) You also tell us that the only way to become wise is to realize that we are fools. (Verse 18) The more we realize how prone we are to make foolish decisions, the more we will be on our face praying for Your wisdom. May we not be proud people who are deceived and see no need to pray for ourselves but may we be humble people who know our great need for Your wisdom and pray before we act or speak.(1 Thessalonians 5:16) You tell us not to boast in men because their wisdom is futile, and You will catch them in all their craftiness, for You reign overall. You give good things to those who live and walk in harmony with Your Son – just as Your Son live and walked in harmony with You. (John 17:22)

Father, we do not want to be like the Corinthians, who trusted in worldly wisdom and exalted themselves and other human leaders. Lord, give us a life devoted to walking in harmony with You and Your Church. May our lives be a passionate pursuit of Your glory in all things. Amen.

Let us read and meditate on John 16:12-15

QUESTIONS FOR REFLECTION AND MEDITATION:

1. How have you come to the end of yourself and learned to trust in the wisdom of God?
2. Why do humble people pray more than proud people?
3. Why are the thoughts and plans of the unsaved futile?
4. In (verse 22), Paul tells us that all things belong to God. Why is this an important truth to remember?

Prayer based on 1 Corinthians 4:1-5

The praise of God is worth every sacrifice.
We must trust in His judgments and not ours.

Father, we praise You, for You are good and just and will make all things right.

Paul calls himself and other faithful brothers who serve with him servants of God and stewards of the mysteries of God. Paul has a clear conscience and knows Whom he believes. (2 Timothy 1:12) Paul sees it as a small thing to be judged by any human Court, for he knows where he stands. His only concern is that he be found faithful. Paul lives for the DAY when he will stand before God: and hear Him say, well done, my good and faithful servant. Paul calls the Corinthian Church to not be premature in their judgment and assures them that Jesus will come and bring light, which will expose the hearts of every man. Everyone will receive what they are due according to their works. (Romans 2:6-8, 2 Corinthians 5:10, 1 Peter 1:17, Revelation 20:12)

Father, forgive us, when we dwell upon and hold too highly the judgment of others. Also, forgive us when we quickly pronounce our self-righteous judgments on others and fail to serve them and You. Thank You for giving us Your commandments and reminders. May we rest in You, for You are the Judge who will bring to light all things and carry out perfect Justice. (Hebrews 4:13) Lord, may we keep our eyes on You and look forward to the DAY when all who belong to You will receive the commendation that You have promised. Amen.

Questions for reflection and meditation:

1. Do you live for the praise and approval of God or others?
2. What desires compete with your desire to serve God?
3. How has your life been changed by believing that the commendation you receive from God will be far greater than anything you could receive from this world?
4. Do you believe the high calling of God is worth the sacrifice? How has that belief changed the way you live?

Prayer based on 1 Corinthians 4:6-13

This passage speaks of two ways to live: foolishly following the ways of the world or being a fool for Christ and looking like the scum of the world.

Father, we praise You for Your wisdom, which You freely give to those who love You!

You do not want us to be proud people who put themselves over Your Word. They trust in their own wisdom and other puffed-up teachers. They decide for themselves what to believe and who to follow. You want us to be humble people who live under the authority of Your Word. You give us a clear distinction between proud people and humble people. (Verses 6b-13) May we have eyes to see and ears to hear. You tell us that proud people are puffed- up, boastful, and divisive, for they think highly of themselves and little of others. You asked us two helpful questions to keep us from boasting about ourselves. Who sees anything different in you? And what do you have that you have not received? You tell us that proud people think they are rich and need nothing, but they are wretched, poor, pitiful, and blind. (Revelation 3:17) You tell us proud people believe they are wise and strong, and those who are not like them are foolish and weak. Proud people cannot grow and learn, for they think they have already arrived. (Philippians 3:12-13) You tell us that humble people know they are spiritually bankrupt and do not trust in their own resources. They know that they are spiritually bankrupt and are blessed. (Matthew 5:3) They also hunger and thirst after righteousness. (Matthew 5 6) You tell us that humble people will labor diligently with their hands, for hard work is not beneath them. You tell us that Your humble people will also bless those who slander and persecute them. (Matthew 5:10-11, Romans 12:14)

Father, may we not be proud people (full of themselves), seeing no need to hunger and thirst after righteousness. Make us more aware of our need for Your keeping and give us a strong desire to press on for the prize in Christ Jesus. (Philippians 3:14) Amen.

Questions for reflection and meditation:

1. What does it mean not to go beyond what is written? (Verse 6)
2. What does it look like to be the scum of the world? (Versus 10-13)

3. What purpose did God accomplish by making Paul the scum of the world?
4. Are you willing, like Paul, to be made the scum of the world and be a fool for Christ? Why or why not?
5. How is your life distinctly different from an unbeliever?

Prayer based on 1 Corinthians 4:14-21

An example of God's love and power at work in the life of a saint.

Father, we thank You for equipping and sending Paul to plant Your Church in Corinth and for giving Paul a heart for Your people.

Paul calls the Church in Corinth his beloved children because You made Paul their spiritual father. As their father, he does not want to shame his children but desires to warn them. Paul's love for the Church is such a reflection of Your Fatherly love that Paul is bold enough to urge the Church to imitate him. Paul also says that he will send his beloved and faithful son (Timothy) to them so Timothy may remind them of Paul's ways in Christ! Father, we thank You for sending Your Son to make Yourself known to us and for saving us through His substitutionary death on the cross. (John 1:14, Hebrews 1:1-4.) Paul warns the proud and calls them to repentance. He wants them to experience Your grace and not Your rod. (1 Peter 5:5b-6) Paul tells them that the kingdom of God is not about talk but power. Paul wants them to repent before he comes.

Father, grant us repentance, so we experience more of Your grace and mercy and less of Your rod. May we please You in all things. Give us a heart for You and Your bride. Bring our hearts more inline with Yours, so we live in Harmony with You and others and enjoy a more fruitful ministry. May we be fully convinced that there is no life apart from You and boldly proclaim Your Gospel with truth and grace. Amen.

QUESTIONS FOR REFLECTION AND MEDITATION:

1. What words and actions of Paul show the love of God for the Corinthian Church?
2. How could you experience more of the grace of God in your life and less of His rod.
3. How does your knowledge and love for God compel you to share the Gospel?
4. Why did Paul tell the Corinthian Church that the kingdom of God is not a matter of talk but of power? (Verse 20)

Prayer based on 1 Corinthians 5:1-8

*Exercising church discipline for the good of an unrepentant
sinner and for the good of the Church*

Father, we praise You for delivering us from the bondage of sin and
giving us new desires to live for Your glory and pleasure.

May we please You in all things. We must love the things, You love –
and hate the things You hate. Those who hate God love death. (Proverbs
8:36) You tell us there are six things that You hate, and pride is at the
top of the list. (Proverbs 6:16-19) The Corinthian Church was proud of
their spirituality. They even tolerated behavior that was a capital crime
according to Roman law. If the Church in Corinth loved You and one
another as they should, they would have mourned over their sins and
lovingly cared for this unrepentant sinner. The Corinthian Church was
proud, arrogant, and ignored church discipline. They disregarded a most
offensive sin that even pagans in Rome would not tolerate! Thank You
for Your servant Paul who patiently and lovingly cared for Your messed
up Church. Paul called the entire Church body to gather together to
excommunicate this man. Father, this is hard to do but help us to see
that this is a most loving thing to do for those with unrepentant sin.
Paul wanted what was best for this man. Paul knew that no earthly
pleasure could compare to the joy found in Christ. Paul knew it would
be better for this man to die to his flesh so his spirit may live. Paul also
wanted what was best for the Corinthian Church. Paul warns them
about the dangers of not practicing church discipline. He speaks of how
a little leaven leavens the whole lump and then calls the Corinthian
Church to purge out the old leaven so they may be a new lump. Since
the beginning, You have called Your people to keep themselves separate
and distinct from the world. (Deuteronomy 7:3-4)

Father, may we be humble people who love You and Your Church. May
we live lives that are holy and distinctly different from the world. May
we lovingly keep watch over one another so that none will be found
outside; of Christ. (1 Timothy 4:16) May all churches be distinct and
separate from the world so that they may be the light You have called
them to be. May Your Church be a city on a hill that puts Your love
on display and compels the lost to seek Your Kingdom. May many

see Your work done in Your Church and give glory to You. (Matthew 5:14-16) Amen.

Questions for reflection and meditation:

1. How is your love for God and your hatred of sin displayed in your life?
2. Do you accept and tolerate sinful behavior in your Church? Do you pray and mourn over the sins in your Church?
3. In what ways, are you lovingly caring for the members of your Church?
4. What is the best thing you can do for an unrepentant sinner?
5. Is it your responsibility to care for your brothers and sisters in Christ. Why or why not?
6. Why must unrepentant sin in the Church be addressed? What is at stake?

Let us read and meditate on Matthew 18:15-20

Prayer based on 1 Corinthians 5:9-12

The call to judge those inside the Church for their good and God's glory.
(Verse 12)

Father, we praise You for calling us to be holy and separate from the world. We thank You for giving us clarity and direction through Your Word.

You are not prohibiting us from mixing socially with unbelievers. Your followers have been crucified to the world (Galatians 2:20), raised to new life (Romans 6:4), and then sent back into the world to share the Good News of what Your Son has done on the cross. (2 Corinthians 5:18). We must love and associate with unbelievers if we are to fulfill Your great commission. (Matthew 28:19-20) In (verse 11), You tell us that we are not to associate with anyone who calls themself a Christian and is willfully sinning and unrepentant. We must care enough to confront them and be careful not to do anything that would condone their behavior. Your Church must judge immorality for three reasons; the health of Your Church, the witness of Your Church, and for the good of the unrepentant sinner. May we love and respect Your Church more and have a greater appreciation for the safety it provides from Satan, our flesh, and the world.

Father, we pray that You will give us the wisdom, guidance, and boldness we desperately need to follow the commands You give us (in verse 12). Make us instruments in Your hand so that we can judge righteously and lovingly care for Your Church. Amen.

QUESTIONS FOR REFLECTION AND MEDITATION:

1. What does being holy and separate from the world look like in your life?
2. Why does Scripture tell us to love those who are in the Church? (Galatians 6:10)
3. How do we love and associate with unbelievers in a manner that pleases God, serves them, and fulfills the Great commission? (Matthew 28:18-20)
4. Why does God command us to be separate from those who calls themselves a Christian and are willfully sinning and unrepentant?
5. Are the members of Your Church called to judge those inside the Church. Why or why not?

Prayer based on 1 Corinthians 6:1-8

Believers should love one another, properly handle disputes, and judge righteously.

Father, we thank You for recording the failings of the Corinthian Church so that we may learn from their failings.

In chapter 5, they proudly judged themselves and others and failed to discipline the unrepentant sinner. In chapter 6, You wisely remind us of who we are and how You call us to exercise righteous judgment. You tell us that Your Church should be able to judge more righteously than the world. You begin by asking us, Why do we go before the unrighteous to settle a dispute and not before the saints in the Church? Father, forgive us when we fail to obey Your Word. You clearly tell us how Your Church should handle disputes among believers. (Matthew 18:15-17) You tell us that we will judge the world and also the angels. If we are qualified to pass judgment on the angels, we certainly should be sufficient to pass judgment on matters that pertain to this life. Lord, You are good, perfect in all Your ways, and You have promised to guide all who look to You. (Psalm 25:9) Surely You will give wisdom to all who humble themselves and ask. (James 4:2b) You are not pleased when believers wrong and cheat one another and are more concerned with their losses than with Your Kingdom.

Father, May we be ashamed when we think so little of You and the reputation of Your Church. May we trust in You to give wisdom to believers that the world does not have. May we see that it is better to be wronged and defrauded than to damage the witness and reputation of Your Church. Give us hearts that truly seek Your Kingdom first, above all things. Amen.

Questions for reflection and meditation:

1. Why should Your Church be able to judge more righteously than the world?
2. How should Your Church handle disputes among it's members?
3. What is wrong with Your Church looking to the courts for justice or to the world for council?
4. How does your life show that the spread of the Gospel is more important than your gains or losses?

5. What argument does Paul use to persuade the Church of their ability to judge righteously?
6. Will God give you wisdom in all matters if you ask Him for it? Why or why not?
7. How important is the witness and reputation of the Church to you?

Prayer based on 1 Corinthians 6:9-11

Those who will not inherit the Kingdom and those who will:

Father, we praise You for every loving warning You give us. You take no pleasure in the death of the wicked. Thank You for graciously imploring us to turn to You and live. (Ezekiel 33:11)

You give us a list of people that will definitely not inherit Your Kingdom. (Verses 9-10) You then assure us that all though we all, at one time, were like those described in (verses 9-10), You have graciously decided to make some new creatures in Christ. (Verse 11) They have been washed (by the shedding of Your blood), sanctified (set apart and made holy), and justified (declared not guilty). (Romans 8-30)

Father, we praise You for the work You have already done in Your children. May we trust in Your faithfulness to complete the work You have begun. (Philippians 1:6) Cause us to recall and affirm these truths every day as we eagerly await the DAY of Your return. Amen.

Questions for reflection and meditation:

1. Why does God have to remind us that sinners will not inherit the kingdom of God?
2. According to this Scripture how is a person saved?
3. According to Scripture, what else does God do for sinners, in addition to atoning for their sin? See (Romans 8:15-17)

Prayer based on 1 Corinthians 6:12-20

All who live in union with Christ become one spirit with Him.

Father, we praise You, for You who opens our eyes, and will grant us repentance.

You warn us that even lawful things may not be helpful. Everything we put before You is an idol and will enslaves us. Paul is determined not to be enslaved by anything. A seemingly good idol is very dangerous. You tell us that our bodies are not for sexual immorality but should serve You. You warned us to flee sexual immorality, for the one joined to a prostitute becomes one flesh with her and can not be one spirit with the Lord. So great is the weight of our sexual sin that You tell us to flee from it and not simply resist the temptation. You remind us that our bodies are a holy temple bought with a price. May we highly value our bodies because they are rightfully Yours and are one with You.

Father, may we accept and embrace these truths so that we may glorify You in all areas of our lives and love You with all our heart, mind, soul, and strength. (Mark 12:30) Amen.

Questions for reflection and meditation:

1. Are you dominated by anything? (Verse 12) If so, What are you called to do?
2. Why does God tell us to flee sexual sin instead of standing fast?
3. What makes sexual sin different from all other sins?
4. How can knowing and believing that your body is not your own, but belongs to another, keep you from sinning?

Prayer based on 1 Corinthians 7:1-9

*Biblical principles will guide the married, the unmarried,
and the widows in the ways of the Lord.*

Father, we praise You for Your Word, which is sufficient to guide us through any situation.

Paul is writing this chapter in response to questions in a letter from the Corinthian Church. Paul wants to agree with them as much as he can and, at the same time, remain faithful to Your Word. The Corinthian Church was very divided. Some were super-spiritual and advocated marital celibacy, while others would engage freely in gross sexual immorality. We thank You for giving Paul Your wisdom and guidance to navigate this difficult situation.

Father, You tell us to be careful not to go beyond Your Word. (1 Corinthians 4:6b) Give us the wisdom and guidance we so desperately need as we study and meditate on this text.

(In Verse 1), Paul wisely agrees with some Corinthians who say that is better for a man not touch a woman, but then Paul shows his strong support for marriage. (Verses 2-7) Paul insists that a husband should have his own wife, and a wife should have her own husband, and they should not withhold affection for one another. You tell us that the wife does not have authority over her body, but the husband does. Likewise, the husband does not have authority over his body, but the wife does. You tell us that it is okay to abstain from sexual relations, but only by mutual consent, only for a set time, and only for devotion to fasting and prayer. After the time set, You strongly encourage husbands and wives to come together again. You know we lack self control and can be tempted to be unfaithful to our spouses. Paul had experienced the joy of living a single life and therefore encourages the unmarried and the widows to remain single, so they can be completely devoted to You, as Paul was. Paul then encourages them to marry if they can not exercise self-control. Should you choose to remain single or should you pursue marriage? In (Verse 7), You teach that both lives are a gift from You.

Father, if we are single may we glorify You in our single life and if we are married may our marriage display Your glory most fully. May we make all our decisions based on what would bring the most glory to You, for You are our Savior, Master, and King forever and worthy of every sacrifice we make. Amen.

QUESTIONS FOR REFLECTION AND MEDITATION:

1. What are your reasons for desiring marriage?
2. What are your reasons for remaining single?
3. What is the key to being content in all circumstances?

Let us read and meditate on Philippians 4:11-20

Prayer based on 1 Corinthians 7:10-16

Biblical principles to guide those unequally yoked.

Father, we praise You for Your faithfulness. You are a covenant-keeping God!

You tell us in Your Word that divorce does not please You. (Malachi 2:16) Since You designed and ordained marriage, any human efforts to dissolve it is an attack on Your design. (Matthew 19:3-6) You used marriage to describe our present and future relationship with You. You tell us that we are Your bride, and You have promised to sanctify and cleanse those who belong to You. (Ephesians 5:22-29) You will never forsake Your covenant no matter what the circumstances. (Isaiah 54:10) Your desire is for Your people to be faithful to the covenant they have made with their spouses. Help us and guide so that our care for our spouses will display Your steadfast, gracious, merciful care for us.

In (verses 10-11), Paul gives Your command not to divorce because Your Son clearly taught on what You desire for marriage. (Matthew 19:7-9) Paul then shares his opinion on how a believing spouse should relate with an unbelieving spouse. (Verses 12-16) Paul calls the believing spouse to do what is right in Your eyes. A believer should honor You in all things and put the best interest of others above their own, even if they have been hurt. (Luke 6:27-28)

Father, forgive us when we want quick, easy solutions, that require no long suffering or sacrifice from us. Lord, we will make a mess of every situation if we proudly do what we think is best in our own eyes. We need to see everything through Your eyes. Lord, may we be a blessing to You and others as we look to You and faithfully live under the authority of Your Word. Amen.

Questions for reflection and meditation:

1. What purpose did God have in mind when He designed marriage?
2. Why is God displeased with divorce?
3. How should a believing spouse treat an unbelieving spouse?
4. What commands of God are the most difficult for you to faithfully follow?
5. Is it okay for you to seek your safety and comfort? Why or why not?

Prayer based on 1 Corinthians 7:17-24

Focus on changing the world through the proclamation of the Gospel and not so much on changing your circumstances.

Father, we praise You, for You are all about Your glory and our good. You have called us to love and serve You. May we focus on living the life You have called us to and not focus on changing our external circumstances. Loving and honoring You through obedience, is what ultimately matters. May we care more about being faithful to Your Word than anything else.

Paul had a general rule for the Churches to remain as they are. Paul does give an exception in (Verse 21). You tell us that those You call to be a bond servant of You are set free, regardless of the circumstances. (Verse22) Paul reminds the Corinthians that You bought them at a great price. They are Your bondservants and warns them not to be a bondservant of another. (verse 23)

Father, You have called each one of us and assigned us our portion. May we be thankful for the gift that You have given us, and may we be faithful to walk in the places that You have assigned us as joyful, obedient slaves of righteousness. (Psalm 16:5-6) Amen.

Questions for reflection and meditation:

1. How have you been focused on changing your external circumstances? What is the problem with that mindset?
2. Are you rejoicing in your current situation? Why or why not?
3. How does being a bondservant of Christ bring you Joy?

Prayer based on 1 Corinthians 7:25-31

The council of Paul to the unmarried and widows, in difficult circumstances.

Father, we thank You for Paul, Your faithful and trustworthy servant, who lovingly speaks to the unmarried and the widows.

Paul continues to answer questions from the Corinthian Church. His answers are consistent with his prior teachings. He tells them to remain as they are. In light of the present distress (possibly severe famine), Paul recommends that the Corinthians not pursue marriage under their current circumstances. In (verse 28), Paul does see marriage as a good choice, but his desire, at this time, is to spare the Corinthians trouble. Father, in (verses 29-31), You remind us that the world is passing away, and regardless of our situation in life, we should be living a lifestyle that shows devotion to You. (Matthew 6:33)

Father, we praise You and thank You for Your many generous gifts. Keep reminding us that all things are from Your hand so that we may rejoice in them as we should. (1 Thessalonians 5:16-18) Although this present world is filled with many pleasures and struggles, You call us to belong to another world which will replace this life forever. (2 Peter 3:13-14)

Father, give us an eternal perspective, for we will be subjected to many concerns and much anxiety when we live for this world and lose an eternal perspective. May we be filled with Your spirit and live faithfully before You and others as we joyfully await Your return. Amen.

QUESTIONS FOR REFLECTION AND MEDITATION:

1. Why does Paul recommend that the Corinthians do not pursue marriage at the present time?
2. Do you believe that this world is passing away? If so how heavily invested in it should you be?
3. What are you anxious about and why?
4. When the Lord comes what will matter the most?
5. Will it matter if you are married or single, rich or poor, famous or unknown, etc.?

Prayer based on 1 Corinthians 7:32-35

The consequences of trusting in our own strength and the wisdom and joy found in abiding in the Vine. (John 15:5)

Father, we praise You for giving us confidence in Your goodness and power.

Lord, forgive us when we are prone, as the Corinthians were to place heavy emphasis on human merit. (1 Corinthians 4:7) Free us from trusting in our own efforts to please You. If our trust is in our own efforts, we will have good reasons to worry about falling from Your grace. May we humble ourselves, submit to Your ways, and rest secure in Your keeping.

Paul wants the Corinthians to be free from anxiety. A single man who desires to lead, protect, and provide for his wife will find marriage a heavy burden if he is trusts in his own efforts. Likewise a single woman who trusts in her own efforts will also try to please her husband in her own strength. Paul, knowing the proud Corinthians and being aware of their current circumstances, believes they would profit better by remaining single at this time.

Father, make us a people who continuously look to You and call upon Your name instead of trusting in our own strength and wisdom. Make us more aware that we are what we are and we do what we do by Your sustaining grace. (1 Corinthians 15:10) Give us grateful hearts that praise and worship You above all things and in all things. Amen.

Questions for reflection and meditation:

1. Why does Paul encourage the unmarried to remain single at this time? (Verse 32, 35)
2. What is the source of anxiety in your life?
3. What would it take for you to be free from being anxious?

Prayer based on 1 Corinthians 7:36-40

Giving, receiving, and acting on godly counsel.

Father, we thank You for the example of the apostle Paul, who gives us pastoral advice in ways that are neither manipulative nor heavy-handed.

Although Paul felt strongly about postponing marriage at this time, he also knew that each individual had to humbly and prayerfully settle this issue before You. Paul does not give them a set of rules but calls everyone to examine their hearts before the Lord. Paul calls on single men to prayerfully consider their motives: and be steadfast before proposing. Some believe that this passage could be addressing fathers, calling them to care for their daughters and give careful thought to giving them away. In (verse 38), Paul assures the single men that if they choose marriage, they have done well, but to choose to remain single is even better. Paul desired everyone to be free from anxiety and serve the Lord without distraction. In (verse 39), You tell us that a widow is bound to her husband as long as he lives, but if her husband dies, she is free to marry any believer that she chooses. Paul believed, at this time, she would be better off if she remained a widow. Under different circumstances, Paul does recommend that young widows be married. (1 Timothy 5:14)

Father, give us the moral courage to take full responsibility for our decisions and actions. Lord, keep us from blaming others and circumstances. May we not choose the easy and comfortable way, nor the hard way of duty. May our decisions and actions be guided by Your love. Lord, help us to press on in prayer until our hearts are conformed to Yours. May we not rest or act until we are assured that our decisions and actions are in harmony with Your Word. (John 17:11 b) You want and deserve our undivided attention and unwavering devotion to You. May we live for Your pleasure, and be quick to submit to Your will and Your ways. Amen.

QUESTIONS FOR REFLECTION AND MEDITATION:

1. When you give council, do you give good advice (rules to follow) or Good News (the Gospel)
2. How are you striving to know God and his will?
3. What does it take to walk in harmony with God and others?

PRAYER BASED ON 1 CORINTHIANS 8:1-3

The knowledge of God should make us humble.

Father, we thank You for another example of love and patience through Paul as he continues to answer questions from the Corinthian Church.

The Corinthians only wanted to know what was permissible and had no concern for what was profitable in serving others and pleasing to You. Paul wisely begins by laying a solid foundation for all teaching. He doesn't want to give them a set of rules to follow – that would only make them more proud and guilty. Paul desires to shepherd them well, see them follow his example, and learn to shepherd one another. Paul tells the Corinthians that if their knowledge makes them proud, they do not know as they should. (Verse 2) We know You only because You first loved us and revealed Yourself to us.

Father, may our awareness of Your love for us increase our love for others and cause us to strive to know You more. (Philippians 3:12-14) May any increase in our knowledge of You increase our love for You, our obedience to You, and make us more amazed and humbled by You. Conform us to Your image, so that we would think more of You and others and less of ourselves. (John 3:30) Amen.

QUESTIONS FOR REFLECTION AND MEDITATION:

1. What is in your life that may be permissible but is not profitable?
2. Why does Paul say that proud people do not know God as they should?
3. What is wrong with trying to live a holy life by following a set of rules?
4. How have you been amazed and humbled by the love and mercy of God towards you? How has that knowledge and experience affected the way you love others?

PRAYER BASED ON 1 CORINTHIANS 8:4-13

The characteristics of a life that is lived to make disciples of Christ.

Father, we thank You for showing us through Paul how to address the hearts of Your people.

Once again, Paul is not going to give the Corinthians a rule to follow but is going to address their hearts as a faithful under-shepherd. Paul could have told the Corinthians to abstain from food offered to idols (Acts 15:19-21), but he loved them too much to overlook the dangerous condition of their hearts. In (verse 4), Paul begins to answer questions about eating food offered to idols. Paul tells them that other gods and lords of this earth are nothing compared to You. For the believer, there is only one Lord for whom they exist. And He is over all things. Therefore, since the false idols of this world are nothing, they are free to disregard them. Paul does not want the Corinthians to be divided on this issue but to live in unity. Paul tells them that all do not have this knowledge and then calls them to have compassion for their weaker brothers. Paul assures them that it is not their keeping of rules that make them righteous or better than anyone else. He then gives them a strong warning. They are not to sin against their brothers by being a stumbling block to them. Paul then proclaims that he is willing to give up anything that would make his brother stumble. (Verse 13)

Father, give us a heart that is willing to put up with anything for the sake of Your Gospel so we may love others as You have loved us. Keep us from being prideful and divisive like the Corinthians. May Your Gospel be more important to us than our rights. Search our hearts, O Lord, so that we may see any divisive way in us that is displeasing to You. (Psalm 139:23-24) Amen.

QUESTIONS FOR REFLECTION AND MEDITATION:

1. Have you ever been guilty of giving someone a rule to follow instead of addressing their hearts?
2. How is it possible to keep all the rules and at the same time displease God?
3. How are you caring for your weaker brothers and sisters in the faith?

4. How have you been a stumbling block to a weaker brother or sister in the faith?
5. What fruit have you seen from being prideful and divisive?
6. What have you given up for the sake of the Gospel?

PRAYER BASED ON 1 CORINTHIANS 9:1-18

All effective ministry will involve sacrifice and care for others.
Ministry is rarely easy and convenient.

Father, we thank You for Paul, who lived according to what he taught in chapter 8.

In chapter 8, Paul taught us that Christians should be willing to forfeit their legitimate rights in loving service to others. Paul goes on in chapter 9 to describe his entire ministry as one of sacrifice and care for others. Paul wants the Corinthians to know that he has rights as an apostle. In (verses 1-10), Paul states his case for his rights and gives examples from life and Your Word. Paul then concludes in (verses 11-12) that he has a rightful claim on the Corinthians. Paul says that he did not exercise his rights, for he would endure anything rather then put an obstacle in the way of Your Gospel. Paul tells the Corinthians that his writing and preaching the Gospel is not for any earthly reward. He tells them that he already has his reward and that he preaches the Gospel willingly out of his love for You, for You have saved him and called him to be an instrument in Your hands. (Acts 9:10-15) Paul forfeiting his right to receive pay shows another distinct difference between him, a true apostle, and the other so called apostles. What a powerful ministry Paul had!

Father, may we also live a life that lines up with what we proclaim so we can have powerful testimonies to Your glory. May advancing the Gospel be our reason for living and more important to us than any gains or losses. Amen.

QUESTIONS FOR REFLECTION AND MEDITATION:

1. Have you ever forfeited your legitimate rights in service to others as Paul did?
2. What stumbling blocks to the Gospel have you incurred? Have you ever been one?
3. How would you describe Paul's ministry? Your ministry?
4. Why did Paul forfeit his rights and preach the Gospel free of charge?
5. Why does Paul's preaching of the Gospel give him no grounds for boasting?
6. Is there a connection between self-sacrifice and powerful ministry? Why or why not?

Prayer based on 1 Corinthians 9:19-23

The sacrificing or your rights and living for the benefit of others is necessary for powerful, effective ministry.

Father, we praise You for Your mercy and grace towards us. We confess that it is impossible for us to live for You alone, apart from Your sustaining Grace. Show us how to please You and be an effective instrument in Your hands.

You show us through the apostle Paul, how we can please You and have an effective ministry by surrendering our rights and being a servant to all. We should not strive for earthly rewards but for eternal rewards. (Philippians 3:14) Although Paul was free and did not have to conform himself to the preferences of others, he did so for the sake of the Gospel. When he was with the Jews he became a Jew and observed their customs and laws, although he was not saved by keeping the law nor under its curse. Likewise, when Paul was with the Gentiles who did not observe the laws of the Jews and had their own rules, Paul would conform to them as much as possible even though Paul disapprove of their pagan lifestyles. When Paul was with the weak, he became weak. For the sake of the Gospel, Paul became all things to all men. (Verse 22) Unlike the Corinthians, Paul limited his freedom. He was determined not to put any obstacle in the path of his weaker brothers.

Father, thank You for the amazing work You have done in and through the apostle Paul. Paul joyfully sacrificed his own rights so that he might share in the blessings of the Gospel. May You work the same way in each of us, according to Your will. Give us the same zeal for Your Gospel as Paul has manifested. Amen.

QUESTIONS FOR REFLECTION AND MEDITATION:

1. Why did Paul, who was free, make himself a servant to everyone?
2. Does powerful, effective ministry need to be self-sacrificing? Why or why not?

Prayer based on 1 Corinthians 9:24-27

Run that you may obtain the prize.

Father, You call us to run a good race and obtain the prize. Thank You for showing us what that takes in these verses.

Self denial in service to others is not easy. Our flesh does not want to surrender its rights for the benefit others. Paul had the same struggles. He tells us that he must discipline his body and keep it under control. He also tells us that he does not run aimlessly or box as one beating the air.

Father, may we also set definite Gospel-centered goals and not run aimlessly. May we be disciplined like an athlete who exercises self-control and joyfully makes the sacrifices necessary to run a good race. (Hebrews 12:1-2) Amen.

May we accept the fact that the cost of following You is great but the cost of not following is much greater.

Questions for reflection and meditation:

1. Have you ever grown weary of disciplining your body?
2. When was the last time you ran aimlessly?
3. How do you live your life with Gospel centered intentionality?
4. What has it cost you to follow Christ?
5. What cost have you incurred from not following Christ?
6. What joyful sacrifices have you made for the benefit of others?

Prayer based on 1 Corinthians 10:1-13

Who will and who will not enter the kingdom of heaven.

Father, we thank You for the strong warnings given in this Scripture. We can be so slow to learn lessons from the Old Testament and so blind to the seriousness of sin.

You compare the experience of the Corinthian Christians to the wilderness wanderings of the Israelites. You delivered the Israelites from Egypt and baptized them into Moses – just like the Corinthian Christians were delivered and baptized into Christ. All the Israelites ate the spiritual food from heaven and drank the water from the Rock – the Corinthian Christians also shared in the Lord's supper, eating the bread of life and drinking at Your table. You go on to tell us that You were displeased with the Israelites and Moses – they did not enter the promised land but died in the wilderness because of their disobedience. In (verses 7-11), You continue to tell us that You will punish idolatry, rebellion, grumbling, and complaining. Through all these examples, it is clear that no one who continues in ungodly practices will escape Your judgment. In (verse 12), You warn us again to be careful and fear falling.

Father, we thank You for (verse 13), which You so appropriately placed after these strong warnings. You remind us that You have provided a way of escape from all sin through the finished work of Your Son on the cross. May we rejoice in Your deliverance and not be like the proud, deceived Corinthians – who did not see their idol worship as an abomination to You. Lord, deliver us from our idols and make us holy, distinct people that follow hard after You. Amen.

Questions for reflection and meditation:

1. Why did all the Israelites who experienced the deliverance and provision of God die in the desert?
2. How have you wandered in the wilderness?
3. Are you currently wondering in the wilderness, or are you resting in God's provisions?
4. What idols have you recognized in your life?
5. What has God done in your life to make it possible for you to follow hard after Him?

PRAYER BASED ON 1 CORINTHIANS 10:14-22

Wholehearted devotion to God is on display
in the practice of servant-leadership.

Father, we praise You for Your faithfulness even when we are not. (2 Timothy 2:13)

You call us to flee from idolatry. May we see idolatry as a serious matter and never flirt or toy with it. We thank You for the example of servant-leadership through Paul. He does not exert his authority but calls on the Corinthians to judge the matter for themselves. Paul wants the Corinthians to understand the mysterious union they have with You and other believers when they participate in the Lord's Supper. We are indeed one body, and we all partake of one bread. You alone are God over all. All other so-called gods, idols, and demons are nothing compare to You, but they do exist. Paul tells the Corinthians that they can not partake of the table of the Lord and of the table of demons. He also warns them not to provoke the Lord, for he is a jealous God. (Exodus 34:13-15)

Father, may we recognize and flee from all idolatry. We want to be humble, loyal, and faithful servants of You and others. Lord, open our eyes and grant us repentance in Your mighty name. Amen.

QUESTIONS FOR REFLECTION AND MEDITATION:

1. Why was it wrong for the Corinthians to eat at the feasts in pagan temples?
2. What activities are not beneficial for you? (Activities that decrease your love and devotion to God)
3. What activities are beneficial for you? (Activities that increase your love and devotion to God)
4. What provokes the jealousy of the Lord in your life?
5. Why is jealousy a just response from God?
6. How often do you recognized idolatry in your life and turned from it?

Prayer based on 1 Corinthians 10:23-11:1

A call to seek the well-being of others, abstain from things that may be lawful but are not beneficial, and make an effort not to be an unnecessary stumbling block to the Gospel.

Father, we praise You, for the earth is Yours and all that is in it. Let us eat and drink and be grateful for all You have given us.

Paul quotes a saying well known among Corinthians. They say all things are lawful for me. Paul agrees that all good things are lawful but then declares that all good things are not beneficial or edifying. Paul continues to call the Corinthians to seek the well-being of others above their own rights. Paul tells the Corinthians they have the right to buy and eat meat sold in the marketplace with a clear conscience. He tells them not to ask any questions about the meat they purchase in the market. If someone tells them that the meat was sacrificed to idols, they should abstain from eating. They should surrender their rights for the sake of not hindering the Gospel. Paul strives not to be an unnecessary offense to the Jews, the Greeks, or the Church, regardless of the cost, to himself. Paul then implores the Corinthians to imitate him as he imitates Christ.

Father, we do not want to be an unnecessary offense to anyone and hinder Your Gospel in any way. Give us the same love for others as You have shown us. Make us more mindful of You so that whatever we do is done for Your Glory. Amen.

Questions for reflection and meditation:

1. What things in your life, although lawful but are not beneficial or edifying?
2. What rights have you surrendered for the well-being of others?
3. Why must God urge us to consider the interests of others above our own? What are the benefits of doing so?
4. Have you ever, like Paul, implored others to imitate you? Why or why not?

Prayer based on 1 Corinthians 11:2-16

Living under the authority of the Word of God. Worshiping Him as we should. And looking to Your Word to establish our beliefs.

Father, we thank You for giving us Your Word so that we can know Your ways and joyfully live under Your authority.

Your Word is eternal and unchanging. To seriously study and live under the authority of Your Word, we must know first and foremost that all of Scripture is from You and never produced by the will of man. (2 Peter 1:20-21) You also tell us that all Scripture is breathed out by You: profitable for teaching, for reproof, for correction, and training in righteousness. (2 Timothy 3:16-17) May we pay attention to these facts as we study and meditate on Your Word and never dismiss anything in Your Word because we think it is irrelevant or uncomfortable. Open our eyes and hearts to see the principles taught in this passage. Paul wisely begins by commending the Corinthians for maintaining the traditions he has given them. Paul wants all to understand that God the Father has authority over Christ: Christ is given authority over all men, and husbands are given authority over their wives. (Ephesians 5:22-30) teaches us how husbands should love their wives and properly exercise their God-given authority. Fallen men are certainly prone to abuse authority, but when men submit to Christ and love their wives as He calls them to, it is beautiful, pleasing to God, and brings glorify to Him. Paul then addresses a serious problem that exists when they gather in worship. They fail to honor You and each other when they gather to worship. (Verse 4) <u>proclaims</u> that every man who prays or prophesies with his head covered dishonors his head (Christ). And every woman who prays and prophesies with her head uncovered dishonors her head. (husband, betrothed, or father) (Verse 10) states that a woman should have a symbol of authority on her head. (Versus 5-9) clearly teach that there is a difference between men and women. May we see that differences exist, but without superiority or inferiority. Persons can be equal and different, as it is clearly shown in the Godhead. God the Son is equal to the Father but different. The Son lives in complete submission to the Father but is not inferior in anyway. (John 5:19) The same is true for the Spirit. (John 14:16) Paul continues to teach that all things are from You and that man is not independent of woman, nor is woman independent of man. Paul then calls the Corinthians to judge for themselves; if it is proper for a woman to pray in Church with her head uncovered. Paul continues to present his argument, calls the Corinthians not to be contentious, and then concludes that this is his practice and the practice of the Churches of God. May we not get caught up in head coverings and miss the principles taught in Your Word. You and Paul are concerned that men live and act like men and that women live like women.

Father, May we look to Your Word and not to our culture to define biblical masculinity and femininity. May we celebrate our differences and be free to honor You and others in all we say and do. When we gather in worship, may everything we do exalt Your Glory and not the glory of man.

Father, give us an awe-inspiring view of Scripture and a humble, teachable spirit, so we will take Your Word as seriously as we should and joyfully live under Your authority. May we give You all the praise, honor, and Glory, You rightfully deserve. Amen.

QUESTIONS FOR REFLECTION AND MEDITATION:

1. What facts about the origin of Scripture, help you to diligently study, obey, live, and boldly proclaim the Gospel?
2. What is the purpose of gathering on Sundays for worship?
3. How are men and women different and equal?
4. How can you increase your faith and your desire to live under the authority of Scripture?
5. Who or what sources do you trust in to form your beliefs?

Prayer based on 1 Corinthians 11:17-33

Celebrate the Lord's supper in a manner that will
please and honor God and serve His Church.

Father, we thank You for giving us the Lord's supper to celebrate. How we celebrate the Lord's supper is extremely important to You. Open our eyes to see the Lord's supper as the weighty matter it is.

Paul, who praises the Corinthians in (verse 2) of this chapter, is now giving them a strong rebuke. He boldly tells them that their gatherings are so bad it would be better if they did not meet at all. In (verse 19), Paul says there must be factions among you, so that those who are genuine among you may be recognized. You have used division in Your Church to provide a backdrop that can make the saints among them shine even brighter! Your designs and Your ways are perfect. May we see this truth and respond well. Paul then continues with the rebuke. He calls them self-centered gluttons that do not love and serve the poor believers among them. They are filling themselves and letting the poor go hungry. Paul then asks them; why do they despise the Church and shame those who have nothing? Paul goes on to teach what he has received from the Lord. Paul tells us that the Lord's supper should be a time of remembering, honoring the sacrifice of Your Son, and proclaiming His death until He comes. Paul then goes on to give a strong warning to those who partake of the Lord's Supper in an unworthy manner. Paul says those who eat and drink in an unworthy manner eat and drink judgement on themselves. Paul calls us to examine our lives prayerfully and judge ourselves. You promised us if we do, we will not incur judgment. We will be chastised but not condemned. It is appropriate to ask our Father to examine our hearts, show us our sins, and lead us in His ways. (Psalm 139:23-24), but for many, myself included, the Lord's Supper was all about me being right with God. This Scripture teaches that the Lord's Supper is more than that. We are to recognize that Your Son selflessly sacrificed His body so we would be a selfless corporate body that puts You on display in all we do. Before we take of the Lord's Supper may our hearts be right before You.

Father, may our hearts be thankful and rejoice in the grace You have freely given – not only to us individually but to Your body (the Church) as well. May we be filled with Your Spirit so we may approach this sacred, wonderful meal in a way that pleases and honors You. Amen.

QUESTIONS FOR REFLECTION AND MEDITATION:

1. How did the Corinthian Church corrupt the Lord's Supper?
2. Is the Lord's supper and individual event or a corporate event?
3. What does it mean to eat and drink in an unworthy manner? What will result if you do?

PRAYER BASED ON 1 CORINTHIANS 12:1-11

There is one God, working through one Spirit to empower
His diverse body to live together, in unity, with one purpose.

Father, we praise You for the wide variety of gifts that You have so wisely given to Your Church through the outpouring of the Holy Spirit.

Paul compassionately addresses the proud Corinthians as brothers and then boldly tells them that he does not want them to be uninformed about spiritual gifts. He reminds them that they were pagans, enslaved to false gods, and could never have been devoted to Your Son without the Holy Spirit making it possible. Only those given the Holy Spirit can honor Your Son and proclaim Him as Lord. Their lives will be a living testimony of Your Lordship. You tell us that there are varieties of gifts given by one Spirit, varieties of ministries given by Your Son, and varieties of activities all given by the Father. All are One – working together to empower all who believe.

Father, may we humbly pray and gratefully receive whatever gifts You have for us. You will wisely and generously give, as You see fit, to each individual who asks. May we rejoice in Your gifts and never be envious of others. May envy be replaced with great joy, as each gifted believer loves and serves one another with the strength and grace that You provide.

Father, may Your Church be built up and fulfill Your calling. Cause us to grow in humility and joyfully accept our dependence on You. May we care for Your Church and strive to live together as one unified body for Your glory. Amen.

QUESTIONS FOR REFLECTION AND MEDITATION:

1. How has God knitted you together with a body of believers?
2. What gifts from the Holy Spirit have you received?
3. How are you using the gifts that God has given to you?
4. How are you joyfully serving and building up the body of Christ?
5. Does (verses 4-6), intentionally teach the Trinity, by showing us the three persons of God at work?

PRAYER BASED ON 1 CORINTHIANS 12:12-31A

The Church is to be one body, with many members, all working together to edify one another and bring glory to God.

Father, we praise You and thank You for individually creating us, redeeming us, giving us spiritual gifts, and knitting us together into one body.

You tell us that we are one body with many members, for You baptized us into one body, and we were all made to drink of one Spirit. Paul reminds the Corinthian Church how diverse they are: some are Jews, some Greeks, some have masters, and some are free. At one time, they were all divided by many things. They are now united together in one body through one Spirit. (Ephesians 2:14) Paul then compares Your Church to the human body, which has many parts that depend upon each other. You tell us that You have arranged each member of Your body as You choose. You also tell us the members that seem to be weaker are indispensable. You have bestowed more honor on the parts that we consider less honorable, so that there would be no division in the body. You tell us when one member suffers, we should all suffer, and when one member is honored, we should all rejoice. (Romans 12:10.) Paul tells us that we do not all have the same gifts and then earnestly encourages us to desire the higher gifts.

Father, may we honor one another and earnestly desire the gifts that will bring the greatest benefit to Your Church. Make us a people who live more for others and less for ourselves. Amen.

QUESTIONS FOR REFLECTION AND MEDITATION:

1. What things can or have separated you from God and other believers?
2. Why does God give spiritual gifts to His Church?
3. Why does God choose to distribute His gifts individually?
4. What are the higher spiritual gifts that Paul is encouraging us to earnestly desire? (Verse 31)

Prayer based on 1 Corinthians 12:31-13:3

God calls us to pursue spiritual gifts and to considering our motives.

Father, we praise You for giving us spiritual gifts. Cause us to pursue them earnestly and with the proper motives.

You command us to desire and seek the higher spiritual gifts and carefully consider our motives. Why would we want to pursue the gift of prophecy: the gift of knowledge, the ability to understand mysteries, the faith to move mountains, and the ability to give sacrificially? Which one of these gifts would be most beneficial and why? Could it be possible to have all these spiritual gifts and miss fulfilling Your greatest commandment? (Matthew 22:37-40) You give us a strong warning in (Matthew 7:21-23).

Father, help us to identify the spiritual gift we most need. May we then fervently pray and carefully think about why we want it and how we will use it if You grant it. (Matthew 7:7-8) Let us all count the cost and weigh the benefits. Lord, give us what we need to be an effective instrument in Your hand. Amen.

Questions for reflection and meditation:

1. What would be some wrong motives for desiring and pursuing spiritual gifts? The right motives?
2. Who does God give His spiritual gifts to and why? (1 Corinthians 12:7, 25)
3. Is it possible to give up everything that you have and still gain nothing? Why or why not?

Prayer based on 1 Corinthians 13:4-7

*The beauty and order of scripture, and the deep-rooted
problems of impatience and indifference are exposed.*

Father, we praise You, for there is no one like You and there is no book
like Yours!

Many poets through the centuries have tried their best to define love,
but none of them come close to Your description of love given here.
May we have ears to hear and hearts that are open and teachable. You
amazingly give us 14 characteristics of love in these four verses. Your
Word is beautiful and perfectly ordered. When You gave us the ten
commandments, the first three are foundational to keeping the rest.
(Exodus 20:3-5) In (Mathew 5:3-12), You give us eight characteristics
of a blessed man, and once again, the first one given is foundational.
Lord, may we pay close attention to Your order in all of Scripture. There
are many characteristics of love. And the first characteristic You list
is patience. An impatient man is not loving, period. May we take our
impatience seriously and ask for repentance. Lord, May we not con-
fuse being patient with being indifferent. Patience is longsuffering and
endures an offense, but indifference disregards the offender and does
not love them. May we see how patient You have been with us so that
we may be more patient with others. May we also see and emulate the
patients that Paul displays when he wisely and lovingly brings correction to the Corinthian Church. Lord You go on to tell us what love is
and what love is not. You tell us that love is not rude, is not self-seeking,
and is not easily angered. Thank You for expounding on three characteristics of an impatient man. How perfect and beautifully ordered is
Your Word!

Father, open our eyes and hearts to see how displeasing self centered impatience is to You. May we experience godly sorrow and Your
amazing grace. Show us Your kindness and lead us to repentance so that
we may honor and please You in all our relationships. Amen.

Questions for reflection and meditation:

1. What separates the Bible from all other books?
2. What happens to a person who takes Your Word seriously, sees
    it for what it truly is, and begins to live under its authority.

3. What is the difference between impatience and indifference?
4. How have you excused your impatience or indifference?
5. What is the root cause of impatience or indifference?

Prayer based on 1 Corinthians 13:8-13

Today, the people of God see dimly, which is better than not seeing at all, but the DAY is coming when they will see clearly.

Father, we thank You for this blessed chapter.

You tell us that love is eternal and never ends. Everything else will pass away, but love will remain forever. There will be no need for the gift of wisdom. or knowledge, or healing, or working of miracles, or prophecy, or the gift of tongues, after the DAY of Your return. You tell us, for now, our knowledge is in part, and we prophesy in part. We see in a mirror dimly, for now, but when You return, we shall see clearly, face to face. May we recognize our current state of seeing dimly and humbly cry out to You for guidance and sanctification. May we eagerly look forward to the DAY when You will come and make all things right. (perfect)

Father, as we live in these last days, looking forward to the DAY of Your return, may we be fully aware of our dependence on You to empower us for Your ministry. May we not trust our dim view of things but look to Your Word for clarity and cry out for Your holy Spirit to empower us for ministry. May we realize that knowing what to do is not enough, for we lack the power to live the life you have called us to live. You have promised to give us everything we need for a life of godliness. (2 Peter 1:3) Thank You for saving us, filling us with Your Spirit, and giving us spiritual gifts to edify Your Church. May we please You by living under Your authority and walking in harmony with You. All this is possible because of Your work. May others see the peace that we have in You and be drawn to You. (Matthew 5:9) Amen

Questions for reflection and meditation:

1. In what way has the perfect already arrived? In what way is the perfect yet to come?
2. Why do we still need to call on the Holy Spirit to equip us for ministry?
3. Are you quick to admit, your dim vision and partial knowledge, or do you trust in your own wisdom? (Proverbs 3:5-6)
4. How and why do you press on to know God more? (Philippians 3:12)

PRAYER BASED ON 1 CORINTHIANS 14:1-5

Earnestly pursue the gifts of the Spirit, especially prophecy.

Father, we praise You for the gift of Your Son, Your Word, and Your desire to empower and equip us to serve You and Your saints.

You tell us to pursue love and earnestly desire spiritual gifts, especially the gift of prophecy, so we will be equipped to speak Your truth into the lives of others.

Father, May are words and deeds be like Yours (filled with Truth and Grace). (John 1:14) May we have more desire to love and edify those You bring into our lives. May You oppose our prideful hearts and give us a humble heart that desires to build up others. (1 Peter 5:5b) Lord, make us more teachable and give us more desire to study and meditate on Your Word. We need to know You more, for we cannot talk about Someone we do not know, and we can not confidently testify about things we have not experienced. Do whatever You must do to make us a people who know You and have a strong desire to make You known. Give us a love for You that compels us to live for You. May we be bold and joyfully speak of Your wonderful works. (Psalm 105:1-2) Make us more mindful of You so we will be a letter read by all. (2 Corinthians 3:2-3) Amen.

QUESTIONS FOR REFLECTION AND MEDITATION:

1. Why is the gift of prophecy considered a greater gift than the gift of tongues?
2. What Spiritual gift do you desire and why?
3. How has God worked in your life to conform you to Himself and cause you to lean on him more?
4. What testimonies do you regularly share about the good work of God?

PRAYER BASED ON 1 CORINTHIANS 14:6-25

Striving to exalt God and not man in our worship so that all will be brought low and God is on display for all to see. (Verse 25)

Father, we thank You for Your spiritual gifts that You individually give to Your body so we may love and worship You as we should.

May we understand that our public worship and daily life should exalt You and benefit others. Paul gives many illustrations, showing the supremacy of the gift of prophecy over the gift of tongues. He tells that prayers of blessings and expressions of thanksgiving are good but can not edify the body if they are unintelligible. Paul commends the Corinthians for their zeal for spiritual gifts and encourages them to pursue a gift that will build up Your Church. Paul tells the Corinthians that if they speak in tongues in their gatherings, their must be an interpretation in order to build up the body. Paul tells them when he prays in tongues, his spirit prays, but his mind is unfruitful. May we, like Paul, prefer to sing and pray with both our minds and spirits engaged. Paul says that when he is with them, in worship, he would rather speak five words with his mind than 10,000 words in a tongue! Paul then affectionately calls them brothers and appeals to them to give up childish ways and grow up into mature Christians. Paul then explains how carelessly practicing the gift of tongues could be harmful to unbelievers and how prophecy could convict both unbelievers and believers and bring them to repentance.

Father, show us the childish self-centered ways that displease You and the childish ways we should exemplify. (Matthew 18:3-4) May we carefully consider what we permit in our worship, for You deserve all glory, honor, and praise. When we gather together to worship, may everything we do exalt You and not ourselves so that all who are gathered will be awestruck and be able to declare that they have been in Your presence! Amen.

QUESTIONS FOR REFLECTION AND MEDITATION:

1. Why does God give spiritual gifts to His Church?
2. How is the gift of prophecy superior to the gift of tongues?

3. Is the gift of tongues a legitimate gift from God or just a strange phenomenon? Give reasons from Scripture to support your answer. (Verse 18)

4. How can the careless practice of the gift of tongues in a church be harmful for unbelievers?

5. How can the gift of prophecy be helpful to all?

6. What childish ways are destructive, and what childish ways should you exemplify?

7. How often are you awestruck by the presence of God in worship?

8. How has experiencing God in worship changed the way you think and live?

Prayer based on 1 Corinthians 14:26-40

Orderly worship that pleases and honors God and builds up the Church.

Father, You deserve all glory, honor, and praise! May You be exalted in our worship of You.

You want us all to come together to worship, with our hearts prepared to praise You and honor You. May we come prepared to share something that will exalt God and encourage others to worship. May we not come as consumers but as participants. May we use the spiritual gifts given to us to build up Your Church and bring glory to You. You are not the author of confusion but of peace and order. Paul emphasizes self-restraint for the greater good of the body. Paul commands that no more than three should speak in tongues and in proper order. Paul also insists that they must keep silent unless there is an interpreter. Prophecies must also be given in turn so that everyone may be encouraged. Paul then instructs others to weigh what was said. This raises an issue for the wives. How should they honor their husbands, and at the same time weigh in on what their husbands said? Paul instructs the women to be submissive and not speak during this time. He wisely instructs wives to encourage their husbands to lead by humbly asking them questions at home. Paul is not against women speaking, in Church, for he encourages women to pray and prophesy. (1 Corinthians 11:5) Paul concludes by imploring the Corinthian Church to seek the gift of prophecy and not forbid people from speaking in tongues, but to do all things orderly and decently.

Father, may we learn from Your Word. Give us a greater love for You and Your body so that our worship of You will give You all the glory and honor and praise that You deserve. Amen.

Questions for reflection and meditation:

1. How would you describe the worship in your church?
2. Do you come as a consumer or do you come as a participant with something to share?
3. Should the Church today strive to follow the New Testament model shown in Scripture? Why or Why not?

PRAYER BASED ON 1 CORINTHIANS 15:1-11

Paul gives a comprehensive description of the Resurrection of Christ.

Father, we thank You for Your Gospel which opens the eyes of the blind and humbles all who have ears to hear.

Before Paul gives the most comprehensive discussion of the resurrection of Christ in the entire Bible, he first reminds the Corinthians of the Gospel, which they had received. He tells them that a believer will remember the Gospel, love to hear it proclaimed, and hold fast to it. You tell us through the apostle Paul that Jesus the Christ died, was buried, and rose again on the third day, according to Your Word. The apostles saw the resurrection of Christ, along with 500 other witnesses. He was last of all seen by Paul/Saul on his way to arrest the Christians in Damascus (Acts 9:1-9) Paul describes the attitudes of a believer by using himself as an example. Paul saw himself as the greatest of sinners. (1 Timothy 1:15) He knew his great need and knew he was saved and kept by grace alone. Paul rejoiced in the great love of God for him and lovingly labored more abundantly with the strength that God provided.

Father, May we see our need to be mindful of the Gospel every day and rejoice more and more in what You have done for us through Your Son. Amen.

QUESTIONS FOR REFLECTION AND MEDITATION:

1. Why did Paul remind the believers in Corinth of the Gospel?
2. What are the benefits of preaching the Gospel to yourself everyday?
3. How does one become aware or their sinful nature? (Isaiah 6:5)
4. What characteristics of a believer are given to us through Paul in (versus 9-10)?

Prayer based on 1 Corinthians 15:12-19

Problems will come if we deny the bodily resurrection of Christ.

Father, we thank You for giving Paul the patience to care for the Corinthians as he addresses yet another serious problem.

Some of the Corinthians did not believe in the resurrection of the dead. They believed that You could restore life as You did with many miraculous healings, but they did not believed in the bodily resurrection of the dead. Like the Corinthians, we can find it difficult to believe because our view of You is too small. Paul patiently explains to the Corinthians the consequences of this unbelief. If Christ did not rise from the dead, then our witness is false: our faith is futile, we are still in our sins, and those who have fallen asleep in Christ have perished and will never receive a glorified body. Paul proclaims if we have hope in Christ in this life only, we are of all people the most to be pitied. (Verse 19)

Father, give us faith and hope in a resurrection like His. (Romans 6:5) Thank You for Your Son, who endured the cross for the joy set before Him. (Hebrews 12:2). May we also see the joy set before us. Everyone You call will know You, joyfully follow after You, and be raised to life on the last DAY. (Philippians 3:10-11) Amen.

Questions for reflection and meditation:

1. If Christ did not rise from the dead what are five sad consequences?
2. Why should Christians be the most pitied if they have hope only in this life?
3. What are the four goals of every believer given in (Philippians 3:10-11)?

Prayer based on 1 Corinthians 15:20-22

Christ was the first to be raised with an immortal and incorruptible body.

Father, we thank You for the life, death, and the bodily resurrection of Your Son.

Jesus, thank You for showing Your disciples Your glorified resurrected body. Your disciples were startled when they first saw You and thought they saw a spirit. You told them to touch You, so they may know that Your resurrected body is flesh and bone. You showed them Your scars and asked them for something to eat. (Luke 24:36-42) You also appeared again for Thomas, who would not believe unless he saw You alive in the flesh. (John 20:24-29) Paul proclaims that Christ has risen from the dead. He is the firstfruits of those who have fallen asleep. (verse 20) Father, we praise You, for long ago, You gave the Israelites seven feasts to be celebrated. (Leviticus chapter 23) Jesus celebrated the Passover feast the night of His betrayal. The Passover was a celebration of deliverance from death by the blood of the Lamb sprinkled on their doorposts. (Exodus 12:1-11) Jesus then appropriately celebrates the Feast of the Firstfruits by rising from the dead on the day after the Sabbath. (Resurrection Day/Easter) (Leviticus 23:10-11) Lord, You were crucified on Passover, buried on the Feast on Unleavened Bread, and rose to life on the Feast of Firstfruits. The next Feast would be 50 days after the Feast of Firstfruits. (Leviticus 23:15-16) We praise You, Father, for You foretold all that would happen. All in Adam would die, but through Christ all shall be made alive. In (Exodus 32:28), 3000 who worshiped idols died in there sins – on Pentecost, 50 days after the Feast of Firstfruits, 3000 repented and were made alive in Christ. (Acts 2:41)

Father, we praise You, for Your Word. May we have ears that hear, eyes that see, and hearts that will respond to Your Gospel. Amen.

QUESTIONS FOR REFLECTION AND MEDITATION:

1. Why does Scripture go to such great lengths to make it clear that the resurrected body of Jesus was flesh and bone.
2. Why is the bodily resurrection of Christ referred to as the first fruits?
3. What does the bodily resurrection of Christ guarantee?

PRAYER BASED ON 1 CORINTHIANS 15:23-34

The events that will occur when Christ returns in glory.

Father, We praise You for raising Your Son from the dead. This first fruit is a guarantee for all Your people. (Romans 6:5)

Paul gives the order in which things will happen. First, Christ, the first fruit, is raised from the dead. Then those who are His at His second coming will be taken up with Him in glory. Next, Your Son will put an end to all rule and authority. He will destroy all his enemies and deliver the kingdom to His Father. Christ will reign until all enemies are put under his feet. The last enemy to be destroyed will be death. All history will end with God triumphant over all evil and the people of God reigning with Christ forever. (2 Timothy 2:1 11-13, Revelation 1:5-6) In (verse 29), Paul then returns to address those who deny the resurrection. Paul asks them, Why do they baptize for the dead if they believe there is no resurrection of the dead? Paul does not believe in their practice. He is just challenging their thinking. Paul tells the Corinthians that he dies to himself every day. Paul then proclaims that all his efforts gain nothing if the dead did not rise and live forever. If Christ has not risen, we may as well eat, drink, and be merry for tomorrow we die. Paul then calls the Corinthians to wake up and know God, for those who know God will repent and live.

Father, may we not be deceived like some of the Corinthians, but may we wake up from our drunken stupor and not go on sinning, but turn from sin and serve You in the righteousness that You provide. Amen.

QUESTIONS FOR REFLECTION AND MEDITATION:

1. When Jesus returns, who will have a resurrection like His and who will not?
2. What does Paul mean when he says he dies to himself every day?
3. What is your response to the imminent return of Jesus?

Prayer based on 1 Corinthians 15:35-58

Everything corruptible, weak, and dishonorable must die in order to raise them incorruptible, powerful, and honorable.

Father, we thank You for Paul who continues his care for the Corinthians by patiently answer their questions.

The Corinthians want to know how the dead are raised and what kind of body they will have. Although their questions may be a cloaked objection to the resurrection of the dead, Paul will answer them and show them how foolish they are because they think so little of Your abilities. Paul tells them a seed planted in the ground does not look like the plant it will become. A seed buried in the earth must die, and You must raise it to life and give it the body that You have determined for it to have. So it is with every seed that is planted. You have done this with Your Son and will do this with everyone who belongs to Your Son. Paul then tells the Corinthians the difference between the earthly body that dies and the glorified resurrected body that You will give to those who are united with You. Two men that had no earthly fathers. The first was Adam, which You made from dust, and the second was Jesus, who came from heaven and dwelt among us. We are all sons of the disobedient Adam, and we have all inherited his sinful nature. Paul tells us that God will raise the body sown in corruption, weakness, and dishonor to be incorruptible, strong, and honorable. We have all borne the image of the man of dust. All who belong to Your Son will reflect the likeness of the man from heaven! You then tell us that flesh and blood can not inherit Your kingdom. On the DAY Your Son returns, the trumpet will sound. And all who belong to You will be changed in the twinkling of an eye. The immortal will put on immorality and death swallowed up in victory!

Father, We must die to ourselves if we are to live. (1 Peter 2:24) May we love and delight in Your Word so that we may be faithful and obedient disciples who remain steadfast, immovable, and unbounding in the work that You have prepare for us to do. (Ephesians 2:10) Amen.

Let us read and meditate on Galatians 2:20-21, 5:24, John 12:24-26

QUESTIONS FOR REFLECTION AND MEDITATION:

1. Why did Jesus have to die?
2. In what ways must you die, if you are going to live a fruitful life for God?
3. How do you experienced victory through death?
4. What does Paul mean when he says he dies daily? (1 Corinthians 15:31, Romans 8:36)

Prayer based on 1 Corinthians 16:1-4

*The love and glory of God are put on display when
His people give sacrificially and generously.*

Father, we praise You for Your love and great sacrifice for poor sinners like us.

Paul begins chapter 16 answering another question from the Corinthians about the collection for the saints in Judea – who are suffering from a severe famine. Paul directs all of them to set aside an offering, on the first day of the week, in accordance with how You have prospered them. Paul wanted no collections taken up when he came. Instead, he wanted the Corinthian Church to be faithfully giving to the poor as a regular part of their corporate worship. May this be so in Your Church today.

Father, may we see our responsibility to care of the poor believers among us. (Galatians 6:10) May we also see it as our responsibility to support Your missionaries and other workers in Your ministry, both local and abroad. Make us a people who imitate You by living out our faith in loving, sacrificial service to others. May we be faithful, generous, and joyful givers like the Macedonians. (2 Corinthians 8:1-4) Amen.

Questions for reflection and meditation:

1. Why does God direct His people to give joyfully, generously and sacrificially to His Church?
2. How does your giving reflect the condition of your heart? (Matthew 6:21)

Prayer based on 1 Corinthians 16:5-7

We are to submit to God, joyfully and gracefully serve others,
and prayerfully set our agendas.

Father, we thank You for giving us an example of a life lived in submission to You May we learn to emulate this example.

Paul does not want his life driven by his will or impose his will on anyone. Paul tells the Corinthians he may remain with them for the winter, and they may support him and send him on his journey if the Lord permits. Paul desires to do Your will, in Your way, and in Your time.

Father, give us the same heart that Paul had so that we may live for You and You alone, as he did. Amen.

Questions for reflection and meditation:

1. When was the last time you imposed your will on anyone?
2. How committed are you to following the Lord instead of your own plans?
3. When was the last time you laid down your agenda and followed His?
4. Do you regularly ask for and receive wisdom from God? Why or Why not?

Let us read and meditate on Proverbs 3:5-7.

Prayer based on 1 Corinthians 16:8-9

*God prepares believers for successful ministry and calls them to obedience.
They must firmly stand where He has placed them.*

Father, Thank You again for Paul, who always wants to be where You are at work.

Paul tells the Corinthians that he will stay in Ephesus until Pentecost because He knows that You have given him a good work to do. Paul knows this is true for two reasons. Hearts are open, and there is opposition. Paul knew that only You open hearts, and he also knew that many opposed Your work.

Father, may we know You as Paul knew You, so that we can know when we are doing Your work, in Your way, in Your time and when we are not. Make us sure, confident, and bold and not half-hearted or doubting in the work that You give us to do. (Ephesians 2:10) May we prayerfully set our priorities everyday, so that we will be faithful to walk in Your ways. (2 Timothy 3:12-13) Amen.

Questions for reflection and meditation:

1. What good work has God given you to do today?
2. How did Paul know his work in Ephesus was given to him by God?
3. Everyday we decide to do certain things and not to do other things. Who or what sets your daily agendas?

Prayer based on 1 Corinthians 16:10-24

*A believer is aware of the grace of God and responds to it
by joyfully living under the authority of His Word.*

Father, we thank You for preserving this letter to the Corinthians. Open our minds and hearts so that we may strive to correctly understand all the instructions You have for us in this letter.

You instruct Your Church in Corinth to honor, support, and submit to Timothy, for he does Your work as Paul does. Paul refers to Apollos as our brother, and strongly urges him to visit the Corinthians. Paul tells the Corinthians that Apollos is not willing to come at this present time. It is likely that Apollos, like Paul, has been given an effective ministry. Apollos may strongly desire to be with the Corinthians, but in obedience, he chooses to remain where he is, for now. Paul mentions the household of Stephen and other faithful ministers of the Gospel and calls the Corinthians to acknowledge, support, and submit to such high character and devotion to ministry. Paul then gives greetings from the Churches in Asia and concludes with a strong warning. Paul proclaims that everyone who does not show love for the Lord is accursed. Paul then prays for You to come and punish those who bring trouble to Your Church with their pretense of faith.

Father, Give us the desire to stay and work where You have planted us or go wherever You call us. You called us: to make disciples, to be watchful, to boldly stand fast in the faith, and to be loving in all that we do. You also call us to acknowledge, honor, and submit to our leaders in Your Church and every fellow worker who laborers for the Gospel. Make us humble submissive servants who live under the authority of Your Word and follow hard after You. Amen.

Questions for reflection and meditation:

1. How are you striving to live for God in the place He has you?
2. In what ways are you resisting His call to go and serve Him?
3. On a scale from 1 to 10, How do you rate your current situation in life? A 1 being unsure of His calling and unaware of the grace of God in your life. A 10 being confident in his calling and overwhelmed by the grace of God in your life.

4. What would have to change in your life, for you to become more aware of God's grace and His calling?
5. How do you support and submit to your church leaders and other fellow workers of the Gospel?
6. How are you growing in your passion to live under the authority of God's word?

Let us read and meditate on Psalm 16. May God meet us as you cry out to Him.

2 CORINTHIANS

Prayer based on 2 Corinthians 1:1-11

God fulfills His purposes through suffering.

Father, we praise You for appointing Paul to be an apostle. You are the source of all blessings and do everything for Your Glory and our good. You have comforted Paul in his sufferings, which equipped him to comfort others in their suffering. You are the God of All comfort, who appoints suffering for those who belong to You, so they would know Your mercy and grace and be able to extend comfort to others. Your ways are perfect and difficult to understand with our fallen intellects. Lord, be patient with us and have mercy on us. May we praise You and never forget that You are perfect in all of Your ways, even when You are chastising us. (Proverbs 3:11-12, Hebrews 12:5-11)

Paul suffered many things and loved the Corinthians deeply. He was rejected by some who denied his apostleship, questioned his motives, and opposed the many instructions that Paul wisely and lovingly gave to them in his first letter. Paul shared with the Corinthians the troubles that he had in Asia. He says he was burdened beyond measure and felt that he had received the sentence of death. You then reminded Paul that You are the One who raises the dead! (Verse 9) Paul praises and gives You thanks for his trials and Your deliverance from them all. (Verse 10) Paul sees his struggles as a means for him to experience more of Your grace. Paul will gladly embrace his sufferings, for his desire is to see Your power on display. He is more concerned about pleasing You than his comfort. (2 Corinthians 12:10) Paul had many powerful testimonies to share with others because of his sufferings. He learned the blessings of trusting in You instead of trusting in his own abilities. Paul believes in prayer and wants to encourage the Corinthians to pray. He knows You answer the prayers of the saints. (verse 11)

Father, may we respond well to our sufferings and learn to praise You and thank You for all things, including our sufferings. You give good gifts to Your children and never withhold any good thing. (Psalm 84:11) You are worthy of all our praise! Amen.

Questions for reflection and meditation:

1. What causes us to miss many of the blessings of God?

2. Why does Paul praise God and thank Him for all the suffering in his life?
3. How has God equipped Paul to comfort others?
4. Is blessing through suffering a common experience in your life?

Prayer based on 2 Corinthians 1:12-14

An example of a saint.

Father, we thank You for the simplicity and sincerity that Paul displays. These qualities are only possible by Your grace.

Paul wrote, by Your grace, with godly sincerity, and not with fleshly wisdom. Paul has a clear conscience, for he knows what he has written is from You and is meant to be plainly understood. The Corinthians and others today try to read other meanings into Your Word. Paul has a clear conscience and is joyfully awaiting the return of Your Son – when He will judge all works. Paul hopes and prays for the Corinthians to understand. He wants to be boasting in them and them to be boasting in him when Your Son returns.

Father, may we have a clear conscience like Paul had and joyfully look forward to Your return, with open arms, minds, and hearts. May we see Your kingdom come and Your will accomplish in Your Church. Amen.

Let us meditate on this example of a saint and ask God to give us a pure heart so that we may see Him. (Matthew 5:8)

Paul had a sincere, passionate desire to live and proclaim the Gospel.

His conscience was clear. He believe that God would always direct the humble in His ways. (Psalm 25:9-10) Paul was confident in God. He firmly believed that everything he said, wrote, and did was directed by God.

Questions for Reflection and Meditation:

1. How confident are you in your walk with the Lord?
2. Do you have a clear conscience? Why or why not?
3. How does your daily prayer life compare to the model Jesus gave us? (Matthew 6:9-13)
4. Are you joyfully awaiting the return of Jesus or are you content or even prefer that He would delay.
5. Are you living for the DAY when you will see Jesus face to face and hear him proclaim, well done, my good and faithful servant, or are you living for something else?

Prayer based on 2 Corinthians 1:15-2:2

A loving Response to opposition.

Father, we praise You and rest in You, for You are consistent in all Your ways.

Paul experienced a painful situation when some within the Corinthian Church questioned his ways. They accused him of being fickle and untrustworthy. Paul assures the Corinthians that he does not make plans according to the flesh. Paul believed his change of plans was directed by God and for their benefit. The charges were so severe Paul had to reinforce his apostleship and his love for the Corinthians. (2 Corinthians 1:18-24, 2:1.) Paul then reminds the Corinthians that God has established them with Paul and Timothy in Christ through the outpouring of the Holy Spirit. Since Paul lived openly and honestly before the Corinthians, they should have known his heart and rejected the accusations made by the false teachers.

Father, make us faithful servants who give careful and prayerful thought before speaking or acting. Conform us to Your ways so that we will keep Your Word and our word. Keep us from all evil so that we would never say or do anything that would cause others to doubt the sincerity of our faith and question what we profess. May we dwell in the shadow of the Most High. (Psalm 91:1) Amen.

QUESTIONS FOR REFLECTION AND MEDITATION:

1. Have you ever experienced a painful problem, like Paul experienced with the Corinthians?
2. Has anyone ever doubted the sincerity of your faith because you did not keep your word?
3. Have you ever been unjustly accused? How did you handle the situation?
4. What reason did Paul give to the Corinthians for not visiting them?

PRAYER BASED ON 2 CORINTHIANS 2:3-11

*Example of a healthy, loving Church that practices
God-honoring church discipline.*

Father, thank You for working in the life of Paul and giving him such a great love for You and the Corinthian Church.

The love of Paul for the Corinthians is evident in (verse 4). The man Paul refers to in (verse 6) could be the man who was excommunicated in (1 Corinthians 5:1-5). Paul instructed the gathered Church to turn this man over to Satan, for through the destruction of his flesh, he would be among the saints in the DAY of the Lord. This restorative discipline has accomplished what it set out to do, and now Paul calls the Church to forgive and comfort this repented sinner so that the man will not be overcome with sorrow. Paul reminds the Church body that they have the power to forgive, and then assures them that whoever they forgive will be forgiven. (John 20:23, Matthew 16:19) Paul tells the Corinthians they should forgive this man and welcome him back into fellowship for the sake of Christ. By doing so, they will also thwart the purposes of Satan. (which are two divide, kill, and destroy).

Father, may we know the great love that You have for us. Give us a gracious, loving heart that desires to show Your love for all in every circumstance. May You keep us from self-righteous judgments and make us quick to listen and quick to forgive. May we be obedient servants who look to You and lovingly watch over our brothers and sisters, which You have placed in Your local Churches. (Hebrews 3:13) Amen.

1. How have you experienced forgiveness? What effect did it have on you?
2. What makes it possible for someone to be slow to speak, quick to listen, and quick to forgive?
3. How is God at work in You and your Church?
4. How is healthy church discipline practiced in your church?

Prayer based on 2 Corinthians 2:12-16

*Our lives are to be a triumphant procession that spreads
the fragrance of the knowledge of God everywhere we go.*

Father, we praise You and thank You for the high calling You give to those who believe in You. You call, equip, encourage, and exhort Your children to follow in Your ways. You guide them daily and give them everything they need to walk confidently in You. And You have prepared every good work for them to do. (Ephesians 2:10) You are great and greatly to be praised!

In the Roman world, the generals would parade into a captive city, towards the palace of the king, with human captives and their treasures displayed behind them. The people taken captive would be killed, and there would be an aroma of death. Also, there would be a sweet incense offered for the victory. Paul gives thanks and praise to You, for Christ always leads His people in a triumphal procession, spreading the fragrance of His knowledge in every place.

Father, may we be the fragrance of Christ wherever we go. You tell us the same scent will produce different results. May we be the aroma of Christ in a lost and dying world, no matter what it costs. Amen.

QUESTIONS FOR REFLECTION AND MEDITATION:

1. How would you describe your walk with Christ?
2. What work has God given you to do today? Are you rejoicing in it?
3. In what ways could you live more intentionally for the Gospel?
4. What has it cost you to be a Christian?

A Christianity without a cross, will, in the end, become a useless Christianity without a crown. Quote from Holiness, by J.C. Ryle.

Prayer based on 2 Corinthians 2:17-3:6

Only God can make us sufficient ministers of the Gospel.

Father, we thank You for Paul and his love for You, Your Word, and Your people in Corinth.

Paul had a clear conscience, and his motives were pure in everything he and his fellow workers did. Paul could confidently say that he and his fellow workers sincerely spoke Your Word and did not peddle it as other false teachers did. Some in Corinth wanted a letter of recommendation from Paul. Paul did not see the need to ask for any letter of recommendation. The spiritual transformation of the Corinthians was endorsement enough for Paul. Paul tells them they are his letter of recommendation to be seen and read by all. A letter written in ink or even stone, in and of it itself, lacks the power to change a life. Written words can only convict or condemn. You tell us that the letter kills, but Your Spirit gives life. We are only transformed into new creatures when Your Spirit writes Your Word on our hearts. We then (and only then) become Your letter to be read by all.

Father, may we know and experience the Truth of Your Word, and may Your Truth be lived out in our lives by Your Power and for Your Glory. Amen.

Questions for reflection and meditation:

1. How could Paul be so confident in everything he said and did?
2. Why did Paul tell the Corinthians that he did not need any letters of recommendation?
3. How is your confidence in God on display in your life?

Prayer based on 2 Corinthians 3:7-18

*The surpassing Glory of the New covenant
compared with the Old Covenant.*

Father, we thank You for replacing the Old Covenant, which brings death to all who sin. Your law is good and has served us well. The Old Covenant brings death because we are sinful and can not keep It. We praise You, Father, for Your New Covenant, gives life to all who believe in Your Son and call upon His name. (Romans 10:9)

Paul contrasts the Old Covenant with the New Covenant. The old Covenant brought death and condemnation, was engraved in Stone, and had a Glory that was both fading and temporary. The New Covenant brings righteousness, is written on hearts by the Holy Spirit, and brings a surpassing and everlasting Glory. When Moses was in Your presence his face reflected Your Glory. Moses put a veil over his face so the people of Israel could not see the fading glory. You tell us there is a veil that remains unlifted until the day one turns to the Lord. (Verse 14) We can only see our sin and repent after we have beheld Your Glory. (Isaiah 6:5, Luke 5:8) Those who repent and believe in You will have unveiled faces, which will reflect the Glory of the Lord. They will continue to be transformed from one degree of Glory to another by the power of the Holy Spirit living in them. (2 Corinthians 3:18)

Father, may we see that growth is normal and healthy for Your children. Give us more desire to grow more and more into Your likeness everyday. (Proverbs 4:18) Amen.

QUESTIONS FOR REFLECTION AND MEDITATION:

1. What is the difference between the Old Covenant and the New Covenant?
2. How have you experienced the removal of the veil describe in (verse 16)?
3. Are you currently experiencing the glorious growth described in (verses 17-18)?

Prayer based on 2 Corinthians 4:1-6

Do not lose heart by following your passions, but repent and joyfully follow the calling of God so that you may walk in His ways and be amazed at the work of God in your life and others.

Father, we praise You, for You and You alone can open the eyes of the blind, to see the light of Your glorious Gospel.

You have called us to be ministers of the New Covenant. You call us not to lose heart but to renounce behaviors that are not appropriate. As Your children, we must hate sin: put it to death, and live for You. You tell us that Satan has blinded the eyes of unbelievers so they can not see the light of Your glorious Gospel.

Father, we praise You, for You chose to reveal Yourself to us and give us the knowledge of Your glorious Gospel so that we may have an intimate relationship with You and be enabled to live for You. Give us compassion for the blind, boldness to speak to them, and the faith to believe that You can remove the veil from their eyes, just as You have done for us. We thank You and praise You, Father, for shining Your light into our darkened hearts and giving us the knowledge of Your glory. May we respond to Your goodness by joyfully telling others of Your wonderful work. (Psalm 40:5) Give us the faith we need to follow You. As we faithfully evangelize, may we be filled with joy, wonder, and astonishment as we see You remove the veil from the eyes of unbelievers. You have called us to be fishers of men. (Matthew 4:19) May we rejoice in the work You give us to do. Amen.

Let us read and meditate on (Matthew 28:17-20)

Questions for reflection and meditation:

1. What motivates you to put sin to death?
2. What testimonies do you have of mortifying sin and living for His glory?
3. What inhibits you from growing in your love for God (Hebrews 12:1)
4. Where do you find your greatest joy?

PRAYER BASED ON 2 CORINTHIANS 4:7-12

*Good work is accomplished, through afflictions, in the
life of a believer. (Psalm 119:71)*

Father, we praise You for in Your wisdom, You have placed Your treasure in jars of clay.

We place our worldly treasures in a secure safe that we believe is impenetrable, but You are not like us. You put Your treasure into easily broken jars; of clay before You harden them in the fire. In Your wisdom, You have chosen to place the priceless treasure of Your unfading Glory into frail ordinary human beings. You allow Your children to be hardpressed, perplexed, persecuted and struck down so that Your children will cry out to You and experience Your resurrection power. You delight in putting Your power and glory on display for all to see. We must be given over to death for Jesus's sake so His life will manifest itself in our mortal flesh. (Verse 11).

Father, help us to understand that dying to ourselves brings life. (Matthew 16:25) Teach us to embrace our sufferings. May we see that suffering is necessary for our growth and an opportunity to put Your glory on display by the way we walk through trials in a manner that pleases and honors You. May we be among those who suffer well and become great ministers of the Gospel. Amen.

QUESTIONS FOR REFLECTION AND MEDITATION:

1. What has been your response to suffering in your life? Who or what have you turned to?
2. Why does God allow His children to suffer? (Romans 5:3-5, James 1:2-4)
3. How can it be possible to rejoice in our sufferings and thank God for them?
4. Have you received more benefits through prosperity or through your sufferings?

Prayer based on 2 Corinthians 4:13-18

*We are to live for the sake of the Gospel and suffering well,
never forgetting the eternal glory found only in Christ.*

Father, thank You for the opportunities You give us to suffer.

You have spoken to us of the sufferings and the blessings we receive when we minister of the Gospel. You gave us (Psalm 116), which describes a man who loves You and experiences sufferings along with Your blessings. May we praise You for Your blessings and the sufferings that come from following You. You have raised Your Son from the dead and You will also raise all those who are united with Him. May we never forget that the glory we will receive through Your Gospel far surpasses the suffering we endure for Your Gospel.

Father, open our eyes, so we may see and rejoice in Your grace, which is new every morning. May we not lose heart as we see our outer body wasting away, but may we rejoice in being renewed inwardly every day. You tell us not to look to the things we see, for all we see is temporary, decaying, and will pass away. May we look to You who is unseen, permanent, and eternal, for only in You will we find life. Amen.

Questions for reflection and meditation:

1. How have you suffered for the Gospel?
2. How have you been blessed by sharing the Gospel?
3. How has suffering cause you to know God more?
4. How can a believe rejoice when their body is wasting away?

Let us read and meditate on Psalm 116.

PRAYER BASED ON 2 CORINTHIANS 5:1-9

God has a plan for His people in this life and after death.

Father, we praise You, for Your plans are perfect, and You will do all that You purpose to do.

We live in a tent, a temporary structure that will weaken and die. Abraham lived in tents, and in faith, he was looking forward to a city that You would build (Hebrews 11:10) Those who know You will earnestly groan and desire clothing in a glorified body, which You will give them at the final resurrection of the dead.

You have given us an intimate relationship with You in this tent through the Holy Spirit living in us. We thank You for this deposit, which You freely give to everyone You choose, as a guarantee of what is to come. As long as we live in this tent, we must walk by faith and not by sight. Those who belong to You yearn for the DAY when they will see You face to face. On that Glorious DAY, their faith will become sight. Lord, You tell us that we must be unclothed (separated from our body) before being clothed in a glorified body. Existing without a body until You return is a strange thought for us. May we walk by faith and not by sight and have the same desires Paul has in (Verse 8). Paul says that he would rather be away from the body and be at home with the Lord.

Father, may we love You more and make it our aim to please an honor You in our life and in our death. Give us the faith to rest confidently in You – knowing full well that You will give us the grace we need to handle every situation so we will be able to glorify You in our life and our death. To live is Christ and to die is gain. (Philippians 1:20-21) Amen.

QUESTIONS FOR REFLECTION AND MEDITATION:

1. How do you deal with the fact that you live in a temporary tent which will weaken and die?
2. How can a believer rejoice and proclaim that their best days are yet to come? (2 Corinthians 4:16-18)
3. What does it look like, in your life, to walk by faith and not by sight?
4. How can you rest and confidently know that you will honor God, in your life and in your death?

Prayer based on 2 Corinthians 5:10-13

*We should know the fear of the Lord and live openly
and honestly before God and others.*

Father, we praise You for saving us and giving us all that we need to follow hard after You.

You remind us that all will appear before Your judgment seat, and all will receive what is due. May we know that we are responsible and will be held accountable for our actions: our words, our goals, our motives, the use of our time, and the use of our abilities. All will be laid bare before You. (Hebrews 4:13) Paul knew the fear of the Lord and the importance of obedience. Paul wanted all of the Corinthians to come to know You as he did. He wanted them to boast in You and Your work and be able to stand and address the false teachers who boast about outward appearances.

Father, may we not sin against You and others. Only You know every heart fully. Lord keep us from making foolish presumptions. We need to see everything through Your eyes. Give us wisdom, insight, and a healthy fear of You so we can please You in all things. Amen.

Questions for reflection and meditation:

1. How do you feel about being laid bare before the Lord and receiving what you are due?
2. If we are saved by grace through faith alone then why will God judge us by our works? (Romans 2:6, 1 Peter 1:17, Psalm 62:12)
3. What are your motivations for doing good? List all, both good and bad.
4. What kind of boasting is sinful and what kind of boasting is pleasing to God? (Verse 12)
5. Have you ever judged someone from what you observed without inquiring about their motives? What makes this so wrong and displeasing to God?
6. Paul was very thoughtful and careful about his actions, for he wanted to represent God well and see the Corinthians come to salvation. How is it with you?

Prayer based on 2 Corinthians 5:14-6:2

God has reconciled us to Himself, making us new creatures,
and given us the ministry of reconciliation.

Father, we thank You for sending Your Son and raising Him from the dead. Your Son died in our place so that we may no longer live for ourselves but for You. You broke the power of canceled sin and set us free from bondage. Your blood can make the foulest clean. You are worthy of all Praise, Honor, and Glory! (Revelation 5:1-14)

Paul says that, from now on, he regards no one from a human point of view. From now on refers to the conversion of Paul as he describes in (Galatians 2:20). All glory be to You, for You made Paul a new creature. The old is gone, and the new has come. Paul then implores the Corinthians to be reconciled to You and calls them to a ministry of reconciliation as ambassadors for Christ. Paul lastly reminds them that today is the favorable day of salvation. (2 Corinthians 6:2)

Father, we Praise You for Your work of reconciliation. You have reconciled us to Yourself through the shedding of Your blood and gave us the ministry of reconciliation. (Colossians 1:20) Open our ears so that we may hear Your call and respond. Give us more desire to represent You well. May we not receive Your grace in vain, but be grateful and live for Your pleasure. Amen.

Questions for reflection and meditation:

1. How would your life be different if God did not salve you?
2. How does the love of God control you and compel you?
3. How does being saved from the wrath of God change the way we regard others?
4. What motivates you to pursue reconciliation with others?
5. What does it mean to receive the grace of God in vain.
6. Why does Paul say that today is the favorable day of salvation? (Verse 2)
7. When will the favorable time for salvation come to an end? (Hebrews 9:27)

Prayer based on 2 Corinthians 6:3-13

An example of Godly character and how God develops it.

Father, we thank You for giving life to Paul and his fellow ministers.

Paul can commend himself and his fellow workers, for You have worked in them and through them. You tell us that You have chosen Paul to bear Your name. You gave him many amazing testimonies of Your power through the hardships that You have ordained in his life. (Acts 9:15-16) You know what it takes to build godly character. You describe the life of Paul in Christ in (Verses 4b-10). Paul embraces and rejoices in his hardships because he loves You more than life. (Psalm 63:3) He sees his hardships as opportunities to put You on display. He loves to please and honor You more than he loves his comfort. He is willing to put up with anything for the sake of making the Gospel known. Paul and his fellow workers have lived open and honest lives with no limits on their affections for the Corinthians. Paul believes that the Corinthians are withholding affections for him and his fellow workers. They will not admit their weakness and will not open their lives for examination. Paul responds by passionately speaking to them as children and implores them to open their hearts.

Father, search our hearts; show us any grievous way in us, and lead us in Your ways. (Psalm 139:23-24) Give us more of a desire to be like You and not like the proud Corinthians. Amen.

Questions for reflection and meditation:

1. What has God used in your life to build godly character?
2. What good work has God done in and through you this past week?
3. What hardships have you embraced this week?
4. How have you come to know and love God more through your trials?
5. Are there others in your life that are withholding their affections from you? If so, How did you respond?

Prayer based on 2 Corinthians 6:14-7:1

We should strive to please God in all our relationships.

Father, we thank You for the New Covenant made possible through the shed blood of Your Son.

We must care for unbelievers to fulfill Your great commission. (Matthew 28:18-20) we should Love unbelievers and desire them to know You as their Savior, but we must never be bound to them as we are bound to Your body (The Church). (Galatians 6:10)

Under the New Covenant, you call us to live lives distinct and separate from the world. We are told not to be unequally yoked together with unbelievers. Paul asked five questions designed to make the Corinthians think, and then he reminds them that they are Your temple. (Verse 16) You have promised that You would make Your dwelling in us and that You would be our God and we would be Your people. (Ezekiel 36:27) You call Your children to depart from all unclean ways. We are to be one with You as Your sons and daughters. (Verses 17-18)

Father, You have chosen Your children and called them to live a holy life (distinct and separate from the world). May we not take Your discipline lightly, and may we not grow weary when You reprove us. (Hebrews 12:5-6) Give us a strong desire to be cleansed from every defilement so that we may experience the joy of being Your sons and daughters now and forever. (Hebrews 12:1-2) Amen.

Questions for reflection and meditation:

1. What freedoms are you rejoicing in, and what bondages still hinder you?
2. How is your investment in unbelievers different from your commitment to your brothers and sisters in Christ?
3. Do You grow weary when God disciplines you, or do you rejoice in His kindness and goodness to you?
4. What does it mean to touch no unclean thing? (Verse 17) And what will be the reward if you obey?
5. What have you lost, or what must you give up to gain Christ? (Philippians 3:8)

Prayer based on 2 Corinthians 7:2-4

To walk by faith and not by sight.

Father, we praise You and thank You, for You have made peace with Your enemies through the shed blood of Your Son.

You comfort the downcast and call us to comfort one another, as You have comforted us. Paul, once again, asks the Corinthians to open their hearts to him and his fellow ministers. Paul wanted all the Corinthians to know their deep commitment to them. They are for them and would never harm them in any way. Even though the Corinthians misunderstood the pure intentions of Paul, he loved them and delighted in them through much tribulation. Paul is overflowing with joy, confident in their salvation, and filled with comfort. Paul is a man who certainly walked by faith and not by sight.

Father, grow us up in You and give us open hearts that love and care for one another as You have loved and cared for us. Lord, may we live by faith, with our eyes on You and not on our circumstances. Amen.

Questions for reflection and meditation:

1. How many characteristics of a saint do you see on display in this passage?
2. What has Paul put up with for the sake of the Gospel?
3. What have you put up with for the sake of the Gospel?
4. When you encounter situations, are you more prone to walk by faith or sight?
5. Are you able to love and delight in your church as Paul did, even when rejected and apposed.
6. What does it take for you to love those who oppose you?

PRAYER BASED ON 2 CORINTHIANS 7:5-16

The difference between godly sorrow and worldly sorrow.

Father, we thank You for You are our rock and salvation. You keep us in the shadow of Your wings and comfort the downcast.

Thank You for comforting Paul in Macedonia. When he was troubled on every side and had no rest, You sent Titus to him to comfort him with the good news of Your work in the Corinthian Church. When Paul hears about the Corinthian's morning and longing and zeal for the Gospel, he overflows with joy. Paul regretted rebuking them and causing them grief, but now he rejoices because their godly grief cause them to seek repentance. You tell us that godly sorrow produces a repentance that leads to salvation without regret, whereas worldly sorrow produces death. (Verse 10) Paul continues to rejoice over the work of God in the Corinthian church. (Versus 13:16) Father, help us to discern worldly sorrow that leads to death from godly sorrow that leads to life in You. May we see that the outcome of our sorrow indicates its true nature. In one verse, You give us at least five results of earnest godly sorrow: an eagerness to clear yourself so that your life would reflect His glory, a love for You and Your righteous ways, a passion to do what is right in Your eyes, a fear of offending You, and a zeal to forsake all and follow hard after You. (verse 11)

Father, may we grow in all these qualities and frequently experience the joy of godly sorrow. Amen.

QUESTIONS FOR REFLECTION AND MEDITATION:

1. How has God comforted you when you were troubled and cried out to Him?
2. How have your brothers and sisters in the Lord shared with you the comfort given to them by God? (2 Corinthians 1:3-4)
3. How have you comforted others with the comfort that God has given you? (2 Corinthians 5:18)
4. What is the difference between worldly sorrow and godly sorrow?
5. When have you experienced worldly sorrow or godly sorrow? How have you come to discern the difference?

Prayer based on 2 Corinthians 8:1-15

Joyfully, sacrificially, and generously giving to all.

Father, we praise You for Your grace is new every morning.

We thank You for pouring out Your grace so abundantly on the Churches in Macedonia. (The churches in Philippi, Thessalonica, and Berea) (Acts 16-17) They first gave themselves wholly to You and then to the ministry of the saints. Even though they were afflicted and had very limited resources, they were filled with joy and had a strong desire to give. In (Verse 4), Paul seems reluctant to take any gift from them, for they were begging earnestly for the favor of taking part in the relief of the saints. What a wonderful picture of a generous, joyful giver. Paul then encourages the Corinthians to abound in this grace also. Paul does not command them to give, for he wants to see the sincerity of their love on display. The generosity of the Macedonians set a high standard, but the sacrifice of Jesus is infinitely higher. He left the riches of heaven and became poor so that believers through His poverty might become rich. (Verse 9) You are worthy of all honor, glory, and praise!

Forgive us Lord, when we struggle to give out of our abundance. You know what is best for us. You warn us that If we feast on the treasures of this world, we will have no appetite for the treasures of heaven. (Matthew 6:19-21) Lord, give us the grace we need to be joyful, sacrificial givers. Open our eyes so that we may see the true needs all around us and joyfully complete the work You have given us to do. (Ephesians 2:10) Amen.

Questions for Reflection and Meditation:

1. Do you give sacrificially or just the leftovers?
2. Have you ever, like the Macedonians, begged earnestly to give to anything?
3. How is the sincerity of your love for God on display?

Prayer based on 2 Corinthians 8:16-24

The signs that prove the Gospel is the central work of the Church.

Father, we thank You for Titus and his earnest conviction to care for the Corinthian Church.

Paul tells the Corinthians that Titus is very diligent and is coming to them of his own free accord. Paul says that he is also sending a famous anonymous brother who is highly praised for the preaching of the Gospel and appointed by the Churches to go with Titus. (Acts 20:4-5) gives a list of many Church members that accompanied Paul. It seems to be common practice for members of the Church to be involved with leadership.

Father, You obviously desire Your Church to be involved with leadership. You command us to do what is honorable, not only in Your sight but also in the sight of men – we should avoid even the appearance of evil. Paul called the Corinthian Church to give proof of their love. May we understand this call and respond to it. Amen.

Questions for reflection and meditation:

1. How do you show your love for your church?
2. How can you be sure that everything you do will be honorable in the sight of God and man?
3. Why did Paul call the Corinthian Church to give proof of their love? (Verse 24)

Prayer based on 2 Corinthians 9:1-7

God is pleased with unbounded, joyful, and generous giving.

Father, we thank You for the wisdom and insight that You have given to Paul.

First, he praises the Corinthians for the generous gift they promised last year for the persecuted saints in Jerusalem. Paul then encourages the Corinthians by telling them how the Macedonians were greatly encouraged because of their generosity. The Macedonians gave sacrificially and liberally. Paul then informs the Corinthians that he is sending brothers to make sure their gift is ready before he comes. If some Macedonians come with Paul and the Corinthians are not prepared to give, both the Corinthians and Paul would be humiliated. Paul wants their gift to be a free-will offering and not look like an extraction. You tell us whoever sows sparingly can not expect much of a crop. Likewise, if we sow bountifully, we can expect to reap bountifully. (Verse 6) God guarantees that all will reap what they sow. (Luke 6:38)

Father, You do not want us to give reluctantly or under compulsion. You delight in a joyful generous giver. Give us grateful hearts that realizes what we deserve is death, and what we generously receive is life. (Romans 6:22-23) May we delight in You and You in us, as we freely give what we have freely received. This is Your plan. (John 17:22-23) Thank you for Your plan! Amen.

Questions for reflection and meditation:

1. How are you sowing, and what are you reaping? what needs to change?
2. Why are we guaranteed to reap what we sow? (Galatians 6:7)
3. Are you a joyful generous giver who gives sacrificially? If so, what motivates you to give? If not, What hinders your giving?

Prayer based on 2 Corinthians 9:8

God is sufficient for all things and we can not abound apart from Him.

Father we praise You for You delight in giving good gifts to Your children. (Luke 12:32) We love You because You first loved us. We are quick to forget Your Love, power, wisdom, and resourcefulness. Forgive us Lord, when our actions and thoughts reflect are unbelief. Thank You for the reminders You give us in this passage. We need them daily because we are so forgetful and unbelieving.

You tell us that You can make All grace (Power and Resources) abound toward us so we may have All sufficiency in All things and an abundance for every good work that comes from Your hand. Lord, in one verse, You blow our puny minds. It is no wonder we forget, for we have no capacity to contain such great thoughts. We need You, Lord.

Father, cause us to walk through this day and every day with our eyes on You – praying and humbly asking for Your guidance in all things. When we fail in difficult situations, may we recall that You are able and willing to deliver us and then quickly turn to You in repentance and prayer. Amen.

Questions for reflection and meditation:

1. When are you most tempted to forget God and act out of unbelief?
2. What truths do you need to hear everyday so that you will not wander from the Truth but abide in Him?

Prayer based on 2 Corinthians 9:9-15

*The submission and joy that comes from knowing, believing,
and confessing the Gospel of Christ.*

Father, we praise You for enriching us in every way so that we may become a generous people who live for Your pleasure.

You set a high bar. In (Psalm 112:4-9) You give us a description of a righteous man. Lord, open our eyes as we meditate on these verses so that we may see the gap between Your righteousness and our own. May we not shrink back because we know we can not fulfill Your righteous demands. May we find ourselves wanting and cry out to You for the imputed righteousness You have provided through Your Son. (2 Corinthians 5:21) You tell us that You are the One who supplies the seed to those who sow and the bread for food. (Verse 10) Your Word is the bread of life, and You give it to all who know You, not only for their comfort and growth, but also for the purpose of spreading Your Gospel. You call Your children to proclaim Your Word, with complete assurance that Your Word will go forth and accomplish all that You purpose. (Isaiah 55:10-11)

We praise You Father, for Your incredible gift and all the opportunities You give us to share it. May our eyes and hearts be open to the physical and spiritual needs of all You bring into our lives. Amen.

Questions for reflection and meditation:

1. Do you shrink back when you fail to meet the righteous requirements of God, or do you rejoice in the fact that Christ has met them and is providing you an opportunity to repent and live for Him and others?
2. Do you feed on the bread of life, or are you starving on the crumbs of the earth?
3. What has consumed you? Do you rejoice and proclaim the goodness of God in your life or are you filled with worldly sorrow and little hope?
4. What is your answer to your guilty conscience?
5. What answer does God provide to your guilty conscience?

PRAYER BASED ON 2 CORINTHIANS 10:1-11

Paul defends his ministry.

Father, we praise You for giving us an example of servant leadership through the apostle Paul.

The apostolic ministry of Paul is challenged; by the false apostles. Paul passionately responds to this challenge. Some accused him of being bold when he was away and lowly and ineffective when he was among them. (verse 1) They obviously did not know Your Son, for if they did, they would have seen that the behavior of Paul was conformed to Your Son and confirmed his apostleship. Jesus spoke boldly, taught with authority, and was gentle, and lowly in heart. (Matthew 11:29) Paul tells the Corinthians that he prefers not to be bold but assures them if a situation requires boldness, he will boldly stand. (Verse 2) Paul tells the Corinthians that he and his company do not wage war according to the flesh. They do not employ intimidation, coercion, or clever arguments, but they have divine power to destroy strongholds. In their travels, Paul and his company destroyed every argument and lofty opinion raised against the knowledge of You. Paul believes that every thought must be taken captive and made obedient to You. (Verse 5) Paul had no doubt that he was in a war, and by Your grace, he would surely win. Paul says that he does not want to frighten them but assures them that there is no contradiction between what he and his fellow ministers say and what they will do in their presence. (Verse 11)

Farther, may we not be weak leaders who try to control and intimidate, but effective servant-leaders like Paul who are meek and serve with humility, for these will be effective in spreading Your Gospel and pleasing in Your sight. (Matthew 5:5) Lord, we thank You for the victory given to those who follow You. May are words and actions be consistent, without contradiction, and in harmony with Your ways. Amen.

QUESTIONS FOR REFLECTION AND MEDITATION:

1. Have you ever been in a situation where you served others by not being bold?
2. Have you ever prayed that you would not have to show boldness when bringing correction to someone?
3. What motivates you to be bold when correcting someone?

4. Why did Paul believe that every thought must be taken captive? (Verse 5)
5. How do you recognize and practice servant-leadership?
6. What does it take for your words and actions to be in harmony with the ways of God?

Prayer based on 2 Corinthians 10:12-18

Paul evaluates, boasts, and rejoices in the work God has given him to do.

Father, we praise You, for the boldness and the clarity of thought that You have given to Paul.

Paul shows the foolishness of the false apostles. Paul declares that they measure and compare themselves to one another and are without understanding. (Verse 12) In contrast, Paul will not evaluate his ministry by comparing it with others. He bases his evaluation on obedience to Your call on his life. The conversion of the Corinthians was proof that Paul obeyed Your call. His boasting was not beyond measure, for Paul brought Your Gospel to the Corinthians. Paul rejoices in the work that You have given him and looks forward to preaching the Gospel in the regions beyond. You command us to boast in You alone. (Verse 17, Jeremiah 9:23-24) You tell us that he who commends himself is not approved, but only those commend by You. (Verse 18) May we learn, like Paul did, to evaluate our life based on our obedience to Your call and not by horizontal comparisons.

Father, we praise You and thank You for Your work through Your faithful servants. Lord, give us more confidence in You so that we may boldly follow You wherever You lead. (Isaiah 6:8) Amen.

Questions for reflection and meditation:

1. How do you evaluate the ministry that God has given you?
2. What work has God given you to do this week and have you found joy in serving Him?
3. Do you regularly boast in the work of the Lord? Why or why not?
4. You tell us that He who commends himself is not approved. Why is this so?

Prayer based on 2 Corinthians 11:1-4

*Paul had God-like jealousy for the Corinthians and wanted them
to have a sincere, pure, and unwavering devotion to Christ.*

Father, we thank You for giving Paul a godly jealousy for the Corinthians.

Paul boldly addresses those who oppose his authority because he desires
to protect Your Church from error. You made Paul their spiritual father,
and he earnestly desires to present the Corinthians as a chaste virgin
to Your Son. He fears this may not happen because he sees how easily
the Corinthians are led astray by false teachers.

Father have mercy on us, for our prone to wonder is no different from
the Corinthians. Lord, turn our gaze to the cross and show us the depth
of Your Son's devotion for His bride. May we fall more and more in love
with You so we may love others as we should. Give us and more love for
the things You love and pure, sincere devotion to You, and god-like jealousy for one another. May we abide and trust in Your sustaining grace
to keep us safe. You are our fortress and strong tower. (Psalm 18:1-2)
May we quickly run to You in times of trouble. Amen.

Questions for reflection and meditation:

1. Have you ever experienced god-like jealousy for another believer?
2. How have you become overwhelmed by the devotion of Jesus
   to His bride?
3. How have you been growing in your love for God and others?
   (Proverbs 4:18)
4. In times of temptation, do you look to God to provide a way
   of escape or to something else?
5. Do you believe that God will always provide an escape from
   temptation? (1 Corinthians 10:13)
6. What matters most to you, escape and deliverance from trials
   and temptation or pleasing and honoring God in how you walk
   through trials and temptations?

PRAYER BASED ON 2 CORINTHIANS 11:1,11:5-15

Paul describes the difference between a true apostle and a false apostle.

Father, thank You for giving Paul a humble heart and patience with the Corinthians.

Paul knows it is foolish to boast in himself, but in order to show the folly of the false teachers, he will. In (verse 1), Paul asks the Corinthians to bear with him in some foolishness. In (verse 5), Paul clearly tells the Corinthians that he does not consider himself inferior to the super-apostles in any way. He may not be as trained in speaking as well as they are, but he does not lack knowledge. Paul was a humble man who faithfully taught the complexities and the mysteries of Your Word, which You had freely revealed to him. The super-apostles exalted themselves and found themselves worthy of being paid. In direct contrast to the super-apostles, Paul love the Corinthians: humbled himself, decided not to be a burden to them in any way, and therefore preached the Gospel free of charge. Paul received funds from the poorer Churches in Macedonia and also supported himself as a tentmaker. The intellectuals in Corinth considered work beneath them and therefore thought less of Paul instead of more of him. Paul continued to preach without pay in order to sharpen the contrast between him and the false teachers. In (verse 13), Paul calls them deceitful self-made apostles and reminds the Corinthians that even Satan can appear as an angel of light. (Galatians 1:8-9) You tell us that these false apostles will receive what they are due, either when Paul and his company arrives or when Your Son returns. (verse 15)

Father, we Praise You for Your Word. May we receive it, understand it, and respond appropriately to it. Give us a heart that is willing to endure anything for the sake of the Gospel. Amen.

QUESTIONS FOR REFLECTION AND MEDITATION:

1. Since boasting in ourselves is sinful, why is Paul boasting in this passage?
2. In what ways are you tempted to boast, privately and publicly?
3. Why does Paul not charge for his service to the Corinthians?
4. How can you recognize false, deceitful workers who disguised themselves as servants of Christ? What warning is given to them (in verse 15)?

Prayer based on 2 Corinthians 11:16-33

*Paul boasts in his sufferings and is willing to be
a fool for the sake of the Gospel.*

Father, we praise You, for You know how to make a godly man.

You gave Paul a heart for Your Gospel. Paul is so passionate about Your Gospel that he is willing to do whatever it takes to make it known to all people. Paul strongly desires that all the Corinthians would come to know You and see the super-apostles for what they really are. Paul knows that all who boast in themselves are fools, but he is willing to be a fool for the sake of Your Gospel. Paul clearly states that he is not speaking as the Lord but as a fool. Paul will boast so the Corinthians will see the difference between him and the super-apostles. Paul asks the Corinthians if the super-apostles are Hebrews, Israelites, and sons of Abraham? He then boldly proclaims So am I. Paul then asked them, Are they servants of Christ? And then boldly proclaims he is more of a servant. Paul then goes on to expound on the difference. (Verses 23b-27) Paul puts the false apostles to shame with his boasting. Paul shows patience, courage, and firm trust in You through all his hardships and learned to rely on You and not on himself. (2 Corinthians 1:9) Paul will only boast in Christ and the things that show his weakness. (Verse 30) God working in and through Paul is what separates Paul from the super-apostles.

Father, help us have the same healthy view of our hardships as Paul had. Lord, take away any bitterness and regrets and fill us with the joy that only comes from knowing You. May we be able to thank You for our hardships and rejoice over the godly character that You have developed in us through our struggles. You know what it takes to build god-like character in men and women – who know You and can rejoice in Your grace and mercy in all circumstances. (1 Thessalonians 5:16-18) May we trust in Your absolute goodness and Your sovereign reign over all. May we fall more in love with You, and learn to trust and rejoice more and more in Your daily provisions. May we be healthy disciples of You that continue to grow into Your likeness. (Proverbs 4:18, 2 Corinthians 3:18) Amen.

Let us read and meditate on 2nd Peter 2: 4-12

QUESTIONS FOR REFLECTION AND MEDITATION:

1. How has God worked in your life to make You a godly man or woman?
2. What situations in your life have caused you to grow the most?
3. Do you praise and thank God for your struggles? Why or why not?
4. Are you willing to be a fool for the sake of the Gospel? Why or why not?
5. What has caused you to grow in humility?

Prayer based on 2 Corinthians 12:1-10

Paul tells us about his heavenly revelation, his thorn the flesh, and gives his response to his thorn.

Father, we praise You, for You are all-knowing and all-wise. All good and perfect gifts are from You.(James 1:17)

You are patient with us and desire that all men would reach repentance. (2 Peter 3:9) You know what is needed for all the Corinthians, including the false apostles, to come to repentance. Paul, a meek and humble man, is compelled to continue to boast about visions and revelations that he has received from You. Paul tells of a man who was taken up into the third heaven fourteen years ago and heard things that no man may utter. Paul has humbly kept this a secret for fourteen years until now. Paul refrains from boasting so that no one would think more of him than what his words and actions convey. (Verse 6) WOW! Because of the surpassing greatness of these revelations, You gave Paul a thorn in his flesh to keep him from becoming conceited. Three times Paul pleaded with You to take away the thorn. You did not remove the thorn but You told Paul that Your grace is sufficient for him, for Your power is made perfect in weakness. (Verse 9) Paul gladly accepts and embraces his weakness, hardships, and persecutions, so that Your power may rest upon him. (Verse 10, 1 Corinthians 1:17)

Father, may we meditate on Your Word and learn much from the example of Paul. Amen.

Questions for reflection and meditation:

1. How has God work in your life to sanctify You?
2. Why did Paul refrain from speaking of a revelation from God for 14 years?
3. When was the last time you were concerned about anyone thinking to highly of you? (Verse 6)
4. When was the last time you corrected someone who thought to highly of you?
5. What weaknesses, hardships, and persecutions have you embraced and accepted?
6. Do you have a thorn in your flesh and how are you responding to it?

7. How have you experience the power of God made perfect in your weakness?
8. How have you encountered opposition to your pride from God or anyone else?

Prayer based on 2 Corinthians 12:11-13

The sacrificial love of Christ is on display in the life of Paul.

Father, thank You for revealing the humble and broken heart of Paul (verse 11-13).

Paul is sad because he had to boast. The Corinthians should of commended him because he lived openly and honestly among them. They should have observed his way of life and acknowledged him as an apostle sent from You. The signs were on display for them to see. Paul loved the Corinthians and served them well. He wisely, patiently and prayerfully rebuke them and taught them Your Word. Everything Paul did and said was for their benefit and for Your glory. He was always for them and would not place any burden on them. In spite of all this, they still thought less of him, for serving them free of charge.

Father, may our eyes not be blind like the Corinthians, but may we see Your power and grace on display in our lives and in the saints that live among us. May we rejoice in Your grace that is new every morning. (Lamentations 3:22-23) Amen.

Questions for reflection and meditation:

1. Why is Paul heartbroken in verse 11?
2. Paul tells us that signs and mighty works were seen and performed among the Corinthians. (Verse 12) What mighty works of God have you seen, know of, and tell of to others? (Psalm 105:1-5)

Let us read and meditate on Psalm 103.

Prayer based on 2 Corinthians 12:14-18

A heart for God that lives for His purposes.

Father, we praise You, for only You can prepare a heart that desires to live for the benefit of others.

You know all things, including how the third visit to the Corinthian Church will go. Will the Corinthians repent and receive Paul and his company or oppose them. In (verse 14), Paul tells the Corinthians that he is ready to come to them. We Praise You, Lord, for that kind of readiness only comes from spending time with You. Paul restates his commitment not to be a burden to them, for he is not seeking their possessions but their very lives. He tells them that parents should take care of their children. As their spiritual father, Paul shows his fatherly care. He declares that he would gladly spend himself for their souls. The desire of Paul is for his spiritual children to respond to his fatherly love. Paul goes on to ask the Corinthians If he or anyone he sent took advantage of them in any way?" Paul hopes and prays for the removal of their blinders.

Father, have mercy upon us and forgive us for being glory thieves. Remove our blinders so that we can see the foolishness of our ways. We are blind and living separately from You when we desire to do our work in our way for our purposes. Draw us into an intimate relationship with You, and cause us to delight in doing Your work in Your way and for Your Glory. (Philippians 2:13)

Questions for reflection and meditation.

1. How can you received the same kind of readiness that Paul received? (Verse 14)
2. What motivates you to spend yourself for others?
3. What drives your daily pursuits?
4. Are you a glory thief, or do you live for the glory of God?
5. How do you spend your time, and what benefits do you receive? (Isaiah 55:2)

Prayer based on 2 Corinthians 12:19-21

Living in Christ is living for the benefit of others,
even when it is risky and uncomfortable.

Father, we praise You for the work You have done in Paul. You have given him much insight into the hearts and minds of the Corinthians. And also great compassion for them.

In (verse 19), Paul asks the Corinthians if they think his boasting was all about defending himself. Paul, can boldly proclaim that everything he said and did was in Christ and for there benefit. Anyone who has an intimate relationship with You can make the same claim! Paul then openly expresses his fear of finding them in need of rebuke when he comes. Paul knows how rampant sin is in Corinth. He wants to rejoice in them, but he is afraid that he will find them in unrepentant sin. Paul sees this as a real possibility and knows if it is so, he will suffer great mourning and will once again have to humble himself before You and the Corinthians so that he would be in a position to benefit them.

Father, open our eyes and hearts so we may see our many failures and mourn over them. May we not be condemned but appropriately convicted. You have promised to comfort those who mourn. (Matthew 5:4) May we experience Your comfort and be overwhelmed by Your grace. You will freely grant repentance and faithfully restore all who confess their sins. (1 John 1:9)

May we read and meditate on the prayer Paul prayed in Ephesians 3:14-19

Questions for Reflection and Meditation.

1. What are the benefits of abiding in Christ? What benefits have you received? (Psalm 103)
2. How can living for others and the pleasure of God become central to everything you do and say?
3. Why is a humble posture necessary for successful ministry?
4. Why does Paul mourn over the sins of the Corinthians? (Verse 21)
5. Why is mourning one of the eight marks of a blessed man? (Matthew 5:4)
6. What sins have you seen in your life and mourned over?

Prayer based on 2 Corinthians 13:1-14

*Paul calls the Corinthians to prepare themselves
for his visit and the DAY when Christ returns.*

Father, we praise You, for You are the source of every good thing. Only You can give us the strength and wisdom that we desperately need to live out what we know and profess. Your ways are not our ways, and Your thoughts are not our thoughts. (Isaiah 55:8) Lord, help us to understand this passage. Give us ears to hear and the wisdom we need to understand Your Word. Having knowledge and understanding is good, but it is not worth anything apart from You.

Paul gives the Corinthians a warning to prepare them for his third visit. Paul begins in (verse 1) quoting Your Word in (Deuteronomy 19:15). You tell us that every fact shall be sustained and confirmed by the testimony of two or three witnesses. In (verses 2-3) Paul warns the unrepentant and assures them they will receive discipline since they seek proof that God is speaking through Paul. Paul is confident that his words will be proven true and his opponent's words proven false. (Romans 3:4) Paul identifies himself with Christ, who was crucified in weakness but now lives by the power of God. (Verse 4) Unlike the false apostles, Paul will gladly boast in his weakness so that Your power may rest on him. (2 Corinthians 12:9) Paul is confident in the authority he has received. Since Paul lived among the Corinthians, they have no good reason for not recognizing the apostolic authority given to Paul. Paul calls the Corinthians to examine themselves to see if they are in the faith. If they do, they will know the Truth (Christ is in them) unless they fail to meet the test. (Verse 5) Paul's life is open to examination, along with his fellow companions. Paul wants the Corinthians to see they have passed the test. Paul and his companions have worked for the Gospel and never against it. They have faithfully done the work God prepared for them. (Verse 8) Paul implores them to do no evil but only what is honorable, regardless of the circumstances. Paul prays for their restoration and rejoices in their growth. Paul once again reminds the Corinthians of his authority given by the Lord to build up the body of Christ, and he sincerely hopes that he will not have to exercise his apostolic authority when he comes. (Verse 10) Paul's final greetings are to encourage and challenge the Corinthians. Paul calls them to comfort one another, aim for restoration, agree with one another, be peacemakers, and to live in harmony with the saints in the Church.

Father, forgive our sins and grant us wholehearted repentance so we can fully obey, adore, and praise Your Name with all the saints, now and forever! Amen.

Questions for reflection and meditation.

1. How can you be confident in the work that God has given you to do?
2. How is God's power on display in your life?
3. Why does Paul call the Corinthians to examine themselves? (Verse 5)
4. What does God command us to do and what does He promise (in verse 11)?

Let us take time to read and meditate on 2 Corinthians 13:4-14 and ask God to examine our hearts. (Psalm 139:23-24)

GALATIANS

PRAYER BASED ON GALATIANS 1:1-5

*Paul was appointed to be an apostle, not by man, but by God,
to proclaim and defend the Gospel.*

Father, we thank You for preserving this letter to the Galatians, which Paul wrote under Your authority, to clarify and defend the truth of Your Gospel.

In (verse 1), Paul claims to be an apostle, chosen and appointed by You. His authority to speak is from You and not from men. Paul proclaims that You have raised Jesus from the dead, along with Paul and his brothers, who are with him. Paul will proclaim the Gospel and defend it until his last breath!

Father, give us more of a passion for the Gospel. May we live and proclaim the Gospel every precious day that You give us, for this is the day that You have made; let us rejoice and be glad in You. You alone are worthy of all our praise! Amen.

QUESTIONS FOR REFLECTION AND MEDITATION.

1. Paul appropriately begins his letter to the Galatians by proclaiming the glory of God in the Gospel of Jesus Christ! How do you start and end your days?
2. Why was it important for the Galatians to know that Paul was appointed as an apostle by God and not by man?

Prayer based on Galatians 1:6-10

Paul has a strong rebuke to those who distort or add to the Gospel.

Father, we praise You and stand amazed at Your love for sinners, such as us. You know how fickle we are and how prone we are to distort Your Gospel by adding our works to Your Gospel. Apart from You, we are bent to live for our glory instead of Yours.

Paul usually has words of thanksgiving after his greeting in most of his letters, but in this letter, he abruptly begins with a rebuke. Paul is amazed and deeply concerned when he hears that the Galatians have turned to a different gospel. Paul begins with this strong rebuke because he knows that a different gospel is no gospel at all. There is only one Gospel and only one name that can save. (Acts 4:12) Jews attending the Churches in Galatia claimed that salvation was impossible for an uncircumcised Gentile. Paul strongly opposes any gospel that requires works for salvation. Paul calls down a curse on all who preach any other gospel but the Gospel he has proclaimed. The false teachers accused Paul of trying to please men by lowering the requirements of salvation. Paul insists that he is not seeking the approval of men and would never lower the standards that God has set. You Word clearly teaches that we must be holy as You are holy. (1 Peter 1:15-16, Leviticus 11:45, Matthew 5:20.)

Father, grant us the wisdom to understand that we are saved by grace, through faith alone, and not by works so no one could boast. (Ephesians 2:8) Holy Father, You are right and just, and You will judge us by our works. (Romans 2:6, 2 Corinthians 5:10, Psalm 62:12) – You can righteously judge us by our works because all believers will bear the fruit of good works. (James 2:17, Luke 6:45) Paul declares if he tried to please men, he could not be a servant of Your Son. Lord, help us to see how this is true for all of us. You tell us, that we can not serve two masters. (Matthew 6:24, Mark 12:30, Deuteronomy 6:5) May we live for You and not for the approval of men.

Father, forgive us for our foolish and dishonoring ways. It is Your glory which we must seek and proclaim. Give us grateful hearts that rejoice in our Master and in all that He has done. May we always look to You, receive from Your hand, and joyfully tell of Your glorious work. May we learn that there is no greater joy to be found than the joy of walking in obedience to You. Lord, we thank You for giving us Your Word and sending Your Spirit to live in us so we can be holy and distinct people who walk in Your ways. (1 Peter 2:9) You and You alone are worthy of all glory, honor, and praise. Amen.

QUESTIONS FOR REFLECTION AND MEDITATION.

1. Why does Paul begin this letter with such a strong rebuke?
2. Paul says that if he is trying to please man he can not be a servant of Christ. Why is this true?
3. Why is teaching salvation by works futile?

Prayer based on Galatians 1:11-24

The effective call of God will transformed lives.

Father, we praise You for Your effective call on the life of Paul and all other saints.

The false teachers desired to discredit Your Gospel, which Paul faithfully preached to Your Churches in Galatia. They question the apostleship of Paul and his authority to speak for You. There are many who do the same thing today, but You will be proven true and every man a liar. (Romans 3:4) The false teachers compelled Paul to boast in You and Your work in him. Paul boldly tells them he did not receive the Gospel he preaches from men but by a direct revelation from Your Son. (Acts 9:1-19) Paul goes on to give his testimony of a transformed life. A transformed life is powerful and difficult to explain away. In (verse 15), Paul declares that You set him apart before he was born and appointed him to preach Your Gospel. Paul did not consult with anyone after his conversion but went to Arabia for three years and was taught directly by Christ. (Verses 17-18) Paul spent as much time with Jesus as the other apostles did. Paul proclaims that many glorified You, when they heard that he who persecuted Your Church is now preaching Your Gospel. (Verses 23-24)

Father, we praise You and thank You for revealing Yourself to Paul and changing his life. You gave Paul a powerful ministry. It is Your delight to make Yourself known and transform lives. May we find our joy in living for Your purposes and not for our own. It is Your will to conform us to Your image. (1 Thessalonians 4:3) Lord, give us more passion for a life lived for Your pleasure: a life that put You on display and reflects Your Glory. (Psalm 119:33-37) Amen.

QUESTIONS FOR REFLECTION AND MEDITATION:

1. When have you experienced the miracle of a transformed life?
2. Why is Paul compelled to boast about the work of God in him?
3. When have you been compelled to boast about the work of God in you?
4. Paul knew that he was chosen and called. How did that knowledge affect his ministry?
5. What work has God prepared for you today? (Ephesians 2:10)

PRAYER BASED ON GALATIANS 2:1-10

Living for the sake of the Gospel by boldly facing opposition and not shrinking back. (Hebrews 10:39)

Father, we are amazed and thankful for continuing to reveal Yourself to Paul and guide him in Your ways, for Your Glory, and for Your purpose.

After 14 years, You instructed Paul to take Titus, an uncircumcised Greek and Paul's son in the faith, to Jerusalem. You told Paul to share the Gospel that You gave to him with the leaders of the Church in Jerusalem so that there would be no division in Your body. Titus was saved by faith alone without works (he was not circumcised). There were Jews in the Jerusalem Church who believed that salvation was impossible for Titus because he had not kept all the laws given to the Jews. Paul stood firm and proclaimed that salvation was by grace, through faith alone, and not by any works done by man. When the leaders of the Church in Jerusalem, (Peter, James, and John) came to see Your mighty display of works done in the Gentiles through Paul, they gave Paul and Barnabas the right hand of fellowship. They praised You for the ministry You gave to Paul for the uncircumcised (Gentiles) and the ministry you gave to them for the circumcised (Jews).

Father, may we stand amazed at the boldness You gave to Paul. You enabled him to go to Jerusalem and face strong opposition. May this give us more confidence to trust in Your leading. May we learn to trust You for the wisdom and boldness we need to face any situation in our lives. You will do this for all who will humble themselves under Your mighty hand and ask. (Matthew 7:7-8) As humble servants, we can stand confident in Your Word. If You are for us who can be against us. Amen.

Let us read and meditate on Romans 8:31-39.

QUESTIONS FOR REFLECTION AND MEDITATION:

1. When was the last time you were amazed at the work of God in your life?
2. What has made it possible for you to trust God to lead you in difficult times?
3. Do you have testimonies of how God provided for you in difficult times, and do you share them regularly?

PRAYER BASED ON GALATIANS 2:11-14

Being bold for the sake of Your Glory and Your Church – having eyes focused on You – humble hearts surrendered to You and living for Your purposes, regardless of the cost.

Father, we thank You for giving Paul the boldness and the authority to confront Peter for Your glory and for the good of Your Church.

Peter is a hypocrite. His actions do not line up with his beliefs. His fearful response was promoting false, legalistic beliefs. Peter is without excuse, for You gave him a vision and a demonstration of Your acceptance of the Gentiles. (Acts 10:9-48) The rest of the Jews were also behaving hypocritically. They were professing to be one with the Gentiles, yet by their actions they denied their oneness. Even Barnabas was led astray. When Paul saw that they were not acting in line with the Gospel, he boldly opposes Peter to his face, in public, because he truly loved him and Your Church. The apostolic authority of Paul is clearly on display here. May this be a strong warning to all – even chosen leaders can be intimidated and fail to be faithful to Your Word.

Father, open our eyes and cause us to see where we are trusting in our own works for salvation. Lord, grant us repentance and give us eyes to see everything through the lens of Scripture. Give us compassion for those who trust in their own works and not Your righteousness. May we see the great danger they are in: and pray for the boldness and compassion that we need to correct those You call us to love. Amen.

QUESTIONS FOR REFLECTION AND MEDITATION:

1. When has your actions conflicted with your beliefs?
2. How does God respond to you, when you are disobedient? (Hebrews 12:5-6)
3. What has motivated you to oppose people and bring correction?

Let us read and meditate on Hebrews 12:5-14.

PRAYER BASED ON GALATIANS 2:15-21

Salvation is through grace alone and not by works.

Father, we praise You for Your salvation. May we rejoice and be glad in what You have accomplished!

We can not fully rejoice, appreciate, and trust in You for salvation if we trust in any of our own works. Salvation by Your grace alone is the main point that Paul is making; not only in this text but in the whole book of Galatians. Since You have devoted one book to teaching us one truth, it must be a hard truth for us to accept and live. We desperately need You, Lord! Open our eyes and our proud hearts so that we may freely receive and rejoice in Your salvation. You make it clear in (verse 16) that justification is impossible through any works of the law. You have declared us righteous through the redemptive work of Your Son. The false teachers who opposed the Gospel of Grace argue that if people are not under the law, they will freely sin and thus make Your Son a promoter of sin. Paul emphatically answers, Certainly Not! Anyone who loves You will hate sin and keep Your Law. Your Word clearly states that only those who have died to sin will live for righteousness. (1 Peter 2:24, Romans 6:14) You tell us that we are a transgressor if we die to the law and then return to it for justification. Only by dying can we be free to live for You. (Verses 18-19) Paul proclaims he has died to sin and no longer under its dominion. (Verse 20) He knows that he no longer lives for himself but for the pleasure of God. He is a new creature with new desires to live for You. Paul will joyfully and sacrificially lays down his life for the benefit of others. The old is gone, and the new has come. (2 Corinthians 5:17) Paul knows Your sacrificial love for him – and believes that You and You alone have the power to save him and keep him forever. (2 Timothy 1:12) Paul then proclaims that if righteousness is attainable by keeping the law, then the death of Your Son on the cross is meaningless. (verse 21, Matthew 5:20)

Father may we humbly admit that we have no righteousness of our own and desperately need righteousness imputed to us through the finished work of Your Son. (2 Corinthians 5:21) Lord, may we live for You, and place our entire hope and trust in what You have accomplished for us, by Your life, death, and resurrection Amen.

Let us read and meditate on Romans 3:20-26

QUESTIONS FOR REFLECTION AND MEDITATION:

1. Why is it impossible to be justified by works?
2. Do you focus more on what Christ has done or more on what you have done or not done?
3. How do you live by faith in the Son of God?
4. How can you nullify the grace of God?
5. How does the grace of God cause you to love the law and keep it?

Prayer based on Galatians 3:1-6

How did you receive the Spirit of God?

Father, we praise You for sending Your Son, who lived the life we could not live, walked in perfect harmony with You, and was obedient to You in all things, even in His death on a cross.

Paul live to exalt You by faithfully preaching Your Gospel. When he was among the Corinthians, he decided to preach nothing among them except Your Son and Him crucified (1 Corinthians 2:2), for he knew that preaching Your Gospel will change lives. Paul is shocked to see how the Galatians became deceived. Paul gave a clear portrayal of the Gospel, and the Galatians received the Holy Spirit. If that were true, how could they possibly believe Your work on the cross was insufficient. Paul asks the Galatians, Did you receive the Holy Spirit through any righteous act or by hearing and believing the Gospel through faith? Paul then asks, How can you be so foolish? If you began your new life in Him in the Spirit, Why are you striving to be made perfect in your own strength? Paul asks them again, Did God give you the Holy Spirit and work miracles among you because you did what the law requires or because you heard the Gospel and believed by faith? Paul goes on to tell them how You counted Abraham as righteous. You called Abraham to leave his family and go to a place You would show him. (Genesis chapter 12) Abraham had faith only because You revealed Yourself to him. Abraham believed, and his faith was counted to him as righteousness. All Abraham did was believe!

Father, may we never forget that every salvation is a miracle, done by Your grace apart from works. You saved us by Your grace, and You will keep us by Your grace. May we be eternally grateful for what You have done and joyfully live for Your pleasure. Amen.

Questions for reflection and meditation:

1. Do you preach the Gospel to yourself everyday? Why or Why not?
2. How is man made right with God?
3. Where, why, and to whom do you proclaim the Gospel?
4. What work do you think you need to add to His? (John 19:30)
5. What can you do to gain more favor with God?
6. Does God love you more on your best days than He does on your worst days? Why or why not?

Prayer based on Galatians 3:7-14

Father we praise You for sending Your Son to redeem us from the curse of the law.

You tell us that the true children of Abraham are not his physical descendants but his spiritual descendants. (Romans 9:6-7) You revealed the Gospel of justification by faith alone to Abraham. You promised that through faith all nations would be blessed, both Jews and Gentiles. (Verse 10) warns us that all who rely on the works of the law are cursed, for no one is made right (justified) before You by keeping the law – living by the law is not living by faith. Those You justify, are the only ones that keep Your Law and live by faith. (Verse 11) They love and obey You, for You chose them and keep them by Your mighty power. You have redeemed them from the curse of the law through Your Son – He became a curse for them so that the blessings of Abraham might come to all nations. (2 Corinthians 5:21) We praise You Father for sending Your Son to take the Wrath that we deserved so that we might receive the promised Spirit through faith.

Father, may we surrender to Your ways and trust in You alone for salvation. There is no salvation apart from You. Open our hearts so that we can receive the Holy Spirit and rejoice daily in Your righteous provision. Amen.

Questions for reflection and meditation:

1. How is it possible to be a physical descendant of Abraham and not be a spiritual descendant of Abraham?
2. How is it possible to be born into a Christian family: do everything things that Christians do, even believe that you are a Christian, and still not know God? (Matthew 7:21-23)
3. How has living by faith and not by works changed your daily life?

Prayer based on Galatians 3:15-18

A covenant can not be a annulled or added to once ratified.

Father, we praise You for Your faithfulness.

You tell us that even a covenant made by a man can not be annulled or added to. You made a covenant with Abraham 430 years before you gave Your Law to Moses. You promised Abraham that all his spiritual children would be blessed, as he was. Just as You counted Abraham righteousness because he believed, You will also count his descendants righteous when they believed in Your promised seed (Christ). All of Israel will be blessed when they believe in the One You would send.

Father, we praise You and thank You for Your unbreakable covenant with Abraham, which You will keep forever. May we come to rejoice and trust in Your promise to Abraham, fulfilled through Christ and not by anyone who tries to keep the law. Christ is our only hope. Amen.

Let us meditate on the faithfulness of God. He has been faithful to keep his promise to Abraham and have saved all Jews and Gentiles – who have believed and lived for Christ through the centuries.

QUESTIONS FOR REFLECTION AND MEDITATION:

1. Is God faithful even when we are not? (2 Timothy 2:11-13)
2. How has God been faithful to you this week?

Prayer based on Galatians 3:19-29

The promise given to Abraham (Genesis 15:9-13) was different from the law given to the Jews through Moses.

Father, we praise You for saving Paul and equipping him to teach Your Word faithfully. You alone can open eyes! Open our eyes to see the difference between the promise made to Abraham and the law given to the Jews on Mount Sinai.

You gave Your Law through Moses to reveal Your standard of absolute righteousness, to convict everyone of their sins so that all would see their desperate need for Your Gospel. Your Law played the necessary role of convicting people of their blindness, ignorance, wickedness, and their disdain for God for the 1500 years between Mount Sinai and the appearing of Your Son. Your Law was given, by an angel to the Jews, through a mediator (Moses). (Acts 7:38) The Old Covenant needed a mediator because there were two parties. (God and the Jews) Both parties had to keep the covenant – You are faithful, but the Jews were not. You gave Your promise directly to Abraham, with no mediator, for there was only one party. (You) Abraham was asleep. (Genesis 15:12) The law was our tutor to show us our sin and our need for a Savior. The Law was never a way of salvation, for no one can keep it perfectly. (James 2:10) You call us to be perfect as You are perfect. (Matthew 5:48) You are our only hope. Those who love You will keep Your Law by the power of Your Spirit living and reigning in them. Your Spirit will convict them and lead them in Your righteous ways. (Psalm 25:9)

Father may we not be deceived by thinking we can come before You justified by our works. Every mouth will be stopped: and no one is justified by their works. (Romans 3:19-20) When Job had his audience with You and tried justifying his behavior before You, his mouth stopped when he saw Your glory. (Job 40:3-5) You tell us in (verses 28-29), that if we belong to Your Son, we will live in union with You and others and be heirs according to the promise that You made to Abraham over 3500 years ago.

Father, You are faithful and will keep every promise that You have made, for You are righteous in all Your ways. May we come to trust and rest in You alone. Amen.

QUESTIONS FOR REFLECTION AND MEDITATION:

1. What was the difference between the covenant made with Abraham and the covenant made through Moses?
2. How was the covenant made through Moses broken?
3. Why is the covenant made to Abraham unbreakable?
4. What was the chief purpose of the law?
5. Why can no one be saved by keeping the law?
6. Who are the true children of Abraham and heirs to the promise?
7. How do you know if you are a child of Abraham and an heir to the promise given?

Prayer based on Galatians 4:1-7

A child, although an heir, lives as a slave, until the time set by the father. Anyone who only knows the law is a child under a guardian and needs to be set free.

Father we praise You, for in the fullness of time, You have redeemed rebellious slaves and made them Your children and heirs to Your Kingdom!

In (verses 1-3), Paul illustrates the immaturity of living under the law. A child who will inherit everything is no different than a slave, for they are under the authority of guardians and managers – until the day appointed by their earthly father. Paul tells the Galatians if they are living under the law (trying to be righteous by keeping the law in their own strength), it is the same as a child being under a guardian. All who only know the law and live to keep the law live in bondage. They are enslaved and need to be set free. The Father, at the appointed time, sent His son to set them.

During the period of Mosaic law. You were setting things up perfectly for the coming of Your Son. The sacrificial system You established, was a foreshadowing of what was to come. (Genesis chapter 22, John 1:29) Therefore, those who try to be righteous by keeping the law will be enslaved to sin. When they believe and call upon the name of the Lord, they will be set free: adopted as sons and daughters and become heirs to Your Kingdom! (John 8:34-36, Romans 8:14-17)

Father, we are Yours for You have created us, and You have redeemed us through the blood of Your Son – and more than that, You have adopted us as sons and daughters, which makes us heirs of Your Kingdom! We praise You, for You have given us everything we need for a life of godliness. (2 Peter 1:3) You have called us out of darkness, and set us free to be holy, distinct people, who live in Your marvelous light, proclaiming and rejoicing in Your excellent work. (1 Peter 2:9)

Father, may we accept and rejoice in Your gracious work. Keep us from foolishly trying to add anything to Your finished work. Amen.

QUESTIONS FOR REFLECTION AND MEDITATION:

1. Describe how you have been freed from the bondage of the law and counted as righteous.
2. How does the knowledge of the grace of God keep you from sinning?
3. How has knowing that you are an heir changed the way you live?

Prayer based on Galatians 4:8-11

We love God because He first loved us, even when we were unfaithful, adulterous people, enslaved to the things of this world. (Romans 5:6)

Father, You knew us, You loved us, and pursued us, even though we did not love You. We praise You for Your faithfulness, long-suffering, and Your patients with us.

You delivered the Galatians from bondage when they believed in Your Son and called on His name. Paul asks the Galatians, Why are they turning back to the bondage of legalism?(trying to be made right with God through works). The Jews, among them convince them that they must observe special days and seasons to gain Your favor. Paul fears for them and urges them to become like him. Paul knew that those who trust in Your work have life, and those who trust in their own works will perish.

Father, search our hearts and enlighten us. We are so quick to try to contribute something towards our justification. Help us to see who and what we are trusting in. Amen.

Questions for reflection and meditation:

1. How have you tried to gain favor with God or man?
2. Describe how God pursued you when you were unfaithful.
3. What does it look like to be fully trusting and resting in His work and not yours?
4. What fruit will believers see in their life? (Galatians 5:22-24)

PRAYER BASED ON GALATIANS 4:12-20

Adding anything to the Gospel is dangerous.

Father, we praise You for Your care for the Galatians, through the apostle Paul.

Paul reminds them of the fellowship they had enjoyed when he was with them. Paul became ill, and they cared for him and even welcomed him, like an angel of God. Paul cares for the Galatians, even though they rejected him and are following false teachers. What an example of Your Love for us! Paul then lovingly asks the Galatians two questions. What has become of the blessings you enjoyed? Have I become your enemy because I tell you the Truth? Paul tells the Galatians why the false teachers are zealous for them. They want to separate them from Paul and strengthen their cause. Paul wants them to see that adding works to their salvation is not a better gospel but a false gospel that will lead to death. Paul then affectionately calls them his little children and tells them that he is committed to labor for them, like a mother in childbirth, until they become conformed to Your Son! Paul then expresses his desire to be with them and his doubts about their salvation. Father, we thank You for the strong warning You give us in this text. The Galatians heard the Gospel preached and saw it lived out by Paul. They joyfully accept the Gospel, but then they were misled by false teachers. (Luke 8:5-8)

Father, may we not look down on the Corinthians with proud hearts. May we all realize that we are prone to wander and leave the One we love. There are many distractions and false teachings all around. Lord, make us diligent. May we be people who go to Your Word to confirm everything that we profess. Give us a humble, teachable heart that desires to know You more. May we see our need to be kept in Your Word everyday and our need to run to a Strong Tower. (Proverbs 18:10, Psalms 18:1-3) We need You Lord! May we spend more time in Your Word and less time with things that will not satisfy. (Isaiah 55:2) May we love You more and be led by Your mighty hand. Amen.

QUESTIONS FOR REFLECTION AND MEDITATION:

1. How do you care for those who reject you?
2. Have you ever experienced anguish as Paul did in (Verse 19)?
3. How can you grow in your love for God and others?

PRAYER BASED ON GALATIANS 4:21-31

Paul gives a final rebuttal of legalism.

Father, we praise You for the passion Paul has for Your Gospel. He is resolved and dedicated to You.

Paul gives a final rebuttal of legalism (trying to be made right with You through works). He uses the example of Isaac and Ishmael. You promised Abram that he would have many descendants and be the father of a great nation. Since Abram and Sarah were old and Sarah could not conceive, they decided not to wait on You to fulfill Your promise to give them a son (Isaac) through Sarah. They decided to have a child (Ishmael) through Sarah's slave from Egypt (Hagar). This disobedience caused many problems that continue today. (Genesis Chapter 16). Paul addresses those who desire to live under the law. He asked them if they understood what the law says. Paul then begins to expound on the Book of the Law. (Genesis 21:8-13) Paul tells them that Abraham had two sons. Ishmael was born to a slave woman (Hagar) according to the flesh (man's plan). Isaac was born supernaturally to a barren woman through Your promise (Your plan). Paul tells us that these are two covenants, one from Mount Sinai and one through the promised Son. Ishmael represents spiritual slavery which comes from being under the law, and Isaac represents freedom found only in Your Son, through Your promise. In (verse 27), Paul quotes (Isaiah 54:1), which speaks of the children of the promised child. Paul then affectionately addresses those who are children of the promise and then those who are children of the flesh (those living in bondage under the law). He tells them that those who live under the law have and will persecute those who live under the promise. (Genesis 21:9). Paul then quotes (Genesis 21:10) which calls them to cast out the slave woman, for the son of the slave woman shall not be an heir with the son of the free woman. Paul then assures his brethren of their freedom that is found in Christ alone.

Father, we praise You and thank You for sending Your Son to set us free. May we not be a bondservant to anything except You. We will remain enslaved to sin until You set us free. (John 8:35-36) Open our eyes and hearts so that we may see who we truly serve. Amen.

QUESTIONS FOR REFLECTION AND MEDITATION:

1. When was the last time you failed to wait on God and acted on your own impulses?
2. Are you content with your plans, or do you press on in prayer until you know the plans of God for You?
3. Are you living in the freedom that is only found in Christ, or are you living in bondage?

Prayer based on Galatians 5:1-15

*We do not eagerly wait for the hope of righteousness,
if we are trusting in our own works.*

Father, we praise You for revealing Yourself to us and keeping us from our foolish ways.

Paul calls the Galatians to stand fast and not to go back into bondage. Paul reminds the Galatians that they have been set free and encourages them not to become slaves to anything. If anyone adds works to their salvation, they proclaim the death of Your Son on the cross was insufficient. Paul warns the Galatians not to accept circumcision, for they will then be obligated to keep the whole law. (James 2:10) Paul tells them they have fallen from grace if they seek to be justified by the law. Those who insist on keeping the law can never be secure because they never know if they have done enough to merit salvation, but those who live by faith in Your Son, will trust and eagerly wait for the righteousness that You will provide. Paul reminds the Galatians that they were running well. He then asked them, Who hindered you from obeying the truth? Paul assures them that a persuasion to keep the law does not come from Him who called them. Paul warns them of the dangers of the false teachers in their midst and then expresses his faith and confidence in the Lord to keep them safe. He then warns the false teachers of the certainty of Your coming judgement upon them and then expresses his anger in (verse 12). Paul then affectionately addresses the Galatians as brothers and reminds them of their calling. You have set them free so that they may live for Your Glory. Paul warns them not to use their freedom to serve themselves but to love and serve others sacrificially, as God loved and served them. Paul then concludes with a strong warning, if they do not love one another, they will be consumed by one another.

Father, open our eyes to see our failings and Your great salvation. Give us eyes to see and a mind to understand the great freedom that is found in You. You do not give us the freedom to do as we please, but the freedom to do Your will. May we not be consumed with ourselves and our own ways. Give us the strength and a strong desire to follow hard after You no matter what the cost. Your ways and Your thoughts are higher than our ways and our thoughts. (Isaiah 55:8-9) Show us our foolish ways so we may turn from them and live for You and You alone. Amen.

QUESTIONS FOR REFLECTION AND MEDITATION:

1. The Word of God tells us that if we seek to be justified by works then we have fallen from grace? Why is this true?
2. What must you do to stand fast and not become entangled with a yoke of bondage?
3. Are you secure in your works, or are you resting in His?
4. Why is Paul so angry with the false teachers? (verse 12)?
5. How have you come to see the foolishness of your ways?

Prayer based on Galatians 5:16-25

The work of the flesh contrasted with the work of the Spirit.

Father, we praise You, for it is Your power living in us, that makes it possible for us to walk in the Spirit.

You tell us that we can walk by the Spirit or walk in the flesh. We can not do both, for they are incompatible with each other. In (verses 19-21), You give us a long list of the works of the flesh, followed by a strong warning. You tell us that all who do these things will not inherit Your Kingdom. Then You give us a list of the fruits on display in the life of a believer. We will either follow our will and our plans or Yours. You tell us that those who belong to You have crucified the flesh with its passions and desires. Crucifying the flesh is not a one-time thing but a daily thing. Victory over sin will not be achieved by living under the law but by actively yielding to the Holy Spirit.

Father, may we obediently submit to Your Spirit and walk in joyful harmony with You. May we never forget to whom we belong and the high calling You have given us through Your Son. May we experience more and more of Your grace. May Your grace cause us to grow in our love for You and gives us more resolve to resist sin. (Romans 6:14) As we grow to love the things You love and to hate the things You hate, we become obedient to righteousness. (Romans 6:16) Father, work more in us privately so that You will be more on display in us publicly. Amen.

Questions for reflection and meditation:

1. As you prayerfully review the list given in (verses 19-21), What works of the flesh has God delivered you from, and what works still hold you in bondage?
2. As you prayerfully review the fruits of the Spirit given in (verses 22-23), how many have you experienced and rejoice in daily? Which ones do you need to grow in the most?
3. How can you experience victory over sin? (Galatians 2:20)
4. In what ways are you yielding to the Spirit and joyfully walking in harmony with God?
5. Are you growing in your love for the things of God and finding yourself rejoicing in Him more and more? If not, What must you do?

PRAYER BASED ON GALATIANS 6:1-10

*The actions, character, and ministry of a Christian
contrasted with the life of a legalist.*

Father, we thank You for giving us Your Word with all of Your instructions, warnings, encouragements, and promises. We praise You for giving us such a treasure!

In (verses 1-2), You speak to believers. Those restored should gently restore others and keep watch on themselves. They should fulfill the law of Christ by bearing the burdens of others. In (verses 3-4), You warned us about being proud: call us to think soberly about ourselves and restrain from comparing ourselves with others – only a humble heart can please You, honor You, and serve others as You intended. (Isaiah 66:2) What a contrast between a Christian and a legalist! The way of a Christian is to restore and bear burdens. The legalist is judgmental, harsh, and condemning. They may know the law, but they do not have the Holy Spirit reigning in them. (Romans 7:5) Only those who have died to the flesh can live in the new way of the Spirit. (Romans 7:6) You tell us how believers should support and encourage their teachers, by sharing the good things they have learned from them. In (verses 7-9), You tell us that we will all reap what we sow. You warned those who sow to the flesh and encourage those who sow to the Spirit. You encourage believers not to grow weary in doing good and assure them that all who are in Christ will persevere and reap a harvest of righteousness. You tell believers to show love for everyone, especially brothers and sisters in their Church. (Hebrews 10:24-25)

Father, You call us to be a light in the world and a city on a hill. (Mathew 5:14) The light of the glorious Gospel will shine brightest when we support and love our brothers and sisters in Your Church. Likewise, Your witness diminishes, when sin reigns in Your Church.

Father, keep us from all self-righteousness and foolish assumptions. May we love others enough to address unrepentant sin in their lives. Make us gentle, lowly, and lovingly firm, so that we will be a humble instrument in Your hand – one who delights in serving You and others, no matter how difficult or costly. Amen.

QUESTIONS FOR REFLECTION AND MEDITATION:

1. According to (verses 1-2), What purpose did God have in mind when He saved you?
2. What is the definition of a legalist?
3. How does the life of a believer differ from the life of a legalist?
4. What must we do to keep your law perfectly?
5. How are you eagerly and regularly sharing the good things that God has given to you with others?
6. When does the light of Christ shine brightest in your life?

PRAYER BASED ON GALATIANS 6:11-18

Final warnings and benediction.

Father, we praise You for Paul's passion for Your Gospel, and his relentless desire to keep it from being corrupted.

In (verses 12-13), Paul once again exposes the motives of the false legalistic teachers, which insist on circumcision for salvation. They want to avoid persecution and boast about the works of the flesh. Paul would not boast about anything except the cross of Christ and his weaknesses. (2 Corinthians 12:9) In (verse 15), Paul declares that the new birth is everything and circumcision is nothing. Paul wants the Galatians to experience the grace and mercy of God, which is only found, by trusting in Him alone, and not in any works of the flesh.

Father, show us how dependent we are on You, so we will be humble men and women of prayer. You must open our eyes, give us understanding, and lead us in Your ways. We are foolish sheep who need a Shepherd. Apart from You, we will do what is right in our own eyes and never know the joy of being on a mission for You. Cause us to walk in Your ways, so we may be spent doing the work You have prepared for us today. May we learn to pursue You and know the joy that comes from knowing You and participating in Your work. Amen

QUESTIONS FOR REFLECTION AND MEDITATION:

1. Why are we tempted to add works to salvation?
2. What boasting can you do that will please God?
3. How does seeing yourself as a sheep in need of a savior cause you to live differently?
4. What does it take to be on mission for God every day?
5. What are the results of choosing to live for him everyday? What do you gain, and what do you lose? (Philippians 3:8)

EPHESIANS

Prayer based on Ephesians 1:1-14

*The spiritual blessings that God has prepared
for those who believe in Christ.*

Father, we thank You for this day. You granted us this day before You knit us together in our mother's womb. (Psalm 139:15-17) May we rejoice and be thankful for You and all You have done.

In (verse 1), Paul proclaims that he is an apostle, not by his own choosing, but by Your will. He is writing to the Churches in the prominent city of Ephesus and addresses the recipients as faithful saints. What Paul proclaims to the faithful saints of Ephesus also needs to be heard by all today. Paul prays for Your grace and peace to abound in the lives of the Ephesians and believes it is necessary to remind them of Your work.

Father, we confess that our intellects are fallen and are so limited. Our finite minds can not comprehend Your infinite worth. Also, our fallen nature wants to think too highly of ourselves and too little of You. Open our minds and hearts, so that we may receive Your Truth, given to us in Your Word today.

You tell us that those who belong to You have every spiritual blessing. (Psalm 103). In twelve verses, You unwrap these blessings for us. Lord, give us ears to hear. You chose us before You created the world to be holy and blameless before You. It was Your decree. No outside influences existed to sway You. You predestined us to be adopted as sons and daughters according to Your will for Your good pleasure and glory. We have redemption through the blood of Your Son, according to the riches of Your grace. You have enlightened Your children and made known to them the mystery of Your will. You will establish a new world with Your Son as the Head: where Your children reign as heirs with Him. (Romans 8:17, Revelation 3:21) You will work out everything according to Your will. Romans (8:28-30) You tell us that You seal all who belong to You with the Holy Spirit, given to them as a guarantee of what is to come. The goal of all this is that Your glorious grace will receive praise!

Father, may our lives be a testimony of Your Grace. Not to us, but for Your glory may we live. (Psalm 115:1) Amen.

QUESTIONS FOR REFLECTION AND MEDITATION:

1. According to this Scripture, When did God choose you, and what are His plans for you and the world?
2. What guarantee of inheritance will God give to all who belong to Him?
3. How can you be sure that your best days are still to come?
4. Are you excited about your future? Why or why not?
5. What attributes of God do you see proclaimed in this Scripture?

Let us study, meditate, and rejoice in the great truths we see in (Ephesians 1:3-14).

Prayer based on Ephesians 1:15-23

The power of God is at work in Paul. And in all who call upon the name of the Lord. (Acts 1:8, 1 Thessalonians 1:5)

Father, we thank You for the example You give us of a faithful servant in (verses15-16.)

Paul rejoices in the faith of the Ephesians and their love for all the saints. He remembers them in his prayers and gives thanks to You for them. May we imitate this example of a faithful servant by living and praying as Paul did. Paul continues in (verses 16-21) to pray for the saints, for he strongly desires for them to know the great spiritual resources that are theirs through Your Son.

Father, give us more desire for Your Word so that we may know You and experience You more fully. May we have the hope of Your calling and know the riches of Your glory! As we trust in all Your promises and believe in the glorious inheritance You have in store for Your children, we come to know and experience Your great power and stand in awe of You! You have demonstrated Your love, wisdom, and ability to free us from the bondage of sin through the finished work of Your Son on the cross. You have raised up Your Son and seated him at Your right hand, far above all rule, authority, power, and dominion! May we be freshly reminded of who You are and what You have done every blessed day You give us. Give us grateful hearts that rejoice in You above all things! Amen.

CS Lewis quote:

If we consider the unblushing promises of reward and the staggering nature of the rewards promised in the Gospels, it would seem that our Lord finds our desires not too strong but too weak. We are half-hearted creatures, fooling about with drink and sex and ambition, when infinite Joy is offered us, like an ignorant child who wants to go on making mud pies in the slum because he cannot imagine what is meant by the offer of a holiday at sea. We are too easily pleased.

Let us take time to meditate on the attributes of the Father: what Christ accomplished by His life, death, and Resurrection, the dominion, power, and authority given to Christ, and the immeasurable greatness of His power toward those who believe. (Ephesians 3:20)

QUESTIONS FOR REFLECTION AND MEDITATION:

1. How have you grown in your knowledge of God and your love for Him and His bride? What hinders you from growing?
2. What desires do you have that are too strong or too weak?
3. How can you press on to the high calling in Christ Jesus? (Philippians 3:12-16)

Prayer based on Ephesians 2:1-10

The depravity of man described, the immeasurable kindness of God exalted, and his plan for his people to flourish proclaimed.

Father, we praise You for raising Your people from the dead. You commanded the light to shine in the darkness of our hearts, and it was so! (2 Corinthians 4:6)

You tell us that we are a walking corpse, dead in our sin until You give us life! While we were enemies and without strength You died for the ungodly. (Romans 5:6) Before You revealed Yourself to us, we were in bondage to sin and objects of Your wrath. We all lived as rebels who rejected Your rightful claim on us. We did all that seemed right in our own minds. Our lives were a passionate pursuit of our fleshly pleasures. Our rebellion deserves Your wrath, but You sent Your Son to become sin and take the wrath we deserved. (2 Corinthians 5:21) We praise You for delivering us from our bondage and forgiving us of our sins. As glorious as that is, Your plan went even further. In (verse 6), You tell us that You will raise up all who are united with Your Son – and make them sit together in the heavenly places with You! (Revelation 3:21) You did all this, so that You might show Your immeasurable, unsurpassed kindness toward all those who belong to You. In (chapter 1), You tell us that You chose Your faithful saints according to Your will and Your good pleasure. In (Ephesians 2:1-3), You tell us that we are dead in our transgressions and sins. In (Romans 3:10), You tell us that there is no one that is righteous not even one. In (Ephesians 2:10), You tell us that we are Your workmanship created in Christ Jesus for good works, which You have prepared in advance for us to do. In light of all this, where is there any room for boasting?

Father, may we all cover our mouths and never boast in anything except Your glorious work and our weaknesses. (2 Corinthians 12:9-10) Show us how to live so Your power will be on display in our lives. May we be rich in mercy and filled with gratitude as we remember who You are and what You have done. (Matthew 5:7) Amen.

Questions for reflection and meditation:

1. How would your life be different if God did not save you?
2. What benefits have you received from God through the sacrifice of Christ? (Psalm 103)
3. What boasting can you do that is pleasing to the Lord?

Prayer based on Ephesians 2:11-22

We were all far off, and God brought us near and made peace by reconciling us to Himself through the shed blood of His Son.

Father, we praise You, for who You are and what You have done. You have killed the hostility and brought peace, through the cross.

Your servant Paul calls the saved Gentiles to remember that they were once without Christ. They were separated from You because of their sins and separated from the Jews without hope. They were not recipients of the covenant given to Abraham. Paul assures them that though they were far off: they have now been brought near. It was the blood of Your Son which put hostility to death and brought unity. (Verses 16-18) Lord, You are our peace. You have done what no man could do. You have broken down the walls of hostility between the Jews and the Gentiles and made them one in You. All who believe in You have peace with You and others though the Holy Spirit, living in them. Your saints are no longer strangers and foreigners but fellow citizens that dwell in Your temple built on the foundation of the apostles and prophets, with Your Son as the chief cornerstone. In Him, we are all are being built together into a dwelling place for You.

Father, may we all believe and rejoice in what You have done and the work You are still doing in Your Church through Your Spirit. May we live in humble submission to You so we can participate and rejoice in Your work and find peace and rest in You. (Matthew 5:9) Amen.

Questions for reflection and meditation:

1. How has the walls of hostility been broken down in your life?
2. How have you seen the power of God at work in those who are fall off?
3. How has God given you the faith to minister to those who appear hopeless?
4. How have you been knitted together with other believers to form a spiritual house? (2 Peter 2:5)

Prayer based on Ephesians 3: 1-8

*The blessings experienced by Paul as a prisoner for Christ
and the mystery revealed to him.*

Father, thank You for revealing Yourself to Paul and giving him eyes to see himself and his circumstances rightly.

He knows he has received Grace for the purpose of serving others. Paul is in prison, but he does not see himself as a prisoner of Rome. He sees himself as a prisoner of Your Son, who has him, in prison, for the purpose of spreading Your Gospel to the Gentiles. Lord, may we all view and embrace our current circumstances as Paul did – if we do, we will experience the unsurpassed joy of knowing You and living for Your purposes. May we not settle for anything less. You appointed Paul as an apostle to the Gentiles. And revealed to him a mystery that was unknown to past generations. The Gentiles are members of the same body and share in the same promise given to Abraham. The Gentiles and the Jews are to be made one body and heirs of Your kingdom; through believing and trusting in Your Son alone for salvation. In (verse 7), Paul rejoices in the grace he has received from You. In (verse 8), Paul is amazed that God would choose him, for he is the least of all the saints.

Father, we thank You for the example of a saint You give through Paul. Give us a bigger view of You and a more accurate view of ourselves. We need You to open our eyes so that we may see You and ourselves correctly. You must open our eyes and sanctify us through Your Word if we are to become the saints You have called us to be. Lord, give us lives that look more and more like a saint – and less and less like a sinner. Have Your full way with us. Amen.

Questions for reflection and meditation:

1. What was the mystery revealed to Paul?
2. Paul was a prisoner in Rome, but he did not view himself as a prisoner of Rome. How does your view of your hardships and trials differ from Paul's view?
3. How does your view of yourself differed from Paul's of himself? (Verse 8)
4. What was Paul's chief purpose for living?

Prayer based on Ephesians 3: 9-13

The purpose and mission of Your Church expounded.

Father, we praise You for giving Paul a revelation of a mystery that was hidden for ages.

Paul sees it as a great privilege to preach the unsearchable riches of Your Son to the Gentiles. You created and established all things, including the Church, which will remain until Your Son returns. (Matthew 16:18). You assure us that You will accomplish all that You purpose to do. (Isaiah 46:10-11) Through Your Church, the manifold wisdom of God will be made known to the rulers and authorities in the heavenly places! You established Your Church to be a divine fellowship and gave it a divine mandate (Matthew 28:18-20) It is the finished work of Your Son on the cross that made it possible for us to enter into Your presence. (Hebrews 4:14-16) What a privilege and blessing to belong to You and Your Church!

Father, may we rejoice more and more in You and experience more wonder and gratitude for Your incredible gift of salvation. (Matthew 13:16-17) And May we not lose heart, for even our sufferings are given to us for our benefit and Your Glory. (Romans 5:2-5, 2 Corinthians 4:7-11,) Amen.

Questions for reflection and meditation:

1. How has, or how is God revealing and fulfilling His purpose in your life?
2. What keeps you from rejoicing in the incredible gift of God's salvation or What causes you to reject it?
3. What makes it possible for you to rejoice even in your sufferings? (James 1:2)

Prayer based on Ephesians 3:14-21

The centrality of prayer in the life of a believer will lead to confident dependence upon the provisions of God and a great discovery of joy in Him.

Father, we thank You for calling and equipping Paul and giving us a great example of a saint who has devoted his life to You.

How appropriate it is that Paul begins this chapter with prayer and ends it with prayer. May every day (You graciously give us) start and end the same way! May we also pray through the day without ceasing, just as You command us to do. (1 Thessalonians 5:17) Make us more aware of our standing before You (justification) and the power of Your Spirit living in us so that we may pray more confidently and fervently. Ask and you will receive, seek and you will find, knock and the door will be open to you. (Matthew 7:7-8) May we acknowledge You in all things, for You are the giver of every good gift. (James 1:17) You bless us with strength, insight, and understanding. Apart from You we can do nothing. (John 15:5) May all that we do be rooted and grounded in love, through the power of Your Spirit.

Father give us a heart for You and Your kingdom. May our souls thirst for You. (Psalm 42:1-2) May we be humble servants, with our eyes fixed on You and Your purposes. Give us a humble heart that can know the love that surpasses knowledge and be complete and content in You alone. (Verse 19a) May we believe that You can do exceedingly abundantly beyond anything that we can ask or think. (Verse 20) Work in us to do Your will for Your good pleasure. (Philippians 2:13) May we all learn to live beyond ourselves confidently dependent on Your provisions so that our lives will be a living testimony of Your power reigning in us. May our days be filled with Your fullness so that You are our All in All. (Verse 19 b) May we be able to exclaim that all of You is more than enough for all of me! Amen.

Let us take time to meditate on the attributes of the Father: the accomplished work of Christ, the dominion, power, and authority given to Christ, and the immeasurable greatness of his power toward those who believe.

Questions for reflection and meditation:

1. How do you find the strength, insight, and understanding necessary to make wise choices that please God?
2. How can you grow and experience more of the love of Christ that surpasses knowledge?

Prayer based on Ephesians 4:1-6

The manner of walking that is worthy of the calling of God.

Father, we praise You and rejoice in Your Word. Your word is complete, without error, beautiful, and in perfect order.

We must acknowledge Your absolute sovereignty, wisdom, and power before we can strive to live the holy life that You have called us to live. Without a big accurate view of You, we will try to live a holy life in our own strength. We shall surely fail in our prideful ways, for You have promised to oppose the proud. (1 Peter 5:5b-6) Therefore, You first give us (chapters 1, 2, 3), which tell us of Your absolute sovereign rule over all events, and then in (chapters 4, 5, 6) You tell us how we must make decisions and strive to live a holy life. We must accept Your absolute rule over us, our responsibility to choose wisely, and our total inability to choose wisely apart from You. (John 15:4-5) To honor and please You, we must be humble children, who live under Your authority and strive to follow hard after You. Your servant Paul declares that he is a prisoner of the Lord – he has given up his freedom in order to follow Your Son. You require all of Your disciples to do the same. (Luke 14:33) Your disciples are new creatures who live in humble submission to You and one another under Your authority. Our daily focus should not be on ourselves but on pleasing and honoring You in all things as we live to serve You and others. You call us to be holy and walk worthy of Your divine calling. (Verse 1) We are to be humble, gentle, and long suffering – while we lovingly keep watch over one another and bear each others burdens. We are also called to be peacemakers who are eager to maintain the unity of the Spirit. (verse 3, Matthew 5:9) You go on to remind us of the corporate unity of all believers. (verses 4-6) You call Your Church to be one unified body, saved by the same Lord, given the same faith, receiving the same Spirit, baptized into the same body, and called to the same hope. You then assure Your Church that You are one, who is overall, and working in and through all. It is this unity that will shine brightly and bring You glory. (Matthew 5:14) Disunity will make a church weak and ineffective. The world needs to see Your powerful unified Church at work.

Father, open our ears so that we may hear and respond to Your call to unity. Give us Churches that are filled with diverse people from every

Tribe and Nation who live in union with You and one another. May we persevere in prayer, until You complete Your work in us! Come Lord Jesus come! Amen.

QUESTIONS FOR REFLECTION AND MEDITATION:

1. What makes the Bible different from any other book?
2. Why is knowledge of God and our depravity necessary for us to live out the calling that God gives us?
3. Why is living in isolation from other believers displeasing to God?
4. Why are unity and diversity necessary for a Church to be a light to the world? (Matthew 5:14-16)

Prayer based on Ephesians 4:7-16

Christ was victorious over all things and now reigns over all things. He wisely and appropriately gives gifts to His saints for the building up of His Church.

Father, we praise You, for Your grace freely given to the saints in Ephesus and to all those who belong to You.

In Your wisdom, You have wisely chosen to divide Your spiritual gifts among Your Church as You see fit. You alone know all things perfectly and will give a spiritual gift to Your children, in Your time, and for Your purposes. May we recognize and humbly receive Your gracious gifts. May we remember that all good things we presently experience are only possible because of Your Son, who made the earth and everything in this world. (Colossians 1:16) He chose to leave the riches of heaven and descend to the earth, even though He knew He would be despised, rejected, and killed. (Isaiah 53:3-5, Matthew 20:18-28 May we also remember that the one who descended also ascended in victory and gave diverse gifts to His captives. You, by Your life, death and resurrection, have delivered us from the bondage of sin and sent the Holy Spirit to live in us. Those who believe in You are no longer held captive to sin but are captivated by You. You tell us that You have appointed pastors to shepherd Your Church so Your body would be well fed and equipped for ministry. You call Your body to use their spiritual gifts to build one other up until Your body reaches unity in the faith. Your desire is for all Your children to attain the full measure of Your Son! You tell us not to be tossed to and fro by every wind of doctrine. You call us to grow up in all things so that we may be one united body with Your Son as our Head. Lord, give us a strong desire to be mature believers who humbly and prayerfully depend on You in all things. May we firmly stand on Your Word, be quick to pray, and be filled with Your compassion. Then and only then will we be able to speak Your Word in love. Give us eyes to see that every part of Your body is precious to You and called to function according to Your plan. Your plan is to knit Your saints together so the whole body will be built up, through love, into a spiritual temple. (1 Peter 2:5) May Your Church be a glorious testimony of Your Grace!

Father, You have been so good to us, and we praise You and thank You for Your Grace and mercy on our lives. You delight in giving good gifts to Your children. (Luke 12:32) May we be open to receiving all that You have for us, so that we may be equipped and empowered to serve You and Your Church. Amen.

QUESTIONS FOR REFLECTION AND MEDITATION:

1. How have you responded to the victory of Christ on the cross? How has His victory changed your life?
2. What authorities do you recognize in your life? Do you submit to them? Why or Why not?
3. How is your submission or rebellion to authority on display in your life?
4. What will it take for everyone to grow up and live in unity with God and His people?

Prayer based on Ephesians 4:17-32

*(Verses 17-20) describe unbelievers and then believers who
live a life in Christ worthy of the Gospel. (Verses 21-32)*

Father, we praise You and thank You for Your Word today. You know
everything that binds us and everything we need to hear and do to be
free indeed.

In this passage, You clearly describe a life lived apart from You. You then
contrast the old life with the new life and command us to put off the
old self, which is corrupt. And to put on the new self which is devoted
to You. You then give us many straight forward examples. Quit lying
and speak truthfully. Do not steal but labor diligently. Let no corrupt
talk come out of your mouth, but only what builds up others and honors
You. Put away all bitterness, anger, and slander and be kind and ten-
der-hearted with one another. Forgive others as God has forgiven you.
Lord, we are so easily deceived. We can convince ourselves that we do
not need to be totally devoted to You. We can foolishly think that all
we need is to do our best and be sincere, and You will accept us on our
terms. This belief is heresy and never taught in Your Word. We must
come to You on Your terms and Yours alone!

Father, open our eyes for us to see how deceitful our hearts are. (Jeremiah
17:9) May we be amazed and convicted, when we see how easily we
can excuse our own behavior and, at the same time, be so critical of
others. Forgive us, Lord, when we make excuses for our behavior and
will not accept our responsibility. We can so easily blame others and
circumstances for our sins. Teach us that others and circumstances do
not cause us to sin – they only reveal the sin which resides in our hearts.
Lord, make us humble people, who live under Your authority and find
peace, rest, and forgiveness in You. Come Holy Spirit, and illuminate
our hearts as we study and meditate on Your Word. Convict us so we
may repent and respond to Your call to live out what we see in Your
Word today. Amen.

Let us read and meditate on Luke 6:43-45

QUESTIONS FOR REFLECTION AND MEDITATION:

1. What contrast do you see between the old self and the new self, created in Christ Jesus?
2. What things have you put off and what things have you taken on?
3. Do you walk in your own ways or do you strive to walk in harmony with His ways?
4. As you prayerfully prioritize your day, what things are you called to lay down and what things are you called to take up? (Luke 9:23-24)
5. How would your life be different, if you took more responsibility for your sins and quit blaming circumstances and others?

Prayer based on Ephesians 5:1-21

God calls us to turn from darkness and to walk in the light.

Father, we praise You for Your love, mercy, and Grace, which You have shown us through Your Son. You are flawless in Your ways and always good and right in all You do.

You call us to be imitators of You. Your Son always walked in humble obedience to You, and You call all Your children to do the same. You want our lives be a sweet, sacrificial offering to You. Your call is for us to walk in Your ways in union with Your Son. In (verses 3-4), You tell us to put off sexual immorality, all impurity, covetousness, foolish talk, and crude joking for they have no place in the life of a believer. You assure us of two things: those who practice the things in verses 3-4 will not enter the Kingdom of Heaven, and wrath upon the disobedient who will not walk in Your ways. Your children are to be discerning and have no part in the works of darkness. You call Your children to wake up and rise from the dead, and as we do, Your light will shine through us and expose the works of darkness in this fallen world.

Father, give us the wisdom we need to make the best use of the time You have given us. May our days be joyfully spent living in submission to You, giving thanks in all things, and submitting to one another out of reverence for You. Amen.

Questions for reflection and meditation:

1. According to this text, What does living for Christ involve?
2. What do you need to put off and what do you need to put on?
3. How have you grown in your desire to know and follow Christ?
4. How have you found submission to God and others more joyful and beneficial than doing your own thing?
5. (Verses 19-21) lists at least five characteristics of a person filled with the Holy Spirit. How many can you identify and relate to and give thanks to God for providing them?

Prayer based on Ephesians 5:22-33

God Fulfills His design for marriage through humble submission.

Father, we thank You for marriage. May we grow in our knowledge and appreciation for Your beautiful design.

You have designed marriage to be a reflection of You. Just as Your Son lived in perfect harmony and absolute, total submission to You (John 5:19), You call wives to submit to their husbands and all husbands to submit to You. When husbands and wives live in perfect harmony, they are a beautiful reflection of You to the world and fulfill Your design for marriage. What a high calling You have given to wives! Submission is very hard, and only holy women filled with the Holy Spirit can do it, and only Your Son did it perfectly. Father, help us see and rejoice in humble submission, for it is beautiful and exalts You. You tell us that the husband is the head of the wife, as Your Son is the Head of Your Church. Your call for every husband is to live lives in submission to You and reflect You in how they lead their wives. As the head, You will hold husbands accountable for how they led or failed to lead there wives. (Genesis 3:9) You call husbands to love their wives as Your Son loved the Church! Jesus dedicated His life for the welfare of the Church and ultimately gave His life for her! In (verse 28), You command all husbands to love their own wife as there own bodies. In (1 Peter 3:7), You remind husbands that their wives are heirs with them and call them to honor their wives. You then give a strong warning to husbands. If a husband does not show honor to his wife, it will hinder his prayers. It would appear that the spiritual health of a husband is affected and reflected in the way he leads his wife. Since the fall, neither the wife nor the husband can fulfill their callings in their own strength. Therefore, You are seen and glorified, every time a husband and wife walk in harmony with You.

Father, empower us through Your Holy Spirit, to live lives in humble submission to You and others. May we put You on display by the way we sacrificially love and serve one another. We must love You above all things. May Your love for us be reflected in the way we love others. (Matthew 6:33) Amen.

QUESTIONS FOR REFLECTION AND MEDITATION:

1. What has shaped your view of marriage?
2. How has your view of marriage changed over the years and why?
3. How does your current view of marriage line up with Scripture?
4. How are you striving to walk in harmony with God?
5. What does living in harmony with others say about your relationship to God?
6. Which call is the most difficult, the calling for wives to submit to their husbands or husbands to love their wives as Christ loved His Church?

Prayer based on Ephesians 6:1-9

*Examples of living for the glory of God in all our
relationships, by loving others as You have loved us.*

Father, we praise You for revealing Yourself to us, so that we may live
for Your Glory.

You have taught the Ephesians to put their relationship with You first
so they can love Your Church and their spouses in the way You have
called them. You now tell us how all our relationships should reflect
Your love for us. Children should honor and obey their parents, just as
Your Son showed honored by His obedience to You in all that He did.
Fathers are to remember how patiently You taught them and how lovingly You disciplined them. You call them to love their children in the
same way You have loved them so that all may see a reflection of You in
their parenting. You tell us that we must respect and honor those who
have authority over us with a sincere heart. Our service to them should
be a reflection of our service to You. In (Romans 12:10), You command
us to be devoted to one another and to outdo one another in showing
honor. You then speak to those who have others under their authority.
Once again, You remind us that we live under Your authority, and we
should reflect You in how we exercise authority over others.

Father, You set a high bar. We have all failed to be the men and women
You have called us to be. Grant us repentance so we may be cleansed
of all our sins and be free to love others as You have loved us. Amen.

Let us read and meditate on Romans 12:9-21. There are at least 28
marks of a true Christian given in these 13 verses.

Prayer based on Ephesians 6:10-23

The need to know your real enemy, your weaknesses, and who you serve?

Father, we praise You for opening our eyes and enabling us to see our sin. Apart from You working in us, we will excuse our sinful behavior and blame others. We will see them as our enemy and fight against them. Thank You for saving us from such a fruitless and pitiful life.

You call us to be strong in the Lord and in His mighty power. We are no match for the wiles of the devil. The only way we will stand is by bowing to You. We must look to You and depend on You for Your provision and strength. You remind us our enemy is not our Church: our brothers and sisters, our children, our parents, our wives or husbands, our employers, or our employees. Our enemy is not any institution in this world; that opposes us and tries to oppresses us. You tell us we do not wrestle against flesh and blood but against the powers and rulers of the darkness in this world and against the forces of evil in the heavenly places! You tell us we must be bound to and sanctified by Your Word (John 8:32, John 17:17) and be clothed in a righteousness that is not our own (Philippians 3:9) and be committed to living in peace (2 Timothy 2:24-25) and above all we need to have faith, if we are going to stand against evil. Your provisions are certain and sufficient to provide for Your children and keep them from falling. (Jude 1:24) You promise to give grace to the humble and oppose the proud. (1 Peter 5:5) We Praise You for Your Righteous ways! May we be humble people who rest confidently in Your sustaining grace in every situation. We must guard our minds by spending more time in Your Word and less time in the world. Our minds need renewed daily. (Romans 12:2) We need to know Your Word and to trust in Your wisdom which You freely give to those who ask. (James 4:2b) We also must abide in Christ, pray in the Spirit, and be watchful, for we have a powerful, deceptive enemy, who hates us, and will not stop wanting to devour us. Our only hope is in a mighty Savior. May we be quick to turn to Him and trust His power to deliver all who belong to Him. (John 10:28) Paul tells us how to pray if we want to share Your Gospel effectively. (verse 19) Paul prays for You to give him Your Words, so he may speak and make known the mysteries of the Gospel. May we all understand how Paul received such a powerful ministry. (2 Corinthians 1:8-10) He learned to embrace his suffering and depend on You.

Father, may we learn to pray before we speak so that our words will be Your Words. Only Your Words that have the power to soften hearts and change lives. Lord, show us how to fight the good fight and run a good race. (Philippians 3:14, 2 Timothy 4:7-8) Amen.

QUESTIONS FOR REFLECTION AND MEDITATION:

1. What do you need to stand confidently against the schemes of the devil?
2. What benefit comes from knowing your enemy is not flesh and blood, but are evil spiritual forces?
3. What are the consequences of spending too much time fighting with Satan and too little communing with God?
4. Can it be possible for us, as finite beings, who see dimly, to think too highly of God?
5. How will a small of view of God and a highly inflated view of yourself affect the how you live and proclaim the Gospel?
6. How are you striving to grow in humility? What benefits have you reaped from doing so?
7. What does Paul call us to do so that we may proclaim the Gospel boldly? (Verses 18-20)

Philippians

Prayer based on Philippians 1:1-11

Thankful, joyful, and confident, in our knowledge and love for God.

Father, we thank You for Your servant Paul, his testimony, his love for You, and his love for the Philippians.

Paul has found his identity in You through Your mighty work in him. Paul humbly introduces himself and Timothy as Your bondservants. Paul rejoices over the Philippians and gives thanks to You, for their partnership with him in the Gospel. Paul testifies that he has experienced great joy from the first day he was with them until now. The first days in Philippi were very hard for Paul. And yet he rejoices in them also. In his first days in Philippi, he and Silas were beaten and thrown in jail. (Acts 16) records the amazing account. Teach us Lord, how to walk through suffering with joy as Paul did. (James 1:2) Paul encourages the Philippians by assuring them that You will complete the work that You have begun in them. Paul tells the Philippians how he longs for them with great compassion given to him through his Lord and Savior. (Versus 9-11) records the prayer Paul prayed for them. May his prayer become our daily prayer for ourselves and one another.

Father, may our love for You abound more and more as we grow in our knowledge of You. May we always look to You for wisdom and insight so we may love and approve what is excellent. Sanctify us, Lord, so we may be the pure and spotless bride You have called us to be. May we be filled with the fruit of righteousness and live for Your glory and for Your praise! Amen.

Questions for reflection and meditation:

1. Paul identifies himself as a servant of Christ. What does it mean to be a servant of Christ?
2. How do you express your love and gratitude for all God has done for you?
3. What trials and hardships do you praise and thank God for bringing into your life?
4. Are you grateful and confident in the power of God to keep You and sanctify you? How did you gain such confidence?
5. Have you grown more through adversity or prosperity? (Psalm 119:71)
6. What hinders you from growing in your love for God? (Hebrews 12:1-2)

Prayer based on Philippians 1:12-18

*A joy-filled life lived for the advancement
of the Gospel, uninhibited by circumstances.*

Father, we thank You for the example of Paul. He lived for the Gospel and trusted You in all his circumstances.

Paul knew that his imprisonment and every trial were from Your hand. Paul was able to rest in Your absolute goodness and sovereignty. Paul did not live for himself but passionately lived for You. He saw all of his trials as an opportunity for the furtherance of the Gospel. Since Paul loved You and Your Gospel more than his own life, he rejoiced in every circumstance. The imprisonment of Paul made it possible for the entire imperial guard to hear the Gospel and made it possible for others to speak the Gospel boldly, without fear. For this, Paul rejoices and praises You! Paul also rejoices when he hears about the Gospel being preached even by those who oppose him. (Verses 15-18)

Father, give us a greater love for the Gospel. May our love for Your Gospel causes us to rejoice in Your Gospel and proclaim it. May we all experience the joy of living for You and the foolishness of living for anything else. Amen.

Questions for reflection and meditation:

1. How did Paul respond to suffering?
2. What enable Paul to be thankful in all circumstances, rejoice in everything, and pray without ceasing? (1 Thessalonians 5:16-18)
3. What would have to change in your life to allow you to experience more joy?
4. Can you praised God and gave thanks to Him for your sufferings? Why or why not?

PRAYER BASED ON PHILIPPIANS 1: 19-30

A life lived for the kingdom of God.

Father, we praise You for You give life and supply the grace we need to live for You or to die for You.

Paul was confident in Your ability to deliver him from every situation. He eagerly expected You to give him the grace he would need (when he needs it) to honor You in his life and in his death. (Verses 19-21) Paul desires to depart and to be with You. Paul knows that death is gain and is eagerly looking forward to the day when he will see You face to face. Paul also knows his calling. For Paul, living meant fruitful labor for others. Therefore, he accepts and rejoices in his calling. (Verses 22-26) Paul calls us to live a life worthy of the Gospel – he calls us to stand firm in one spirit, with one mind, striving side by side with one another for the faith of the Gospel and tells us not to fear anything. (Verses 27-28) Those who fear You will fear nothing else. (1 John 4:18) In (verses 29-30), Paul proclaims that all who believe in the Gospel will suffer for the Gospel. They will experience the same conflict which Paul described in (versus 23-26). All of this is a clear sign of God's saving work.

Father, search our hearts as we study and meditate on this Scripture. Make us a fearless, unified people that will astonish the world by living and dying for You. Amen.

QUESTIONS FOR REFLECTION AND MEDITATION:

1. What did Paul mean when he said: To live is Christ and to die is gain?
2. Have you ever face the dilemma that Paul describes in (verses 23-24)?
3. If Paul believed that to die is gain, Why does he desire to remain in the flesh?
4. Why are all believers called to suffer? (Verse 29)
5. What made it possible for Paul to face life or death courageously?
6. What made it possible for Paul to find joy in his daily work?

Prayer based on Philippians 2: 1-11

A calling to have the same mind as Christ.

Father, we praise and thank You for Your Word. You want us to live in harmony with You: by being open, loving, and humble. Only You can open our ears and give us soft hearts. Lord, You want us to live under Your authority in harmony with You and Your bride: enlightened by Your thoughts, filled with Your love, and empowered by Your Spirit. We praise You for all of Your ways!

In (verse 3), You tell us to do nothing from selfish ambition or conceit but in humility to count others more significant than ourselves. You tell us not to look out for our own interests but for the interests of others. You then remind us of the example You have given to us in Your Son. He being God, emptied Himself, and took on the form of a servant. He humbled himself and walked in perfect obedience to You, even to His death! You then exalted Him above every name in heaven and on Earth, so that every knee will bow and every tongue will confess that He is Lord, to Your glory forever and ever!

Father, You have promised that You will exalt everyone who humbles themselves under Your mighty hand. (1 Peter 5:6) May You show us our sins and grant us repentance, so we will turn to You and live for Your Glory, now and forever! Amen.

Questions for reflection and meditation:

1. Why should we count the cost before we decide to follow Christ?
2. What will you gain if you follow Christ, and what will you lose?
3. What has it cost you to be a Christian? (Luke 14:33)
4. What are the consequences if we do not humble ourselves and believe that Jesus is who He says He is? (John 8:24)
5. What makes it possible for you to embrace and endure suffering?

Let us read and meditate on Philippians 1:27-2:11

A wise man once said, the cost of following Christ is high, but not following is much higher.

Prayer based on Philippians 2:12-18

God calls us to work out our own salvation in the midst
of a crooked and twisted generation – we are to shine like
lights as we walk through situations.

Father we praise You, for You work in us to do Your will for Your good pleasure. (Verse 13)

You called us to become innocent children, holy and blameless, shining like stars in a corrupt world. We are not to grumble or complain, but to strive to do Your work, even if our labor appears to be in vain – for we know we will reap a harvest, in do time, if we do not give up. (Galatians 6:9)

Father, may we trust You to give us everything we need for a life of godliness. (2 Peter 1:3) You have promised to be faithful to complete the work that You have begun in us. (Philippians 1:6) Instead of grumbling and complaining, may our eyes be set on You. You want us to act like Your children. Your desire for us is to be without blemish, so that we will shine like stars in the darkness of this fallen world. Keep us from grumbling and complaining and make us a humble people, who joyfully live under the authority of Your Word, so that this fallen world may see Your glory reflected in our lives and repent. Lord, cause us to live lives that are devoted to You so that we may not dread the DAY of Your return but eagerly look forward to seeing You face to face. Amen.

Questions for reflection and meditation:

1. How are you resting and trusting in God?
2. How are you striving to work out your salvation?
3. How has God worked in you to do His will for His good pleasure? Today, Last week, Last month.
4. On a scale of 1 to 10, how would you describe your life? A 1 being grumbling and complaining and a 10 being proclaiming and rejoicing in God's work. What must happen in your life to move you closer to a 10?
5. Are you looking forward to the DAY that Jesus returns? Why? or why not?

Prayer based on Philippians 2:19-30

Paul's desire is to honor and make known those who are Christ-like models.

Father, we praise You, for Your calling and equipping. You call us to be imitators of You. (Ephesians 5:1-2) Thank You for giving us so many examples of a saint in the following verses.

You want Your people to be saints that shine like stars in this dark fallen world. You conclude (Chapter 2), by giving us great examples of a saint. In (verse 19), Paul is in prison facing death and is willing to send Timothy (who is a great comfort to him) to the Philippians for their edification and progress in the faith. A saint does not seek their own comfort over the good of others. A saint rejoices in the growth and success of others. A saint has a sincere interest in the well-being of others. A saint has proven character. (verse 22) A Saint shows great faith and hope in God. A saint finds great joy in knowing that others are following Christ. (2 John 4) A saint longs for the fellowship of other saints? (Verse 26) A saint honors and rejoices in his brothers and sisters who are fellow workers and fellow soldiers. A saint will take risks and suffer for the sake of the Gospel. (Verse 30)

Father we thank You for the many examples of a saint which You set forth for the Philippians and us to emulate. Amen.

Questions for reflection and meditation:

1. What are the characteristics of a saint given in this Scripture?
2. What is your definition of a saint? Have you been called to be one?
3. How have saints in your life helped you to grow in your knowledge and love of God?
4. What does God promise to those who hunger and thirst after righteousness? (Matthew 5:6)

Let us read and meditate on 2 Chronicles 16:9

PRAYER BASED ON PHILIPPIANS 3:1-11

The method by which we may know God and the power of His resurrection.

Father, we praise You for sending Your Son. Only You can set us free from the bondage of sin, and give us life.

You warn us to look out for false teachers who want to put us in bondage, and then You give us three characteristics of believers. Only those whose hearts are circumcised can worship You in Spirit and Truth: glory in Your Son, and be able to refrain from putting confidence in the flesh. Those who are confident in anything or anyone besides You are foolish. Paul says he has more reasons to have confidence in his flesh than anybody and then backs it up with a long list. Paul has impressive credentials but does not trust in them for his salvation. Paul knew there was nothing he could do to make himself righteous. Paul had to suffer the loss of all things, so that he may gain Christ. (Luke 14:33) Paul knows that he has no righteousness of his own. His only hope is in the finished work of Your Son. Above all things, Paul wants to experience the closest possible relationship with You. Therefore, Paul longs to share in the sufferings of Christ, so that he can know You and the power of Your resurrection. (Romans 8:17)

Father, make us willing to be crucified with Christ, so that we may live life in Him by faith. (Galatians 2:20) Amen.

QUESTIONS FOR REFLECTION AND MEDITATION:

1. What qualifications are you tempted to trust in for salvation?
2. What have you sacrificed and counted as rubbish in order to gain Christ?
3. Describe your relationship with Christ and how He is making it richer and fuller day by day. (Proverbs 4:18)
4. Do believers need to suffer persecution and loss? Why or why not?
5. Do you have a righteousness that can overcome sin? If so, How did you receive it?

Prayer based on Philippians 3:12-21

Pressing on to the high calling in Christ Jesus.

Father, again we praise You and thank You for the example of Paul.

Paul knows that he is not perfect, but he continues to press on because he knows he belongs to You. His confidence is in Your promises and Your power and not in himself. Paul forgets what lies behind (his persecution of the Church, his beatings and imprisonment, and all of his hardships) described in (2 Corinthians 11:24-29) Paul knows that he has not arrived but presses on for the prize that awaits him and he encourages other mature believers to think and act this way. Paul is looking forward to the DAY when his race is complete. Paul encourages the Philippians to imitate him, and others who walk according to Paul's example. Paul compassionately warns the Philippians by telling them that many live as enemies of the cross of Christ. Destruction is sure for all who set their minds on earthly things, but all who live for Him, and joyfully awaiting their Savior's return will be citizens of heaven and receive a glorified body!

Father, guide us and keep us safe so we will not live as enemies but faithful servants of You. Amen.

QUESTIONS FOR REFLECTION AND MEDITATION:

1. What is it that you need to lay aside, so your focus can be on the finish line?
2. What is hindering you from running a good race?
3. On a scale from 1 to 10, how would you describe the race you are running. 1 being a mind set on earthly things and 10 being joyfully awaiting Jesus's return.
4. What would have to happen in your life for you to move up to a 10?

Let us read and meditate on Hebrews 12. Especially verses 1-6 and verses 14-15. May God conform us to His image as we cry out to Him.

PRAYER BASED ON PHILIPPIANS 4: 1-7

*A holy delight that comes from living in harmony
with Christ and His Church.*

Father, we thank You for giving Paul a love for You and Your Church. He wanted the Philippians to Know the joy and peace found when living in harmony with You.

Paul has a holy delight in You that rises above his hardships. See (Acts 16:24-25) for an example. Paul tells the Philippian Church that he longs for them and implores them to stand fast in the Lord. Paul then gives an example of standing fast. There is a disagreement between two women, and Paul asks them to agree; in the Lord. He encourages others, in Your Church, to come alongside these women and help them. Paul's desire was for all disputes to be settled within the Church, for it is the unity of Your Church that puts Your glory on display. You command us to always rejoice in the Lord and not to be self-centered and self-righteous, but respectful and gentle with others. You remind us that You are near, and call us to turn to You and pray, when we are anxious about anything. And You promise that if we do, we will experience a peace which will surpass all understanding.

Father, give us more desire to live lives that please and exalt You. May we be quick to give up our ways and humbly submit to Your ways, so that we may know the peace that surpasses all understanding, which will only come from living in harmony with You. Amen.

QUESTIONS FOR REFLECTION AND MEDITATION:

1. What examples of standing fast in the Lord do you see in your life and in the life of your church?
2. Paul took the disagreements between two women in the Church very seriously. Are there any disputes in your church that you excuse or take lightly?
3. How does knowing the fact that the Lord is near change the way you live?
4. How much anxiety do you tolerate before you humble yourself and pray?
5. Have you ever experienced a peace which surpasses all understanding?
6. Is it possible to live a life in harmony with God? What would it take?

Prayer based on Philippians 4:8-20

The confidence and peace that comes from walking in the ways of the Lord
– and having a mind full of God and things worthy of praise.

Father, we thank You for Your instructions. You tell us to only think about things that are worthy of praise and call us to put into practice those things which we have learned from You. And if we do, You promise that we will know Your peace! Paul is rejoicing over the concern the Philippians have shown him. Paul assures the Philippians that he has learned to be content in every situation. Paul can face plenty or hunger with full confidence in Christ. Paul continues to express gratitude to the Philippians and he assures them that he is well supplied. Paul is trusting and resting in Your provisions.

Father, give us the confidence that Paul had in Your ability to supply every need according to Your riches in glory, through Your Son. Amen.

QUESTIONS FOR REFLECTION AND MEDITATION:

1. What thoughts occupy your mind most of the time?
2. What weeds need pulling from the garden of Your mind?
3. What things have you learned from God and put into practice?
4. What is the source of your anxiety?
5. What is the secret to being content in all situations?
6. In what ways and by what means has God provided for you in the past?
7. Are you able to trust in God's future provisions? Why or why not?

COLOSSIANS

Prayer based on Colossians 1:1-14

Paul's fervent prayer for the spiritual growth of believers.
(Colossians 1:9-12)

Father, we thank You for this letter that proclaims the good fruit that will result from knowing and focusing on Christ.

Paul addresses the faithful saints in Colossae, which he never met, but dearly loved. Paul rejoices in the hope that is laid up for them in heaven because he knows that they have heard, understood, and believed the Gospel. Paul knows they are believers. Their faith and their love for all the saints are clearly on display. Paul rejoices when he hears that the Gospel is bearing fruit and spreading all over the entire world. Paul knows that many false teachers inside and outside Your Church oppose him and Your Gospel. Paul then prays fervently for Your Church. He prays for You to fill them with knowledge, spiritual wisdom, and understanding. Paul reminds them of their high calling and prays for them to bear fruit in every good work and continue to increase in their knowledge and love for You. Paul continues to pray for them to be strengthened with all power and have the endurance and patience needed to run a good race. He reminds them to give thanks to You, for You have qualified them to share in the inheritance of the saints. In (verse 13-14), Paul concludes with reminding the Colossians of the glorious work of the Gospel.

Father, We are so forgetful and so prone to distractions. We need a daily reminder of who You are and what You have done. Open our eyes so we may see our great need and Your great calling. May we cry out to You for the power to live the life You call us to live. Equip us and empower us to pray great prayers and accomplish the works You have prepared for us to do. (John 14.12-13) Thank You for Paul's example, which You give to us to spur us on! Amen.

Questions for reflection and meditation:

1. Why is Paul rejoicing over the Colossians?
2. How many people in your church pray the way Paul does? Are you one of them?
3. What keeps us from praying big God-centered prayers?

4. Is it possible for believers to grow spiritually, so that they can pray big God-centered prayers instead of man-centered prayers? If yes what would it take? If no Why not?

Prayer based on Colossians 1:15-20

The infinite worth and Glory of Your Son proclaimed. And His glorious work described.

Father, we praise You, for sending Your Son, who is preeminent.

You tell us that Jesus is an exact imprint of Your nature. (Verse 15, Hebrews 1:3) You tell us He is preeminent over all creation: for all things were created by Him and for Him, all things are held together by His power, He is the Head of the Church, He is before all things, the first born (preeminent) over all creation. (John 1:1-5) In Him all of Your fullness was pleased to dwell. (Verse 19, John 1:14)

May we meditate on these Scriptures and rejoice in the infinite Worth and Glory of Your Son.

Father, may Your Word have its full effect on us, as we spend more and more time with You in Your Word. May we be awestruck as we see Your Power and Glory! (Revelation 4:9-11) Lord, Give us a greater love for You and more desire to submit to Your ways, so that we may please and honor You in all our words and deeds! Amen.

Let us study and meditate on (Colossians 1:15-20)

Questions for reflection and meditation:

1. When someone asks you, who is Jesus, what will you tell them?
2. How important is it that you proclaimed the truth about God? (Romans 1:18)

PRAYER BASED ON COLOSSIANS 1:21-23

Everyone God has reconciled is kept by His mighty power,
and presented blameless and holy on the last DAY.

Father, we praise You, for You are our only hope.

We were all rebels, alienated from You and hostile in our thoughts and actions. We all rejected Your ways and followed our own ways. We worshiped created things, instead of You. Therefore, You sent Your Son to reconcile us to Yourself. It took Your Son's death to make it possible for us to have peace with You and to be presented blameless and above reproach in Your sight. You promised that all who call upon Your name are kept safe.. By Your grace they will continue to abide in You. They will grow in their knowledge and love for You and will be grounded and steadfast in the faith.(2 Corinthians 3:18) You will keep them from moving away from the hope of the Gospel. (Philippians 1:6) You have saved Your children and You will keep them by Your mighty power. Not one will be lost! (John 6:39)

Father, Cause us to rejoice daily in Your salvation, and be full of gratitude and praise for the work You have already done in our lives. Make us more aware of the grace we have already received, so we can rest securely in You and be confident in Your future Grace. Amen.

QUESTIONS FOR REFLECTION AND MEDITATION:

1. What did Jesus accomplish on the cross?
2. Can every believer rest in God's salvation? Why or why not?
3. What fruit in your life shows that you are resting in God's salvation?
4. What fruit in your life shows that you trust in your own works and not in God's power to keep you?
5. What makes you confident in God's future grace?

Lord, You are beautiful. Your face is all I seek, for when Your eyes are on Your child, Your grace abounds to me! Lyrics from a Keith Green song.

Prayer based on Colossians 1:24-29

Pleasing and honoring God by the way we walk through suffering.

Father, we praise You, for Paul's successful God-centered ministry.

Paul is rejoicing in his sufferings, for he knows that You are put on display in the way he walks through the sufferings that You have given him. For Your sake and for the good of the Colossians, Paul gladly embraces his sufferings and rejoices in them! Pleasing and honoring You means everything to Paul. He is grateful for the ministry You have given him and acknowledges that all he has is from You. He lives for one purpose, to make You known to all the saints. He wants all to have the hope of glory, living in them through the Holy Spirit. He proclaims Your glorious work and warns of Your judgment, for His desire is to bring all the saints to maturity in Christ – to this end he struggles with all the energy that You have worked in him.

Father, we thank You for Your Word and the wonderful ministry that You have given to Paul. We need You to open our eyes and our hearts, so we may see all the glorious work that You have done and desire to do in all of Your saints. You want to bring them all to maturity. Lord, make us a holy distinct people who live for Your Glory to be seen and known! Amen.

Questions for reflection and meditation:

1. Why does Paul rejoice in his sufferings?
2. What does Paul mean by saying that he filling up what is lacking in the afflictions of Christ. It can not mean that there was something lacking in Christ's atoning work. Any true interpretation of Scripture must align with the rest of Scripture.
3. What made Paul's ministry to the Colossians so effective?
4. How is the joy of Christ living in you most effectively displayed?
5. Does your sufferings suppress your joy in Christ or magnify it?

Prayer based on Colossians 2:1-5

Paul tells of his great struggles and desires for Your Church.

Father, we praise You for Your desires for us are far above our weak desires. Thank you for giving us this long list of loving encouragements in this passage.

You want our hearts to be encouraged and Your Church to be knit together in love. You want us to know the riches of full assurance and to desire the treasure that is found only in Your Son. You hate deception and desire order and firmness in faith. You know what we need and how we must strive to live a holy life, for we are easily deceived and led astray by this world because of the desires of our flesh.

Father, keep us safe and confidently abiding in You and when we fall may we fall on You! Amen.

Questions for reflection and meditation:

1. Why does Paul want the Churches to know how great his struggle is for them?
2. How do your desires for your Church align with Paul's desires for the Church?
3. In what ways do you need to be conformed to God's image and be kept by His grace?

PRAYER BASED ON COLOSSIANS 2:6-15

*To walk in Christ, being rooted and built up in Him,
and abounding in thanksgiving.*

Father, we praise You, for we have so many reasons to be abounding in thanksgiving. The more we live in harmony with You, the more reasons we will see. We praise You for all the incredible gifts which You freely give us in Christ!

You call us to be rooted and grounded in Him. We are not to be tumbleweeds who have no roots and are blown around by every wind of doctrine. We are to be knit together into one body, under one Head. You warn us not to be captivated by a hollow deceptive philosophy of false teachers. May we not be entertained by false teachers who tickle our ears. We praise You, for You are the True Teacher who knows what we need. You have sent us true teachers, who will continually remind us of Your Gospel. To be eternally secure, we must know and believe that Your divine nature dwells fully in Christ. If we have Christ, we have it all. He is good and there is no good apart from Him. (Psalm 16:2) You go on to remind us of what You have done. Everyone You have called is circumcised not physically, but spiritually through the power of the Holy Spirit. They are dead to there old ways and raised to new life in Christ. All of their sins are forgiven and paid for by the blood of Christ. Their slate is made clean, and they are free to live a new life in Christ. Knowing this, how can we not be thankful and filled with joy and love for You? We Praise You Jesus, for You have triumphed over all principalities and powers. You made it possible for us to be free from the bondage of sin and to live for You alone! May we be eternally grateful. Amen.

QUESTIONS FOR REFLECTION AND MEDITATION:

1. What good teachers do you have in your life?
2. How do you recognize good teaching?
3. How have you been freed from the bondage of sin?
4. Describe how repentance and faith are part of your daily life.
5. What is your definition of a great day?
6. How many great days have you had this week?
7. What would need to change to make all of your days great?

Prayer based on Colossians 2:16-23

True treasure is found in Christ alone.

Father, we praise You for revealing Yourself to us through Your Son. Only through Your revelation, can we know You and love You.

You instituted Your laws, holy days, and rituals. You tell us they were only a shadow of what is to come, and the substance is found in Your Son. You warn us not to be seduced by false legalistic teachers who tell us that we must observe certain days and rituals to be right with You. We must reject those who delight in false humility and insist on asceticism and the worship of angels. (Galatians 1:9) You tell us that the proud have lost connection with the Head. You command us to hold fast to Christ (our Head), from whom the whole body is nourished and is knit together, so we may grow in our knowledge and love for You and one another. Paul asks us, if you have died with Christ and are set free from the bondage of sin, then why would you live by human precepts and teachings? (Verse 20) They may appear wise, but they can not deliver us from the indulgences of our flesh. Why do you look to things that are ineffective, temporary, and will pass away? Christ is the real eternal treasure! What would cause you to look to anything else? Christ is the fullness of God, and all those who belong to Him have been given fullness in Him! Only He can break the power of canceled sin and set the prisoner free! (Luke 4:18-19)

Father, open our eyes, grant us repentance, and cause us to walk in Your ways? Amen.

Questions for reflection and meditation:

1. How has your pride caused you to lose connection with the Head?
2. What is your definition of legalism?
3. What rules or codes of conduct are you trusting in?

Let us meditate on Christ and how He is a great treasure. (Matthew 13:44-45)

Jesus the Christ is the only source of righteousness and deliverance. He is worthy of our full devotion. (Luke 14:33)

PRAYER BASED ON COLOSSIANS 3:1-17

*Set your mind on things above and not on the things
of the Earth. And be ready for the return of Christ.*

Father, we praise You, for You are all about Your glory and our good.

You encourage all to set their minds on the things above and not on the things of the earth. You assure us that Christ will return, and all whose life is in Christ will appear with Him in glory. You call us to put to death everything earthly and to put on the new self, which is renewed and made into Your image. You tell us clearly in (verses 8-9), what we must put off and in (verses 12-14), what we must put on. You call us to be united in one body and to be thankful. You assure us that if we obey Your commands, we will know the peace of Christ and He will rule in our hearts.

Father lead us and guide us in the way of Your Truth. (John 17:17) May Your Word be our delight, and may it dwell in us richly. Give us thankful, grateful hearts that love and rejoice in You and Your bride. Give us Your compassion, patience, and wisdom, so that we may teach and admonish others in Your Church. Fills us with Your Grace and Truth. Guide us and direct us in Your ways. May we learn to humbly and prayerfully submit to You in all things. May we live for Your pleasure and Your Glory. Amen.

QUESTIONS FOR REFLECTION AND MEDITATION:

1. What have you set your mind on today?
2. What fruit are you bearing in your life?
3. According to this passage, What will determine the harvest you will reap in your life?
4. What will it take to for you to follow the command to do everything in the name of the Lord Jesus? (Verse 17)

Prayer based on Colossians 3 18-4:1

A call to honor God and please Him in all our relationships.

Father, we praise You, for You have taken rebellious enemies and turn them into obedient servants that love You and follow You!

You have given us these nine verses, because You want us to know and experience Your pleasure and Your glory. You command everyone to live a life that pleases and honors You. You speak to wives, husbands, fathers, and children. You tell us how to righteously respond to the authorities in our lives and administer our God-given authority in a way that pleases and honors You. (servant-leadership) You remind us that those who belong to You, work to please You and not to please men, for they know it is You who will ultimately reward and punished.

Father give us a sincere heart and a reverent fear of You. May we remember that we were created for Your pleasure, and may that knowledge affect how we live and work. Keep us from being man-pleasers, who only work for earthly rewards. Father, we thank You for reminding us that those who follow You have a great inheritance. We also thank You for giving a strong warning to those who only work for earthly rewards and have no thoughts of You. Father, Keep us abiding in You. May we never forget who we belong to and who we are working for. Amen.

Let us meditate on these nine verses and ask God to search our hearts, teach us, and lead us in the way everlasting. (Psalm 139:23-24)

PRAYER BASED ON COLOSSIANS 4:2-6

A life lived for the spread of the Gospel.

Father, we praise You for all the encouragement and instructions in Your Word.

You call us to be persistent in prayer, watchful, and filled with thanksgiving. Paul, who knows that he is in prison for the Gospel, is not focused on his circumstances but lives and prays for opportunities to make known the glorious mysteries of Christ You revealed to him. Paul asked the Colossians to pray for You to open a door for Your Word, and give him the words to speak boldly and clearly. What a great example You have given to us of a humble man who is diligent in prayer, thankful, and encouraging.

Father, You have called us to walk in wisdom and to make the best use of the time You give us. May our speech be gracious and full of truth, and may we be obedient and faithful to tell others of the hope in us. (1 Peter 3:15) May our days be filled with prayer, faithfulness and compassion, so that we may share Your Gospel often and with clarity, wisdom, and grace which You generously provide for all who ask for it. (James 4:2) Amen.

QUESTIONS FOR REFLECTION AND MEDITATION:

1. What instruction or encouragement in this Scripture do you find helpful?
2. What hinders you from sharing the Gospel regularly?
3. Where does sharing the Gospel fall in your list of priorities?
4. Are you equipped to share the Gospel? If not what should you do?
5. What made the ministry of Paul so successful? (Verse 3) gives us one answer.

Prayer based on Colossians 4:7-18

More examples of godly men.

Father, You give us more examples of humble men through Paul. Paul gives credit to You and others for his powerful, fruitful ministry. Paul honors seven men – who have worked faithfully with him. He calls them faithful, beloved brothers and fellow workers for Your Kingdom. May we imitate them and Paul as we persevere in our prayers for others, just as they did. May we fervently pray for ourselves and others: to stand mature, be more obedient, more confident, and steadfast in His ways. Amen.

Questions for reflection and meditation:

1. Are you in the habit of giving credit to God and others for your success?
2. How are you striving to outdo others by showing honor? (Romans 12:10)
3. What examples of godly men and women do you have in your life?
4. Are you more mature, more obedient, and more assured of the will of God today than you were last week, last month, or last year? Why or why not?

1 THESSALONIANS

Prayer based on 1 Thessalonians 1:1-10

The Thessalonians had the assurance of faith and the joy that comes from knowing God through the power of the Holy Spirit.

Father, we praise You, for the work that You have done in the Thessalonian Church through Paul, Silas, and Timothy.

Paul, Silas, and Timothy ministered to the Thessalonians with one voice. You have answered their prayers, and they are rejoicing as they recall the work of faith, the sacrificial labor of the saints, and the steadfast hope of the Thessalonians. They all have assurance because the Gospel did not come to them by words only but also in the power of the Holy Spirit. Despite much affliction, the Thessalonians received Your Word and became followers. Their Church became a model to all believers in Macedonia and Achaia. They turned from their idols to serve You and are eagerly awaiting the return of Your Son. They are rejoicing, because they know that Jesus has deliver them from the wrath to come.

Father we thank You for this model of a healthy Church. May we have eyes to see, ears to hear, and hearts that will respond to Your call. You will enlighten those who honestly seek You and love You. (Matthew 7:7-8) Amen.

Questions for reflection and meditation:

1. How many characteristics of a healthy Church can you find in this passage?
2. How many of these characteristics are on display in your Church?
3. In what ways do you and your Church need to grow?
4. Why did the Thessalonians have an assurance of faith?
5. How can you, like the Thessalonians, be certain of a future in heaven with Christ?
6. How have you grown this past week, month, or year in your love for God? (Proverbs 4:18).

Prayer based on 1 Thessalonians 2:1-12

A faithful ministry leads to the salvation of many.

Father, we thank You for Paul, who boldly proclaims Your Gospel, even in great conflict and at great cost to himself. He does this with a clear conscience because his motives are pure. He shares the Gospel with confidence because he knows it will powerfully change lives.

Paul, Silas, and Timothy have been approved by You and entrusted with Your Gospel. They are not seeking the glory of man, but they seek Your Glory in all they say and do. They were gentle among the Thessalonians, as a nursing mother cherishes her children. They sacrificially lay down their lives for the benefit of the Thessalonians. They exhorted, comforted, and charged the Thessalonians to walk in a manner worthy of the calling they have received from You.

Father, We thank You for this fine example of ministry. May we not just hear Your Word, but be doers of Your Word. (James 1:22) Make us faithful ministers, who live to serve You and others. Amen.

QUESTIONS FOR REFLECTION AND MEDITATION:

1. According to this passage, what are the requirements of a faithful minister?
2. How does knowing you are approved by God and entrusted with the Gospel change how you do ministry?
3. What gave Paul, Silas, and Timothy the confidence to live for God and to boldly minister to others?
4. How has God given you the confidence to live for Him and to boldly minister to others?

Prayer Based on 1 Thessalonians 2:13-16

*Receiving the Word of God for what it is and
learning to trust in God through persecution.*

Father, we praise You, for it is Your power that changes lives.

You tell us how the Thessalonians received Your Word proclaimed by Paul, Silas, and Timothy. They accepted it and embraced it, not as words of men, but as a Word directly from You. They became imitators of Your Church In Judea and suffered attacks from those who oppose the spread of the Gospel. Paul assures the Thessalonians that God will only tolerate a certain amount of sin before His judgment falls. (Romans 1:18, Psalm (75:7-10) Holy Righteous Father, we praise You, for You are perfect in all of Your ways. You promise to carry out perfect Justice and to make all things right. (Romans 12:19) No one will get away with anything. (Hebrews 4:13) You are beautiful and perfect in all Your attributes, even Your Wrath, for it is Your just response to sin.

Father, give us an accurate view of ourselves and a bigger more accurate view of You so that we may live in reverent fear under the authority of Your Word. Amen.

QUESTIONS FOR REFLECTION AND MEDITATION:

1. How have you come to accept and embrace the Word of God for what it is?
2. Do you suppress the Truth or proclaim the truth?
3. How does knowing that God will carry out perfect Justice (make all things right) affect how you respond to persecution?

Prayer based on 1 Thessalonians 2:17-3-10

Many attributes of a saint are listed: the longings, struggles, afflictions, comforts, hopes, joys, and the prayer life of a saint.

Father, we thank You for giving us this glorious picture of a saint.

You continue to show us the life of a saint: they have a great desire to gather with other saints face to face, know they are in a glorious war against the powers of darkness, their hope and joy are found in Your presence, their boast is in their spiritual family. They desire to establish and encourage others in the faith and rejoice when they see the saints stand through persecution. Paul wanted to be with the Thessalonians but he chose to remain in Athens. Paul sends Timothy (his fellow labor in Christ) to the Thessalonians to establishing them and encourage them in the faith. You tell us that a saint knows his appointment and joyfully accepts his portion. (Psalm 16:5-6) They are willing to suffer tribulations and put up with anything for the sake of the Gospel. They care about other saints and want to know how they are doing. They rejoice in and are comforted by other saints, who stand fast in the Lord. They pray night and day for other saints and strongly desire to speak Your truth into their lives.

Father, as we look at this long list may we not be discouraged or condemned, but appropriately convicted. May we set our eyes on You and pray for You to do all You desire to do in us! Amen.

Questions for reflection and meditation:

1. As you meditate on this Scripture, what attributes of a saint do you desire to grow in?
2. What work has God done in your life or in the life of other saints that causes you to rejoice?

Prayer based on 1 Thessalonians 3:11-13

Paul's prayer for the Thessalonians reveals the plan of God for His people.

Father, We praise You and thank You for Your plan of redemption for lost sinners. You are holy, faithful, and just!

Father, we are so easily distracted and led astray. We can easily turn from You and pursue things of this world that will not satisfy. (Isaiah 55:1-2)

Father, may You direct our ways and cause us to abound in joy for You and one another. Do whatever You must do to make us holy and blameless in Your sight. Establish our hearts so that when Your Son returns, we will be the spotless and blameless bride of Christ. (Colossians 1:22) Amen.

Questions for reflection and meditation:

1. When are you tempted to pursue your satisfaction apart from Christ.
2. What is wrong with being satisfied with worldly things?
3. How is it possible for us to be holy and blameless in His sight?

God is most glorified in us when we are most satisfied in Him.
John Piper.

Let us read and meditate on 1 Thessalonians 3:11-13

Prayer based on 1 Thessalonians 4:1-8

God reveals His plan for His bride.

Father, we praise You for all Your ways are good. You are so gracious and patient with us.

You have loved us and revealed Yourself to us while we were yet sinners. You have given us Your Word to instruct us, so we may know how to live in a manner that pleases and honors You. Father, You are all wise and You know we need more than instruction, for we are weak and unable to do what we know is right in our own strength. (Romans 7:18) Lord, we praise You and thank You for Your grace and mercy. You tell us that it is Your will (desire and delight) to conform us to Your image (verse 3) You then describe a life lived to reflect Your image. We must abstain from sexual immorality and all lusts of the flesh. We must know how to control our own bodies in holiness and honor, and we must flee sexual immorality. You lovingly warn us that You are an avenger who must punish all sin because You are Holy and Righteous in all of Your ways. You then remind us that You did not call us to be impure, but to live a holy life through the power of the Holy Spirit!

Father, we praise You for Your saving and keeping power. Have Your way with us and do whatever You must do so that we may abide in You, today and forever more. John (15:4-5) Amen.

Questions for reflection and meditation:

1. What does God want to do for you? (Verse 3)
2. Why is God an avenger in all things? (Verse 6)
3. How does God want you to live? (Verse 7)

Prayer based on 1 Thessalonians 4:9-12

*Abide in Christ and walk in a manner that will
be a powerful testimony to unbelievers.*

Father, we praise You for revealing Yourself to us so we may know You and be able to love others as You have loved us.

You want us to have a willing and obedient heart. You taught the Thessalonians to love one another. (verse 9) And the Thessalonians responded by loving all the brethren in Macedonia! Paul then encourages the Thessalonians to love more and more. Your healthy children will continue to grow. (Proverbs 4:18) You call us to live a quiet life, mind our own business, and work diligently with our hands so that we will lack nothing and be a living testimony for Your Glory. May we intentionally live and work for Your glory. (1 Corinthians 10:31) Amen.

Questions for reflection and meditation:

1. How does abiding in Christ affect the way you love others?
2. How is your Love for God on display?
3. How is your love for unbelievers on display?
4. How can you avoid evil or even the appearance of evil?

Prayer based on 1 Thessalonians 4:13:18

Paul's revelation from God about the end times. (verse 15)

Father, we praise You for Your Word. We can not know Truth apart from Your revelation.

You tell us that the death of a believer is very different from the death of an unbeliever – a believer lives for Christ and when they die their is much gain (Philippians 1:21) – an unbeliever lives for the world and when they die there is much loss. Paul is not just giving the Thessalonians a lesson on eschatology. His words are Your Words and are meant to encourage and give hope to believers. He did not want them to grieve over the fate of those who have died in Christ. You tell us that all believers who die before You return will be at home with You. (2 Corinthians 5:8) Paul boldly declares by Your revealed Word to him. Those who are still alive will not go before those who have died. Jesus will descend from heaven with many loud noises. He will bring with Him all the believers who have died in Christ. Then all believers who are alive will arise and meet the Lord in the air. What a DAY that will be! All the saints will be together rejoicing with You for all eternity.

Father, may we all believe in Your Word and respond to Your call. Amen.

Questions for reflection and meditation:

1. Do these words give you great hope or great fear?
2. What must you lose to gain Christ?
3. Are you ready and eagerly looking forward to Jesus's return or is there something that you want more than His coming?
4. Do you pray for His kingdom to come? Why or why not?
5. How can you be sure that when the role is called up yonder you will be there?

Prayer based on 1 Thessalonians 5:1-11

We are called to be awake, sober, and prepared for the coming of the Lord.

Father, we praise You, for You give us everything we need to know in Your Word.

You tell the Thessalonians that they do not need to know the times or the seasons. They were obviously already taught about these things just as Your Son taught His disciples in (Matthew chapter 24) You teach us clearly in (Matthew 24:36) that no one knows the DAY of Your coming. You proclaim that the DAY of the Lord will come like a thief in the night. (Luke 12:39-40) You tell us that those who belong to You are children of the day and not children of the night. Therefore, You call us not to sleep as others do, but to keep awake and be sober, for Your Son will surely come at a time least expected. You tell us that Your children of the day are not destined for wrath, but will obtain salvation through Your Son, and live with You through all eternity.

Father, may we encourage one another and build one another up, by sharing the good news of the Gospel. May we joyfully proclaim His wonderful works. Amen.

Questions for reflection and meditation:

1. How does the goals and the motives of the people of darkness differ from the goals and motives of the people of the light?
2. Do you live and operate in the shadows, or do you live openly and honestly in the light? (1 John 1:7)
3. How does the promised certainty of Christ's return affect your daily life and decisions?
4. Are you ready for Christ's return? If not what must you do?
5. How can you prevent spiritual snoozing and stay awake and alert?
6. When was the last time you lovingly warned someone of Christ's imminent return?

Prayers based on 1 Thessalonians 5:12-16

Honor your leaders and thank God for them – for they lovingly keeping watch over you – strive to do the same for your brothers and sisters in the faith.

Father we praise You for these many mandates, given to us, for our good and Your glory.

Father, May we esteem those who labor among us. May we comfort and edify one another with the comfort You have given us. May we warn the unruly and the idle, comfort the feeble minded and the faint hearted, support the weak, and be patient with All. May we realize that we can not do any of these things in our own strength. You have reconciled us to Yourself and entrusted to us the message of reconciliation. (2 Corinthians 5:19)

Father, show us Your glory so that we will see our great need and be quick to call on Your name and not trust in our own wisdom and resources. Amen.

Questions for reflection and meditation:

1. What keeps you from abounding in the works of God given in these verses?
2. How can you see more of the grace and power of God and be amazed by it?

Prayer based on 1 Thessalonians 5:16-28

*A transformed life pleases God and is a powerful
testimony to the reality of God.*

Father, we praise You, for You lifted us out of a slimy pit, planted our feet on a rock, and put a new song in our hearts. (Psalm 40:1-3)

We want to be the people You have called us to be. A people who give thanks in all things, rejoice in all thing, and pray without ceasing.

Father, show us what a life like this looks like and give us the wisdom and power we need to live it. Teach us how to pray without ceasing so that we will always talk with You before we act or speak. May we be quick to acknowledge that Your ways are not our ways and Your thoughts are not our thoughts. (Isaiah 55:8-9) May we never quench the Holy Spirit or despise prophecies. May we test everything by Your Word; hold fast to what is good; and abstain from every form of evil. Increase our desire to be conformed to Your image as we eagerly await Your return. May we be prepared to see Your Glory, which will be fully displayed when Your Son returns. You are faithful and You will surely do all that You have promised. (Philippians 1:6) Amen.

Questions for reflection and meditation:

1. Are you quick to recognize that God is the source of all true wisdom, and how do you respond?
2. What makes it possible for you to be thankful and rejoice in all things?
3. What benefits have you received from loving God more than the world?
4. What problems have you encountered from loving the world more than God?
5. How has God's revelation to you changed the way you live?

Let us take time to meditate on the attributes of God. And rejoice in His ability and desire to care for us in every situation.

Lord, give us a soft, humble heart that will quickly submit to You. May we never grieve You, but rejoice in living for Your pleasure. Amen.

2 THESSALONIANS

Prayer based on 2 Thessalonians 1:1-4

Paul boasts and rejoices in the work God has done in the Thessalonians.

Father, we praise You for Your faithful work in the Thessalonian Church.

May faith, hope, and love abound in us as it did in Your Church in Thessalonica. May we be patient and persevere in our hardships as we walk through them in a manner that pleases and honors You and brings You glory. May there be undeniable evidence that shows we belong to You and have been counted worthy of Your kingdom. (Verse 5)

Father, we give thanks to You for Your work in our lives. May we pray for ourselves and our Churches in the same manner as Paul did. Lord, give us the grace we need to suffer well and live for Your glory! Amen.

Questions for reflection and meditation:

1. How can you abound in faith, hope, and love in your current circumstances as the Thessalonians did?
2. What cause Paul to boast about the Thessalonian Church?
3. In what ways do you desire to grow and be united with Christ?
4. How is God filling you with more confidence and desire to pray? (Luke 11:9-10)
5. What has kept you from asking for great things from God?

PRAYER BASED ON 2 THESSALONIANS 1:5-12

On the DAY that Jesus returns, all who believe will marvel at His appearing – those who do not know Him and obey Him will suffer eternal destruction.

Father, we thank You for reminding us of Your Power, Your Righteousness, and the imminent and glorious return of Your Son.

Your mighty power guarantees that You will do all You said You would do. (Isaiah 46:9-10) Your Righteousness guarantees that You will repay those who oppose You and reward those who love You and obey You. Those who rebel against You and refuse to acknowledge Your authority and bring affliction on Your people will most certainly receive their just punishment. They will live in outer darkness, experience everlasting destruction, and eternal separation from You. Your Righteousness also guarantees that Your afflicted children who love You and obey You, will have rest in You, both now and for all eternity. In (verse 5), Paul calls this, evidence of Your Righteous judgment. You tell us that Your Son will appear with His mighty angels on that DAY. And He will be glorified in His saints and admired by all those who have believed. (Verse 10) What a DAY that will be! The saints will rejoice and those who refused to live under Your authority will hide under the rocks. (Revelation 6:16) May we all pray as Paul prayed in (verses 11-12)

Father, May You be glorified in our lives, as we live for Your pleasure and do the good work You have prepared for us and called us to do. Make us more aware of Your glory and worthy of Your calling. Fill us with every resolve we need for every good work You have for us. Amen.

Let us read and meditate on Paul's prayer in 2 Thessalonians 1:11-12

QUESTIONS FOR REFLECTION AND MEDITATION:

1. How does your life reflect your belief in God's sovereign authority over all things?
2. How does the fact that God is perfect in all of his ways and will carry out perfect Justice affect how you respond to injustice?
3. In this passage, some are actively living for Christ and joyfully awaiting His return and another group will dread His

return. Why is there no mention of a third apathetic group? (Matthew 12:30)

4. Is the degree to which we long for the return of Christ a measure of our spiritual condition? Why or Why not?

Prayer based on 2 Thessalonians 2:1-5

*Paul's addresses the rumors and false teachings about the coming of the
Lord – and reminds the Thessalonians of the truth he taught them.*

Father, we praise You, for establishing Your unshakable Word.

Your love and patience are once again on display through the ministry of Paul to the Thessalonians. Paul is deeply troubled because the Thessalonians are deeply troubled by false teachers who proclaim that Christ has already come. Paul clearly taught them in his first letter that they could not possibly miss His coming. It would be a very public event, like the day of Pentecost, but global. Jesus would descend with a shout and would bring with Him all those who have died in Christ. All who are alive and believe will meet the Lord in the air. And be united with Him and all the saints for all eternity. (1 Thessalonians 4:13-5:3, Acts 1:11) Paul then assures them of two events that will occur before Christ comes. There will be a great falling away within the organized Church. Those who claim to believe in You will abandon the faith. And then the man of lawlessness will be revealed. He will take his seat in the temple of God, proclaiming himself to be God. Paul also proclaims that the DAY of the Lord will come when one least expects, like a thief in the night.

Father, whenever Your Son returns may we be ready, awake, and about Your business. Amen.

QUESTIONS FOR REFLECTION AND MEDITATION:

1. When was the last time you were troubled by false teachings that are so dominant in our society?
2. When Jesus comes what will you gain and what will you lose?
3. How can you be content and secure knowing that the return of Christ is imminent?
4. How is God making you ready for His return?

Prayer based on 2 Thessalonians 2:6-12

The removal of the restraining one, the revealing of the lawless one, and the false signs, wonders, and wicked deceptions that will occur before the Lord returns.

Father, we praise You, for You and You alone are sovereign overall things.

You tell us, in (verses 6-8), that Someone is restraining the work of lawlessness. The revealing of the man of lawlessness will not happened until He is taken away. Paul, writing to the Thessalonians, does not say who He is because Paul is sure that the Thessalonians already know. What candidates are there that can restrain the power of Satan? Father, only Your sovereign power can restrain Satan. You have chosen restraint of the lawlessness one through Your Holy Spirit working in and through Your Church. You have established Your Church and have promised that the gates of hell will not prevail against it. (Matthew 16:18) The lawless one will be released when the Holy Spirit is taken away – this means Your Church will be taken out of the world, as well, because without Your Holy Spirit, there is no Church. A church without Your Holy Spirt is dead. After the removal of the Holy Spirit, the work of Satan will be unrestrained and the man of lawlessness will be released. You tell us there will be counterfeit miracles, signs and wonders, and every kind of evil that will deceive those who are perishing. All who delight in evil and hate the Truth will perish. What a terrible time that will be! Only those who turn from their evil ways and run to You will escape Your wrath. You are our only hope, for in You alone can we find refuge and strength. (Proverbs 18:10, Psalm 91:1-2) Amen.

Questions for reflection and meditation:

1. What would the world be like without the restraining power of the Church?
2. How would your life be different if God did not save and restrain you? Have you ever trembled at that thought?
3. What is the difference between a dead church and one that is alive?
4. Does God send people to hell or do they choose it?
5. Why do some people choose life and other people choose death? What makes the difference?

Prayer based on 2 Thessalonians 2:13-16

Those who are called through the Gospel, will obtain the glory of their Lord.

Father, we praise You, for it was Your plan (from the beginning) to save and sanctify the elect.

Paul is giving thanks to You and rejoicing over the Thessalonians, for they received Your Gospel. Paul encourages the Thessalonians to stand fast and hold on to sound teachings. Paul prays that they would be established in Your Word and in every good work that You have prepared for them. Father, You call all of Your children to rejoice and give thanks for choosing them for salvation. It is You who opened their eyes and regenerated their hearts so that they could hear and respond to Your Gospel. Only through the sanctifying work of Your Holy Spirit living in Your people can cause them to die to themselves and live for You.

Father, We praise You for all that You have done so that all believers may stand glorified in Your presence. (Romans 8:29-30) Cause us to stand firm on the teachings we have heard. We need You to establish us, both in Your Word and in every good work. Amen.

QUESTIONS FOR REFLECTION AND MEDITATION:

1. What are you most thankful for in your life?
2. How and when do you express your thankfulness to God?
3. How has God established you in His Word and good works?
4. Are you confident that you will stand firm and live a life that will please and honor God and bring Him glory, both in death and life? If so, How have you obtained such confidence?
5. What steps do you need to take to have more confidence in God?
6. How often do you humbly share your confidence in God with others?

Prayer based on 2 Thessalonians 3:1-5

Paul requests prayer and encourages the Thessalonians.

Father, we praise You for Your work in Your elect.

You show us, through the apostle Paul, what our attitudes and prayers should be. May we pray that Your Word would spread rapidly and be honored, celebrated, and glorified. when we see opposition to Your Word by unreasonable and wicked men, may we not shrink back but boldly and humbly ask for deliverance as Paul did. Paul reminds us that You are faithful to guard, deliver, and establish Your people.

Father, give us more confidence in Your power and faithfulness. And also the love, wisdom, perseverance, patience, and strength that we need every day so we may live and die for You. Amen.

Questions for reflection and meditation:

1. How would you describe your prayer life?
2. Are you prone to shrink back or are you quick to ask for deliverance?
3. What has hindered you from following hard after God?

Prayer based on 2 Thessalonians 3:6-18

Paul calls the Thessalonians to avoid idleness and to imitate him, Silvanus, and Timothy. And to not grow weary of doing good.

Father, we thank You for Your warnings, commandments, encouragements, instructions, and patience.

You command us to withdraw from every believer who is idle and does not live according to Your teaching. Father, give us a healthy view of work and a love for the work You have given us to do. You created a wonderful garden and placed Adam in it to work it and keep it. (Genesis 2:15) It was Your design for man to work. May we receive Your commands rightly and take them seriously, for all of Your commandments are good and should be rightly understood and obeyed. We need You, Lord, for we quickly forget that we are fallen creatures with a fallen intellect. We are prone to rebel and trust in our own wisdom. Lord, have mercy on us. Give us eyes to see, a mind that understands Your ways, and a heart that desires to follow hard after You.

The Thessalonians knew how they should live because Paul modeled it for them. He labored and toiled day and night and did not eat any food without paying for it. Although Paul had the right and authority to charge for his work, he decided to forgo his rights to set an example of how one should live. Paul gives a warning to those who are idle and undisciplined. He tells them to work to supply their own needs and the needs of others. Father, You tell us that everything we do should be for Your glory? (Colossians 3:17) In (verse 13) You tell us to not grow weary in doing good. And in (verse 14), You tell us not to keep company with anyone who does not obey Your Word, so that they may be ashamed and repent. You tell us not to regard them as an enemy. And then command us to admonish them as a brother.

Father, make us disciplined in our thinking and quick to listen to You, so that we may know Your grace, fall more in love with You, and joyfully obey all You command us to do, regardless of the cost. Amen.

QUESTIONS FOR REFLECTION AND MEDITATION:

1. How can withdrawing from another believer, who is not living according to the Word of God, serve them and please God?
2. When have You forgotten that you are a fallen creature with a fallen intellect and foolishly trusted in your own wisdom? What was the result of your foolishness?
3. How often do you pray to know God's thoughts and His ways?
4. Is it possible for you to love the work that you do? Why or why not?
5. When was the last time you surrendered your rights?
6. When have you admonished a brother or sister in the Lord?
7. What evidence of the grace of God do you see and rejoice over in your life and other believers?

1 Timothy

PRAYER BASED ON 1 TIMOTHY 1:1-7

Paul confronts false teachers and cares for Your Church.

Father, we thank You for preserving these pastoral letters to Timothy and Titus. We praise You for the way You worked Your will, in them, for Your good pleasure. (Philippians 2:13) You put Timothy in Ephesus and Titus in Crete to confront and encourage believers not to turn from the Gospel. We praise You for Your work in them and in everyone else who will die to themselves and live for You.

In (verses 1-2), You tell us that Paul is Your apostle by Your command and that grace, mercy, and peace come from You through Your Son. Paul urges Timothy, who he left in Ephesus, to confront the false teachers that were troubling Your Church with a pure heart, a good conscience, and a sincere faith. False teachers promoted useless speculation and meaningless arguments and were causing disputes rather than godly edification in the faith. Some had wondered away into vain discussions. They are without understanding and they make confident assertions about things they do not understand.

Father, give us a humble, compassionate heart, a sincere faith, and the patience we so desperately need to love and care for those who are proud and have no understanding of You. Open our eyes and our hearts as we meditate and pray through Your Scriptures, and then call us to action. May we rejoice in pleasing and honoring You as You work in us to draw many to Yourself. Amen.

QUESTIONS FOR REFLECTION AND MEDITATION:

1. How does knowing that Paul is appointed by God affect how you receive his words?
2. Are you guilty of promoting useless speculation and meaningless arguments?
3. What is your response to the false teachers who live among you?
4. What motivates you to study God's Word?
5. What is your purpose for living and how is it being seen by others? If you asked others what they thought your purpose for living is, What do you think they would tell you?

Prayer based on 1 Timothy 1:8-11

The law is good. The law should be feared by the lawless and disobedient and kept by those that God has declared righteous.

Father, we thank You for giving us Your law. May we know it is good and use it lawfully and appropriately.

We know that Your law is good, but it is not the basis of Christian living. You gave us Your law so we could see that we are ungodly sinful rebels, unable to keep Your law. Thank You for opening our eyes so that we may acknowledge Your law and turn to You for deliverance. Without Your intervention, we would be blind and lost forever. (Verses 9-11) describes the sins that Your law addresses, given in the order that You gave it to Moses on Mount Sinai. (Exodus 20:12-16). Paul remembers Your deliverance and praises You for Your glorious Gospel which You have entrusted to him. (Verse 11)

Father, may we also praise You and be committed to Your Gospel, which You have entrusted to all who believe in Your name. Lord, may we never forget what You have accomplished on our behalf. Amen.

QUESTIONS FOR REFLECTION AND MEDITATION:

1. Do you fear the law? Why or why not?
2. Do you keep the law? Why or why not?
3. How often do you experience the weight and the glory of the Gospel like Paul did? (Romans 11:33)

Prayer based on 1 Timothy 1:12-17

*God gives strength to His children, declares them
righteous, and appoints them to His service.*

Father, we thank You for the miraculous work You do in all Your saints.

In (verse 12), Paul thanks You for the strength that You have given him.
He praises You for Your faithfulness. He humbly accepts his calling
and is filled with gratitude, for You appointed him to be an apostle.
He never forgot the depths of his sin and the Love You poured out so
abundantly on him. He knew that Your Son came into this world and
laid down his life to save sinners, which he believed he was the foremost.
Paul saw himself as the greatest sinner he knew. (Verses 15-16) You
tells us that those forgiven much love much, and those forgiven little
love little. (Luke 7:41-48) Paul then explains why he received such great
mercy from God and breaks out in praise. (Verse 16-17)

Father, open our eyes and hearts so that we may see the depth of our
depravity and become more aware of Your immeasurable power and
love toward those who believe. Amen.

Let us read and meditate on Ephesians 1:16-23 and Ephesians 3:14-21

Questions for reflection and meditation:

1. What has caused your love for God and others to grow deeper;
   over the years?
2. Do you regularly express gratitude for having the privilege of
   being a bondservant of God?
3. Who is the greatest sinner that you know?
4. How does the awareness of your sinfulness cause you to love
   God and others more?
5. If someone asks you, why did God save you, what would be
   your answer? What answer would Paul give? (Verse 16)
6. In what ways are you growing in your faith and service to God
   and others?

Prayer based on 1 Timothy 1:18-20

Hold fast to the faith and fight the good fight.

Father, we thank You for Your wisdom and strength, which keeps us abiding in You. We would be lost apart from Your keeping. (Proverbs 18:10)

Paul reminds Timothy of how God set him apart for ministry by speaking through others. Paul encourages Timothy to persevere in the faith that he has been given with a clear conscience so that he may run a good race and fight a good fight. Paul then gives an example to Timothy of two men who made a shipwreck of their faith. He then gives an example of how to pray for these men.

Father, may we take all this advice that You have given to us through the apostle Paul and apply it to our lives. Amen.

Questions for reflection and meditation:

1. When was the last time you saw the transforming power of God at work in your life? or the life of another?
2. Do you regularly speak the Word of God into the lives of others? Why or why not?
3. How has God led you to pray for the lost all around you?

Prayer based on 1 Timothy 2:1-7

Prayer is the first and consistent indicator of a changed heart.

Father, we praise You, for You strongly support and delight in the prayers of Your saints. (2 Chronicles 16:9, Psalm 16:3)

You emphasize the need for everyone to pray. You know we can only grow in our love for You and in our love and service for others if we have a vibrant, healthy prayer life. In (verse 1), Paul implores Timothy, to put prayer before all things. He tells him to pray, intercede, and give thanks for all. You tell us that prayer is good, acceptable, and necessary for all who desire to live a holy life. You will use our prayers to change us and draw others to Yourself. You tell us that Your desire is for all to be saved and to come to the knowledge of Your truth. Father, Make our desires like Yours and give us the privilege of partnering with You in Your great work. Paul then goes on to proclaim the Gospel, which he was appointed to preach in faith and truth.

Father, open our ears so we may hear and respond to the Gospel preached in faithful Churches. Lord, remind us daily of our desperate need for the Gospel and our commission to share it. Matthew 28:18-20 Amen.

Questions for reflection and meditation:

1. How does your lifestyle display your desire to see all come to know Christ?
2. How would you describe your prayer life?
3. What are you most consistent in praying for and why?
4. When was the last time you were cut to the heart when you heard the Gospel?
5. Do you think that preaching the Gospel to yourselves every day is excessive or necessary?

Prayer Based on 1 Timothy 2:8-15

God desires for His people and rules for their conduct.

Father, we praise You for making Your desires known to us through Your Word.

You first and foremost desire is for all men everywhere to pray. You also desire order, peace, and holiness in our lives, so we may reflect Your character in all we do and say. You are all-wise and know the necessary order of all things. We confess that we need guidelines, and we thank You for Your rules, particularly the ones You give us in this text on public worship. You tell us that godly prayer comes from godly men and women who know You, love You, and live for Your Gospel. You tell us that a godly woman will dress modestly and decently and will be clothed with good deeds: in keeping with her professions of faith. (1 Peter 3:3-4) Paul encourages men to lead; and for women to be submissive and not to exercise authority over a man in Your Church. Paul reminds us that Adam was created first and then Eve. You disapproved when Eve usurped the authority given to Adam in the garden. It was Adam who You called into account for his failure to guard and protect the garden, not Eve. (Genesis 3:9) You appointed Adam to care for the garden. He should never have allowed a lying snake to remain in the garden to tempt his wife.

Father, show us how to live lives that reflect Your character. May we not trust in our fallen wisdom, but look to Your Word for Your wisdom, in all things. (Proverbs 3:5-7) Amen.

Questions for reflection and meditation:

1. What does God desire in your life and in His Church?
2. How does your worship gatherings exalt God?
3. How does your conduct reflect the character of God?
4. Do you do things to draw attention to yourself or do you live to serve others and exalt God?
5. In what ways are you striving to live under the authority of the Word of God?
6. Who or what sets the agenda for your days?

Prayer based on 1 Timothy 3:1-16

Qualifications for pastors and deacons are listed. And a call for saints to know how to conduct themselves in the household of God.

Father, we thank You for the gift of Your Word, which is the source of all that is true and all good counsel.

You have given us a long list of qualifications for pastors and deacons. Except for the ability to teach and not being a recent convert, the qualifications for deacons and pastors are very similar. As we meditate and pray over this list, may we see how ordinary these qualifications are and how they apply to every member of Your Church. You want Your Church to be a light, a city on a hill that shines brightly. (Matthew 5:14) You clearly show us in Your Word today what is required, not only of the leadership in Your Church, but of every member of Your Church. You call Your Church to be a city on a hill and to uphold and undergird the Truth of the Gospel. You have given us Your Word, so we know how to conduct ourselves in Your Church. Thank You for revealing the mystery of godliness. (Verse 16) You call us to be a holy: a distinct people, set apart from the world, a people called out of darkness into Your marvelous light and who live to declare Your praises. (1 Peter 2:9)

Father, may we meditate on (1 Timothy 3:1-13) and pray that You will open our hearts to Your Word. May we rejoice in the ways You has worked in our lives, and may we repent from the ways we have failed to love, honor and obey You. You promise us if we confess our sins, You will forgive us and cleanse us from all unrighteousness. (1 John 1:9) Amen.

Questions for reflection and meditation:

1. What are the requirements for the leaders and the members of your church?
2. What are Paul's reasons for writing chapter 3?
3. What is the mystery of godliness that Paul shares with Timothy?

Prayer based on 1 Timothy 4:1-5

In the last days some will depart from the faith. Everything created by God is good if received with thanksgiving and prayer.

Father, we praise You, for You will keep Your children from falling.

You give us a strong warning through the apostle Paul. You tell us in latter times (from the time Your Son ascended until His return), some will depart from the true Gospel and devote themselves to false, deceitful teachings that are demonic. Paul gives us two examples of demonic teachings: those who forbid marriage and those who require abstinence from foods; as a means to be made right with You. Paul tells us these demonic teachings are a direct attack on Your Gospel. (See Galatians) Paul tells us these false teachers have a seared conscience guided by their appetites. (Romans 16:18) A good conscience is submitted to and guided by Your Word. You created marriage and food, which are good gifts from Your hand; meant to be received with prayer and thanksgiving.

Father, may we recognize and reject false distorted teachings and be quick to turn to You and embrace Your Gospel. Amen

QUESTIONS FOR REFLECTION AND MEDITATION:

1. Why is trying to find favor with God through works a big problem?
2. Have you ever had a problem with enjoying the gifts of God more than God himself? If so, How did you resolved that tension?
3. What does (verse 5) mean?

Prayer based on 1 Timothy 4:6-16

The training and discipline that is necessary for developing godly character.

Father, we praise You for giving us Your good, perfect, and sufficient instructions in Your Word.

You tell us that it is good for us to be nourished in Your Word so that we can know and practice sound doctrine, reject irreverent foolish teachings, and live for You. You call us to trust in You and to follow hard after You. You make it clear that to grow in godliness will require effort. (backsliding is a natural default) You call us to train ourselves for godliness just like athletes discipline and train their bodies. You remind us of the great value of godliness, both in this life and in the life to come. You tell us that all who have set their Hope on You will toil and strive to follow You. (verse 10) You are the only hope and the only Savior for all people. (Acts 4:12) Paul implores Timothy to set an example for all believers in speech, in conduct, love, faith, and purity. (verse 12) Paul encourages Timothy to immerse himself in preaching and teaching and to keep a close watch on himself and his doctrine, so all may see his progress and be saved. (Verses 13-16)

Father, give us more desire to live for Your Glory. May we practice and immerse ourselves in sound doctrine, so that our growth in godliness may be evident to all. Conform us to Your image so that we may walk in Your ways and have the great privilege of being fishers of men. Amen.

Questions for reflection and meditation:

1. How have you grown in godliness this past week, month, or year? Describe the part God played and your part.
2. Why are training and discipline necessary for a life of godliness?
3. How does your life reflect your desire to be conformed to the image of God?
4. What has hindering you from sharing the Gospel?

Prayer based on 1 Timothy 5:1-16

Paul gives instructions for caring for Your Church.

Father, we thank You for all of the instructions You faithfully give us in Your Word.

(Verses 1-2) gives good counsel to Timothy on how to shepherd those under his care. Your Word is very explicit. (Verse 3) tells us to honor those who are truly widows and please You by providing for our families. (Verse 8) gives a strong warning – anyone who does not provide for their own family has denied the faith and is worse than an unbeliever! (Verse 5) describes a true widow as a godly woman, who is left alone with no one to care for her. (Verse 6) describes an ungodly woman who is self-indulgent, living for her own pleasure, and is dead in her sins, even while she lives. Father, You call Your Church to take care of the true widows. Paul give us specific requirements for placing widows on a care list: over sixty years of age, been faithfully devoted to one man, and have a reputation for good works – such as raising up children in the Lord, showing hospitality, and caring for the afflicted. (Verses 9-10) Paul warns Timothy not to put younger widows on the list, for he fears they would become idle busy bodies who say and do things they should not say and do. (Verses 11-13) Paul would prefer younger widows to remarry and live a godly life for the benefit of others. (Verse 14) Paul then addresses women who have widows in their families and calls them to strive to be in a position to care for them. (Verse 16)

Father, we need Your wisdom to guide us so we may strive for the right things, in the right ways, and with the right motives. Give us a pure heart and a stronger desire to follow hard after You. Amen.

Questions for reflection and meditation:

1. How are you caring for older men, older women, younger men and younger women that God has placed in your life?
2. What widows do you and your Church support? (James 1:27)
3. What are the characteristics of a true widow?

Prayer based on 1 Timothy 5:17-25

*More instructions for caring for pastors. And a strong
charge for them to shepherd well.*

Father, we thank You for Your Church and the pastors that lead them well.

You tell us that Your under shepherds are worthy of double honor. They are to be respected by the congregation and paid well. In (Deuteronomy 25:4), You tell us not to muzzle an ox when it turns out grain. And in (Luke 10:7), You tell us that a worker deserves his wages. Paul tells Timothy an accusation against a pastor must be supported by two or three witnesses. You gave this wisdom to Your chosen people thousands of years ago. (Deuteronomy 19:15) Your Son also stated this principle in (Matthew 18:16) Paul tells Timothy to rebuke publicly all who persist in sin as a warning to all. Paul, aware of the extreme difficulty of following You faithfully, solemnly charges Timothy before You and Your Son and the elect angels to observe all things without prejudice and show no partiality. Paul tells Timothy not to share in the sins of others but to keep himself pure. Paul warns Timothy not to be quick to lay hands on someone to dedicate him to the Lord, for not all sins are evident but may remain hidden.

Father, may we never take Your commandments lightly or elevate our wisdom above Yours. May we never forget how You destroyed all flesh, except Noah and his family, because all men were wicked and did what was right in their own eyes. (Proverbs 14:12) Lord, may we not be like them. Make us humble people who look to the hand of our Master and strive hard to follow Your ways, regardless of the cost. Amen.

Questions for reflection and meditation:

1. In what ways are you grateful for the under shepherds that God has given to you? In what ways have you supported them?
2. How have you experienced the benefits of being rebuked in your life?
3. Why does Paul use such strong words with Timothy in (verse 21)
4. Can you recall a time in your life when you have taken the Lords Commandments lightly? Why did you decide to do so? What was the result?

Prayers based on 1 Timothy 6 1:10

*The pursuit godliness in all our relationships. A description
of false teachers and a call to godly contentment in all things.*

Father, we praise You, for You have provided everything we need in
Your Word.

You call us to a pursuit of godliness in all our relationships, both inside
and outside Your Church. You tell us we should show honor to unbelievers who have authority over us so no one would revile Your name.
(Romans 13:1-2) You call us to never be disrespectful, especially to those
who believe. (Galatians 6:10) Paul urges Timothy to teach these things
and then describes false teachers that do not embrace sound teachings
that promote godliness. Paul tells Timothy that false teachers are proud
and know nothing. They are obsessed with disputes and arguments over
words, which do not lead to godliness but lead to quarrels and divisions.
They are corrupted in their thinking and deprived of the truth of God
They see godliness as a means to financial gain. In (verse 6), You tell us
that godliness with contentment is great gain. You remind us that we came
into this world with nothing, and we will not take anything out of it. You
call us to be content with what we have and not spend our lives striving
after things that will perish. You assure us that ruin and destruction await
those who do not live for You but live for their lusts and comfort. You
warned us that the love of money led some away from the faith. (Verse 10)

Father, we need Your wisdom and discernment, to see what we are living
for and identify any false teachers or teachings. Have mercy on us, Lord,
and grant us the power we need to repent so that we may turn from all
that is false and worship You alone. Amen.

Questions for reflection and meditation:

1. How are you pursuing and growing in godliness?
2. Who do you have in your inner circle of friends that spurs you
   on to godliness?
3. How do you recognize false teachers? or true teachers?
4. What characteristics of false teachers do you find in this Scripture?
5. Where do you regularly receive sound teaching and good counsel.
6. (Verse 6) proclaims that godliness with contentment is great gain!
   Has this been your experience?

PRAYER BASED ON 1 TIMOTHY 6:11-16

A call to fight the good fight of faith and to run the good race. And a reminder of the absolute power and infinite grace of God.

Father, we praise You, for You are sovereign over all things, and You delight to give life to all who cry out to You.

You call us to flee all ungodliness and to joyfully pursue righteousness, godliness, faith, love, patience, and gentleness, (Galatians 5:22) And to lay aside everything that hinders you from fighting the good fight of faith so that you may take hold of eternal life. (Hebrews 1:2) Father, we thank You and praise You for Your calling. We are grateful and confident in You, for You will complete Your sanctifying work in us. (Philippians 1:6) Paul, urges Timothy to keep the good confession that he made in the presence of many witnesses. Paul then reminds Timothy of the good confession Jesus made before Pontius Pilate: For this purpose, I was born, and for this purpose, I have come into the world that I should bear witness to the Truth. (John 18:37) Paul then charges Timothy to keep this commandment unstained and free from reproach, until the DAY Your Son return. What a charge! Paul then appropriately reminds Timothy of who You are! You are the Sovereign One, the King of kings and the Lord of lords, who alone has immortality and dwells in unapproachable light. All Honor, Glory and Power belong to You and You will bring about all that You decree!

Father, may we not give up because the bar is so high or foolishly believe that all we need is sincerity and hard work. May we realize that our best works can not meet Your righteous requirements. May we rejoice in the righteousness that You provide to all who humbly live under Your authority, in the power of Your Holy Spirit. Amen.

QUESTIONS FOR REFLECTION AND MEDITATION:

1. What was the charge that Paul gave to Timothy in (verses 13-14)?
2. Why did Paul remind Timothy of the great character of God in (verses 15-16)?
3. What purpose did Jesus have for living? (John 18:37)
4. How do you bear witness to the truth or suppress the truth?

5. Do you tell others of the mighty works that God has done? (Psalm 105:1-2)

6. What ungodliness have you fled from, and what fruits of the Spirit have you experienced?(Galatians 5:22)

7. What makes it possible for you to rest confidently in God's salvation? (2 Timothy 1:12)

Prayer based on 1 Timothy 6:17-21

We need to strive to be rich in good works and not to trust our temporary worldly riches.

Father, we praise You for saving us and giving us meaning and purpose. You are eternal and only work done for You will last.

You warn us never to be proud and never set our hopes on the uncertainty of riches. May we always rejoice and rest in You, who richly provides for us. Make us generous people, rich in good works, and always ready to share the blessings You have freely given us. Give us wisdom so we will not participate in foolish babblings and false teachings that have led many astray.

Father, we need to kept by Your mighty power. You are our greatest treasure. May we guard that which You have entrusted to us. Amen.

QUESTIONS FOR REFLECTION AND MEDITATION:

1. Where do you find your hope and security?
2. How have you learned to trust in the provisions of God?
3. How are you storing up a treasure for yourself as a good foundation for the future?(verse 19)
4. How do you guard the deposit God has entrusted to you? (Verse 20)

2 Timothy

Prayer based on 2 Timothy 1:1-2

Paul gives his last words to his beloved son in the faith.

Father, we thank You for appointing Paul, who boldly proclaims the promised life, found only in Your Son.

Paul writes his last letter to Timothy while he is in a Roman prison awaiting his impending execution. Father we thank You for preserving these last words from Paul to his beloved son in the faith. His heart is clearly on display in his last days. He will not speak of trivial things but only of his chief desire to communicate Your Gospel for Your glory and for the benefit of others.

Father, may we all live out our final days like Paul. Give us a strong desire to finish well. Amen.

Let us meditate on Philippians 1:20-21.

Question for reflection and meditation:

1. How would you live your life differently if you lived like you were in your final days?

PRAYER BASED ON 2 TIMOTHY 1:3-7

*This text gives us six characteristics of a saint and calls
us to fan into flames the gift of God we have freely received.*

Father, we thank You for Your Word. In (verses 3-4), You give us six characteristics of a saint.

Paul is thankful, has a clear conscience, is consistent in prayer day and night, longs to be with other saints and is filled with Joy. Timothy is sensitive, open and honest, and not afraid to show emotion. Paul being confident of the conversion of Timothy; encourages him to fan into flames the gift that was given to him when Paul laid hands on him. Paul then reminds Timothy that You have given him a Spirit of power, love, and a sound mind.

Father, we praise You, for You alone know how to make godly men and women. (2 Peter 2:9) Come and stir up the gift that You have given us and remind us that You have not given us a spirit of fear but a Spirit of power, love, and self-control. Amen.

QUESTIONS FOR REFLECTION AND MEDITATION:

1. Why is Paul so confident in the salvation of Timothy?
2. What are the signs of true conversion, according to this passage?
3. How have you been stirred up to serve God?
4. How are you stirring up others?
5. In what ways are you tempted to live in fear?
6. In what ways are you living in the power of God?

Prayer based on 2 Timothy 1:8-18

The benefits of embarrassing suffering.

Father, we praise You for all the ways You work in our lives to conform us into Your image.

Paul sees himself as a prisoner of Your Son and not a prisoner of Rome. Paul calls Timothy not to be ashamed of him and the Gospel: but to join with him in suffering for the Gospel. Paul then reminds Timothy of the power of God and the holy calling he freely received and not earned. Father, before time began, it was Your good pleasure and purpose to manifest Yourself through the appearing of Your Son. You planned to abolish death and bring everlasting life to those who believe in Your Gospel and obey Your Son. Lord, You appointed Paul to be a preacher, apostle, and a teacher to the Gentiles. Paul wholeheartedly embraced his appointment and the many sufferings that came with it. Paul tells Timothy that he is not ashamed, for he knows whom he has believed, and is confident in His keeping power. (Verse 12) This confidence only comes from knowing Your grace and mercy through suffering. Paul chose to suffer for the Gospel and experience shame rather than be disobedient and ineffective for Your kingdom. Paul embraced his sufferings for the joy set before him and encouraged Timothy to do the same. Paul knows that Timothy is aware of the cost of following You. They both knew that all of Asia turned against Paul. (Verse 15). Paul then mentions Onesiphorus to encourage Timothy. Onesiphorus was not ashamed of Paul's chains and diligently sought Paul out in Rome and also served him in Ephesus.

Father, may we be grateful to You; for the many saints that have gone before us. You have kept them by Your mighty power! May we know You as they did. Adam, before the fall, only knew You in part, even though You walked and talked with him in the garden. After the fall, Adam experienced the curse and Your Grace and mercy in a way that he never did before the fall. Your saints today, know You better because of the suffering that You have permitted in their lives. We praise You for You desire to make Yourself fully known to Your people. It is only through suffering that Paul came to know whom he believed and was fully convinced that You would keep him until that final day. (Verse 12)

Father, may we all come to know You like Paul did. May we experience Your grace, mercy, and provisions in our sufferings and grow in our love and knowledge of You. May our sufferings draw us to You and equip us to be good soldiers of Christ. Amen.

In our military, a wounded soldier receives a purple heart and is sent home. In Christ's army, only the wounded soldiers are fit to serve!

QUESTIONS FOR REFLECTION AND MEDITATION:

1. Why does Paul want Timothy to join him in suffering?
2. What was the greatest good that came out of the greatest suffering; of all time?
3. What has cause you to embrace sufferings instead of mitigating them?
4. What role has suffering played in your sanctification?
5. Is there any correlation between fruitful ministry and suffering in the life of a saint? (Hebrews 12:11, 2 Corinthians 8:2)
6. Why was the fall necessary for God to make himself fully known?

Prayer based on 2 Timothy 2:1-7

This passage gives us the requirements of a good soldier of Christ..

Father, we praise You, for You have saved us from Your wrath, strengthened us by Your grace, and entrusted us with Your Gospel. We praise You, for You have called us to suffer for the sake of Your Gospel so we may have the joy and privileged of pleasing and honoring You, by sharing Your Gospel with others.

In this Scripture, You tell us what is required to be a good soldier of Christ – one who lives a life that is worthy of imitation. Good soldiers of Christ must share in His sufferings (in a death like His) to live with Him in glory. (Verses 11-12, Romans 6:5) Good soldiers aim is to please the One who enlisted them, whatever the cost – and will not get caught up in the pursuit of anything unrelated to the business of their Master. You tell us that a hard-working farmer who diligently toils in the field must be the first to partake of the crops. You also tell us that an athlete will not receive a crown, unless he obeys the rules – so how can we expect to receive a crown of righteousness, unless we know and obey the rules of God. You then promise that if anyone meditates on Your Word, You will give them an understanding of all these things. (Verse 7)

Father, may we faithfully serve You and others with complete confidence in Your reward, regardless of our current circumstances, for You never fail to do what is right and just. Make us humble instruments in Your hand, who joyfully proclaim Your good works. Give us a strong desire to equip others for Your glorious work. Lord, help us to embrace our struggles and see them as opportunities to put You on display by the way we walk through them. May we be good soldiers for Your kingdom, one who is constantly looking to You for our marching orders and not following our fleshly desires. Keep us from being entangled with other pursuits and give us a single-minded focus on pleasing You. Make us obedient servants that obey You, reap a harvest of eternal life, and never grow weary of doing it good. (Galatians 6:7-9) Amen.

Questions for reflection and meditation:

1. How is God using you as a humble instrument in the lives of others?

2. What does it take to endure hardships as a good soldier in Christ's army?
3. Why should a good soldier of Christ not get entangled in civilian pursuits?
4. Whose rules are you following and what kind of a harvest are you reaping?
5. Are you confident in your salvation and rejoicing in the holy righteous judgments of God? Why or why not?

Prayer based on 2 Timothy 2:8-13

You call us to live for the Gospel and suffer for the sake of the elect.

Father, we thank You for the commitment of Paul to live for the Gospel regardless of the cost.

Once again, Paul reminds us of the Gospel. You know what we need to hear everyday. May we remember Your Son today – who He is and what He has done. Make us a people who rejoice in You and proclaim Your Word, knowing that Your Word is powerful and can not be bound. Paul was bound in prison, but the Gospel was not. May it be the same for us today. Paul, in his last days, shares some trustworthy sayings with Timothy. (Verses 11-13) His final words of encouragement are a treasure.

Father, may we endure all suffering today; for the sake of the elect so they may see and obtain the salvation that is on display in us as we walk in Your ways. Lord, may we know the joy of being united with You in suffering and raised, with You in glory. (Romans 6:5-8) Amen.

Questions for reflection and meditation:

1. No outside circumstances could keep Paul from proclaiming the Gospel. Although he was bound, the Word of God was never bound. How is this good news for you?
2. What made it possible for Paul to have a powerful ministry in difficult circumstances?
3. Do you struggle with fully trusting and believing in God as I do? I struggle with believing in God for he is so unbelievable. I am constantly being amazed at His work in a sinner such as I. How is it with you?

Prayer based on 2 Timothy 2:14-19

The Lord knows who are His, and He calls them to depart
from iniquity and rightly handle His Word.

Father, we praise You, for You have called rebellious sinners to live for You.

Paul charges Timothy to be diligent and to present himself as one approved by You, rightly handling Your Word. You call us to lead and so we will. We do not want to be ungodly leaders. Many false teachers are leading Your people in ungodly ways. You tell us not to be one of them. You do not want us to participate in profane foolish babble which leads to death but to speak Words that will lead to life. You know those who belong to You and have set them on a firm foundation and called them to depart from all inequity.

Father, may we all hear and obey Your call. May our words be Your Words. Give us Your wisdom and boldness to say no to ungodliness and to live for Your Kingdom today and forever. (Titus 2:11-12) Amen.

QUESTIONS FOR REFLECTION AND MEDITATION:

1. How does God's call on your life affect where you go, what you say, and what you do?
2. How can you be sure that your words are His Words?
3. What has made it possible for you to depart from iniquity and live for God?
4. How have people benefited from your example?

PRAYER BASED ON 2 TIMOTHY 2:20-26

Youthful passions fled and righteousness pursued.

Father, we praise You, for You have given new desires to Your children. Only You can turn wood and clay into gold and silver!

You tell us that all dishonorable vessels made clean become a vessel for honorable use. You tell us to flee youthful passions, pursue righteousness, have nothing to do with foolish, ignorant controversies, be kind to everyone, be able to teach and correct opponents with gentleness, and patiently endure evil. And if that is not enough, You call us to be holy as You are holy. (Exodus 19:5-6, Leviticus 20:17, 1 Peter 1:16)

Father You are good, and all of Your words are true. If we could do what You command in (verse 21), we would be holy and ready for every good work. Who has this kind of righteousness and power? (Revelations 5:3-5)

Father, we thank You for providing us the righteousness we require through Your Son. Only You can make us new creatures, with a new desire to be honorable vessels, set apart as holy for Your use, and ready for every good work You have prepared for us. We need a strong desire for a pure heart and a strong love for Your saints. Fill us with Your Spirit so we will be able to flee youthful passions and pursue righteousness, faith, love, and peace. May we die to ourselves and live in harmony with You and with other believers who call upon Your name with a pure heart. Lead us in Your ways and conform us to Your image so we may gently and patiently correct those who oppose You and us. Fill our hearts with faith and love for the lost so we may be as kind to the wicked as You are. Luke 6:35-36. Lord, give us confidence through faith to pray big effective prayers that please and honor You. You have the power to open the eyes of the blind. Those who have been blinded by Satan and been held captive for years are not beyond Your reach. If You grant them repentance, they will come to their senses, know Your truth, and escape the snares of the devil.

Father, make us a distinct people who participate with You in Your supernatural work in others. Take us, mold us, and make us all You have intended for us to be. Amen.

QUESTIONS FOR REFLECTION AND MEDITATION:

1. Are you an honorable vessel fit for good works? How did that happen?
2. What evil desires of youth have you fled from or embraced?
3. In what ways are you growing in your love for God and others?
4. Why is God kind to the wicked and ungrateful? why should you be the same? (Luke 6:35-36)
5. Do you believe that God can save the vilest of people? Why or why not?
6. How often have you been amazed at the supernatural work of God in your life or in the life of another?

Prayer based on 2 Timothy 3:1-9

This passage gives us a description of ungodliness in the last DAYS.

Father, we praise You for saving Your people and keeping them until the last DAY.

(Verses 1-9) describe a life lived apart from You. Some people are always learning but never arrive at the knowledge of Your Truth. You strongly warn us to avoid these people. You assure us that men with corrupt minds will oppose You, but they will not get very far and their folly will become plain to everyone.

Father, we need You to open our eyes and enable us to see as You see, speak as You speak, and do as You do. Give us more desire to live in harmony with You. Only through abiding in You can obedience be possible for us. If we obey, You will give us the strength to stand in the faith. Apart from You, we will be taken in by the foolishness of this fallen, corrupt world. May we tremble at the thought of being apart from Your salvation. We thank You and praise You because we are what we are by Your Grace. May this truth inform us and allow us to see everything through Your eyes. Keep us from self righteousness and give us compassion for those who live apart from You, so we may serve them and love them – knowing full well that apart from Your sustaining grace we would live just like them.

Father, make us humble and faithful servants that continue to look to You and call upon Your name instead of trusting in our own wisdom. Father, keep us from vain pursuits. May we live in harmony with You and others so that many will see and desire a life that is lived for You. (2 Corinthians 3: 2-3) Amen.

Let us read and meditate on John 17:14-26

QUESTIONS FOR REFLECTION AND MEDITATION:

1. Does reading the list in (verses 1-9) cause you to remember and rejoice in your deliverance from the wrath of God?
2. How would your life be different apart from the saving power of God?

3. How are you growing in your compassion for others and awareness of your need for God?
4. What vain pursuits have you laid down and what worthy goals have you taken up?

Prayer based on 2 Timothy 3:10-14

A description of a life lived for the Gospel
contrasted with the life of an unbeliever.

Father, we thank You for the free gift of life in You.

You show the strong contrast between the life of an unbeliever, described in (verses 1-9) and the life of a true saint, described in (verses 10-12). Paul boldly puts himself forward as an example of a saint and encourages Timothy to follow him as he has followed You. Paul reminds Timothy of all the ways he saw Paul suffering. Paul boldly proclaims that You have delivered him from all of his sufferings! Paul wants Timothy to know that suffering is a common experience in the life of a Christian. Paul assures Timothy that all who desire to live a godly life will suffer persecution. Paul warns Timothy of the many false teachers that will come, and will actively oppose him and the Gospel. Paul then calls Timothy to continue to follow what he has learned and firmly believes.

Father, conform us to You so we can be faithful to You. Cause us to remember and rejoice in Your deliverance. May we thank You for our trials – knowing that they are all from Your hand and are for Your glory and our good.

We thank You for Your good and perfect work in us. You care more about our sanctification than our comfort. Help us to understand that suffering is necessary for all of those You chose to save. Just as Jesus was a Man of sorrows and acquainted with grief, so shall it be in our union with Your Son. May we rejoice when we suffer, for You have opened our eyes and made it possible for us to see sin. It is better to suffer than be blind to sin. You tell us that those who mourn over sin are blessed. (Matthew 5:4) As we walk through this day may we rejoice in our union with You – knowing that every good gift is from You. (James 1:17) You are good in what You give, and You are good in what You withhold. (Psalm 84:11) Keep our eyes on You, so we may stand firm in our union with You. Amen.

Questions for reflection and meditation:

1. How can Paul rejoice and proclaim the goodness of God while experiencing such severe suffering? (2 Corinthians 1:9)

2. Why must believers be prepared to suffer?
3. What has God used in your life to conform you to His image?
4. If God took all the sufferings out of your life, how would that diminish your love and knowledge of Him?
5. When God opens the eyes of an unbeliever, what do they see and how do they respond? (Isaiah 6:1-5, Luke 5:8)
6. Is there any good thing that God has withheld from you?

Prayer based on 2 Timothy 3:15-17

All of Scripture is from God and written for our benefit.

Father, We praise You, for giving us this high view of Scripture.

Paul tells Timothy that all Scripture is given by You and is profitable. May we accept all of Your Word as relevant and worthy of serious study. May we never put ourselves over Scripture and reject Your clear teachings or twist and distort it to say things the Author never intended. May we realize the great danger of trusting in our fallen intellects. Make us humble, teachable people who delight in Your Word and live under Its authority. Your Word is complete, sufficient, and without error. Surround us with Your good teachers who faithfully expound on Your Word so that we come to know You and love You more. May we be so familiar with Your Word that we will quickly recognize and reject false teachings. You have given us Your Word to equip us thoroughly for every good work.

Father, may we live every day under the authority of Scripture, knowing it is Your infallible Truth. Let us not lean on the understanding of the world but look to Your Word, which is able to make us wise and pleasing to You. May all that we believe, and do, and say be guided and directed by Your Word. Amen.

What you believe about God is the most important thing about you? A. W. Tozer

Questions for reflection and meditation:

1. How does what you believe about God affect the fruit that you bear?
2. What would change in your life if you took the Word of God more seriously?
3. Who are your teachers, and what effect have they had on your life?
4. Are you like a noble Berean? They were open and eager to be taught, and they examined the Scriptures daily to see if their beliefs line up with the Word of God. (Acts 17:11)

Prayer based on 2 Timothy 4:1-8

This passage shows us a life filled with passion for the
Gospel and warns us of the persecutions that will come.

Father, we thank You for the faithful example of Paul in his finale days.

Paul knows his death is near. He is not consumed with that thought but still continues to strive to live for You and others. He has a love for Timothy and a concern for his well-being. Paul solemnly charges Timothy to preach Your Word. Paul knows what it takes to finish well and implores Timothy to continue Your work regardless of the opposition. Paul warns Timothy that many will not embrace sound doctrine but pursue their own passions and desires and follow false teachings. He encourages Timothy to be patient with them: to be long suffering, sober-minded, and to live and proclaim the Truth that God has given to him. Paul calls Timothy to finish well and tells Timothy that the time of his departure has come. Paul will continue to pour himself out as an offering to God in his last days. He is determined to finish well. Paul then describes the crown of righteousness that awaits him and all who love him and long for His return.

Father, we are prone to wander and follow our own passions and live for our glory instead of Yours. Lord, conform us to be people who love You more than life itself and look forward to Your appearing. May we live for that DAY, when we see You face to face and hear You say, well done, my good and faithful servant. May we live this day in light of that DAY when You appear. At the end of every day may we be able to say: I have fought the good fight, I have finished the race, 1 have kept the faith. May this day and all our days be devoted to You. Amen.

A God-centered life is a string of God-centered days.

Build a cross centered life, one day at a time. C. J. Mahany, The Cross Centered Life 2002

Let us read and meditate on Matthew 16:24-28

QUESTIONS FOR REFLECTION AND MEDITATION:

1. Paul's first command to Timothy is to preach the Word. Why should preaching the Word be a primary goal?
2. Who do you have in your life that encourages you to run a good race and finish well?
3. Are you living for the joy of that DAY or have other things captured your gaze?
4. What does it take to run a good race and receive the crown?
5. Are you determined to finish well?

Prayer based on 2 Timothy 4:9-18

God equips us to joyfully proclaim the Gospel,
even in times of great sorrow and opposition.

Father we praise You for Your all-sufficient grace in our times of need. (Hebrews 4:16)

Father, keep us from being crushed and captivated by this world like Demas was. May we not fall in love with this present world, but more and more in love with You. May we delight in Your Word and rejoice in every opportunity that You give us, especially when we face betrayal and opposition. May we be more aware of those who oppose the Gospel. Give us more compassion for them and a greater trust in Your righteous power to change lives so we may pray for them as Paul did for Alexander. Strengthen us, Lord, by the power of Your Spirit so that through us the Gospel is proclaim. May we not shrink back, either in fear of man or in sorrow, but may we have great confidence in You – who can rescue us from every evil deed and bring us safely into Your heavenly kingdom. To You be the glory forever and ever! Amen.

Questions for reflection and meditation:

1. How have you responded two betrayal and opposition?
2. What opportunities has God given you this week to love and care for others?
3. Are there any Alexanders in your life? How are you praying for them?
4. How is your confidence in God or lack of it reflected in the way you live?
5. How is faith in God gained or lost?

TITUS

Prayer based on Titus 1:1-16

Qualifications for elders are listed. Paul charges and encourages Titus to appoint elders, rebuke the unruly Cretans, and bring the light of the glorious Gospel into a very dark place.

Father we thank You for the high calling, the joy, and the rewards given to those who love You and obey, even to the vilest of sinners.

Paul knew that he was appointed and entrusted to preach the Gospel to the elect. Paul desires to see the truth that leads to godliness preached everywhere, even in Crete. Creek was a very dark and treacherous place, and Paul had the faith to leave Titus in Crete to establish a Church. Paul calls Titus to raise up and appoint elders and lists their qualifications. (Versus 5-9) Paul sets the same high bar for the Church in Crete as he did for the healthy Church in Ephesus. (1 Timothy 3: 8-13) Paul knew that a lower bar would not please God or be effective in the conversion of the Cretans. It is obvious Paul did not believe in the seeker-friendly church method. Paul describes the depravity of the Cretans and calls Titus to rebuke them. (Versus 10-16)

Father, give us faith in the power of the Gospel to change lives so that we may boldly go into the darkest of places and bring the hope of the Gospel to all. May we not be discourage and give up when we encounter the hopeless, empty talkers and deceivers, the arrogant, the greedy, the self-centered, the violent, the detestable, and the disobedient. Father, give us compassion for all and confidence in the power of Your Word to save the vilest of sinners. Make us eager and bold to obey You and do Your work wherever You send us. May we not shrink back but be driven to our knees in humble dependence on You. You tell us that obedience will produce good fruit, not only in those we minister to, but in our own hearts as well. Amen.

Questions for reflection and meditation:

1. Why does Paul believe in setting a high bar for the Church?
2. How does your belief in the power of the Gospel to change lives, affect how you evangelize?
3. How has God prepared you to go into dark places?
4. When have you been driven to your knees in humble dependence on God?

5. Do you boldly live for him or choose to operate within your limited abilities?
6. Why do some people experience more of God's mercy and power?
7. What makes a Church powerful, effective, and pleasing to God?

Prayer based on Titus 2:1-15

Believers are to live a holy life as they eagerly wait for the appearing of their great God and Savior, Jesus Christ.

Father, we thank You for giving us all the sound teachings we need in Your Word?

Paul gives instructions to Titus to teach sound doctrine. Older men are to be dignified, self-controlled, and stead fast. (Verse 2) Older women are to model reverence and kindness, be submissive to their husbands and teach the younger women to do the same. (Verses 3-5). Paul commands Titus to urge younger men to be self-control and then charges him to model good works, integrity, dignity, and sound speech. Verses 6-8) Bondservants must be submissive to there masters, well-pleasing, not argumentative, or deceitful. (Verses 9-10)

Father, thank You for sending Your Son to die in our place. You have redeemed us, and we are Yours. You have called us to renounce worldly passions and live self-controlled, upright, and godly lives in this present world as we eagerly await the glorious appearance of Your Son. May we, by the power of Your Spirit reigning in us, live as people who have been set apart for Your purpose. (1 Peter 2:9) Knowing our calling and Your power, may we be willing and zealous to do the good works which You have prepared for us today. (Ephesians 2:10) Amen.

Questions for reflection and meditation:

1. Why does God command our worship and praise?
2. What demands does God place on your life, and how have you responded?
3. What has God done in your life to cause you to rejoice in Him?
4. What has God allowed or not done in your life that cause you to question His perfect ways?
5. What makes you zealous for good works? (Verse 14)

PRAYER BASED ON TITUS 3: 1-15

The unrighteous and ungodly are equipped
and made ready for every good work.

Farther, we praise You for delivering us from our hopeless, miserable condition. You not only provided forgiveness for our sins, but freedom from the bondage of sin. We became heirs, not because of any works of our own. We were saved and adopted by Your grace which You freely and richly poured out on us through Your Son. We praise You for saving us and keeping us, by Your grace.

Apart from You, we are foolish, disobedient, easily led astray, enslaved to our passions and pleasures, and unable to love You and others as we should. Our condition was hopeless until You revealed Your Son to us. The moment we saw Your righteousness and beauty, we saw our unrighteousness and ugliness. We were undone and cried out as Isaiah did. (Isaiah 6:5) When Isaiah confessed his sin, You took his guilt away. (Isaiah 6:7) The same is true today. Every believer who confesses their sin will experienced Your amazing grace instead of Your just wrath. If we confess our sin, You are faithful and will cleansed us from all unrighteousness. (1 John 1:9)

Father, we thank You for what You have done through the merit and sufferings of Your Son. Because of His work and not ours, we can be free from those things that are unprofitable and worthless, and we can spend our days devoted to the good works which You have prepared for us. By Your grace we can joyfully look forward to Your return and to spending an eternity with You. Amen.

QUESTIONS FOR REFLECTION AND MEDITATION:

1. How were you equipped and made ready for every good work?
2. When someone sees the Holiness of God, how do they respond?
3. How would you describe your conversion?
4. How has God's love for you equipped you to love others
5. What can capture your gaze and tempt you to seek your good apart from God?
6. Are you joyfully looking forward to Christ's return? Why or why not?

PHILEMON

PRAYER BASED ON PHILEMON 1-23

This letter gives us wise instructions on caring for others.

Father, we thank You for preserving this letter from Paul to Philemon.

Every word of this letter is so wisely put. There is much for us to learn from Your Word, as we take time to meditate on it.

Father show us how to be a blessing to You and others as we live for the furtherance of Your Kingdom today. Amen.

QUESTIONS FOR REFLECTION AND MEDITATION:

1. Do you pray for others as Paul prayed for Philemon in (verse 6)?
2. Do you encourage others as Paul encouraged Philemon in (verse 7)?
3. Do You prefer to appeal to others in love as Paul did in (verses 8-10)?
4. Are you willing to sacrifice for the benefit of others as Paul did in verses (11-15)?
5. Do you receive others as Christ has received you, as modeled by Paul in (verses 17-20)?

Continuing story and prayer for the reader

I HAVE SPENT 24 months reading, studying, and writing prayers from the Epistles. I spent 19 of the 24 months in Paul's letters. I am more confident in the rewards and goals, which I spoke of in the introduction after spending over 3,000 hours studying, writing, rereading, and editing these prayers. You would think these prayers would become stale, and the constant editing would have become a chore. That was not the case. These prayers remained fresh and have been a great blessing to me, over and over again. It was, and is, my joy and privilege to write them. They continue to speak to me and remind me of God's sovereignty and goodness. I pray that they would also have the same affect on you. God's grace is nothing short of amazing.

I submitted my first manuscript to my publisher on July 30, 2021 for review. The review was very encouraging, and their three suggestions were very good.

They suggested that I write a few lines to introduce a prayer. That helped me to identify the main point of the Scripture and stick to it.

They suggested that I organize the prayers. That turned out to be a brief outline of the 13 letters. I believe that will serve the reader well by giving them an overview of the letters and a quick page references to topics.

Their last suggestion was to write a conclusion, which I am now attempting to do.

I plan to spend the next few months, or whatever it takes, proofreading and prayerfully editing these prayers. I expect to make hundreds of changes. Every time I read these prayers, I can find room for improvement. My goal is to make them meaty, accurate, easy to read and understand, and hard to misinterpret. I have spent many hours editing these prayers to accomplish this goal. I know this is a lofty goal that I could never achieve in my own strength, but I can not stop trying to achieve it. I have tried hard to cut out all the bones and leave the meat. Despite my best efforts, some bones may remain. I pray that you will chew carefully, eat the meat, and spit out the bones.

I pray that God will use these prayers to awaken ordinary people; to the high calling of God. I believe that God has called all His people to be saints as described in (1 Peter 2:9) May these prayers serve you well and bring the appropriate conviction; necessary for growth. May they challenge you and spur you on to the high calling in Christ Jesus. Take care, my friends; I pray that you will continue to grow in your knowledge and love for our Lord and His bride. Amen.

God tells us that we must walk by faith and not by sight. (2 Corinthians 5:7)

I leave you with an old southern African-American Gospel song, composed by an unknown author, which beautifully expresses what I believe should be the continuing heart cry of every believer.

I am weak, but Thou art strong

Jesus, keep me from all wrong

I'll be satisfied as long

As I walk, let me walk close to Thee

Just a closer walk with Thee

Grant it, Jesus, is my plea

Daily walking close to Thee

Let it be, dear Lord, let it be.

CPSIA information can be obtained
at www.ICGtesting.com
Printed in the USA
BVHW032123100622
639494BV00009B/154

9 781662 846977